Frank Lloyd Wright

ESSENTIAL TEXTS

Frank Lloyd Wright

ESSENTIAL TEXTS

Edited by Robert Twombly

W.W. Norton & Company

New York • London

Copyright © 2009 by Robert Twombly

All rights reserved
Printed in the United States of America
First Edition

Manufacturing by Edwards Brothers, Lillington
Book design by Jonathan Lippincott
Production manager: Leeann Graham

Library of Congress Cataloging-in-Publication Data

Wright, Frank Lloyd, 1867–1959.
   [Selections]
   Frank Lloyd Wright : essential texts / edited by Robert Twombly. —
1st ed.
      p.   cm.
   Includes bibliographical references and index.
   ISBN 978-0-393-73261-0 (pbk.)
   1. Architecture. I. Twombly, Robert C. II. Title.
   NA737.W7A35   2009
   720—dc22   2008045685

ISBN 13: 978-0-393-73261-0 (pbk.)

W. W. Norton & Company, Inc.
500 Fifth Avenue
New York, NY 10110
www.wwnorton.com

W. W. Norton & Company Ltd.
Castle House, 75/76 Wells Street
London W1T 3QT

0 9 8 7 6 5 4 3 2 1

For Jeanne Chase
1939–2007

Contents

Preface and Acknowledgments

From out of the blue, my editor at W. W. Norton & Company called one day to ask if I would consider assembling a collection of Frank Lloyd Wright's essential texts. My immediate reaction was "No," but I told her I would think about it. "No" because after two books, and dozens of essays, reviews, public lectures, and college classes on Wright, I was bored with him, had long ago moved on to other things in teaching and writing, and did not want to be part of what I once described in *Design Book Review* as "the Frank Lloyd Wright cottage industry that ... has now become an assembly-line." At that time there were fifty-five Wright entries in *Books in Print: Titles* but only twenty-six for Franklin Roosevelt. Enough was enough, I thought, and often still do.

But I said I would think about it, to be polite, because working with her on a previous book has been a terrific experience and besides, a few extra dollars wouldn't hurt. When I did think about it, I realized that the Wright "word glut"—that was my review's title— did not include a volume such as this. There are anthologies too inclusive for classroom use, or with inessential material thrown together with the essential, with tiny snippets culled from lengthy pieces, with unidentified texts, partial texts, and texts grouped by themes that weren't Wright's. In short, what is available or is now out of print is user-unfriendly. So at the risk of adding to the glut, I did this book.

There are lacunae here, to be sure, most obviously the overtly political writings: Wright's strong endorsement of the Soviet Union in the 1930s, his advocacy of conscientious objection during World War Two, his heated postwar opposition to the House Subcommittee on "Un-American" Activities and to Senator Joseph McCarthy's "anti-communist" witch hunts, and his (initially enthusiastic) approval of Franklin Roosevelt's New Deal and then of Adlai Stevenson. A more comprehensive reconstruction of Wright's intellectual spectrum would have included these and other writings. But since this editor decided they would not illuminate his thinking about architecture, they are omitted.

The objective here is to bring together Wright's most important statements in chronological order so that students of architecture may trace the evolution and maturation of his design philosophy. Those preceding United States entry into World War One are the most important because by then the theory and practice that so strongly affected world architecture was fully developed. After that, his thinking does not so much reveal conceptual change as confront matters he cared about personally, or that were less theoretical: the significance of his "master" Louis Sullivan, the International Style's challenge to organic architecture, his Broadacre City decentralization project, and updating his residences in light of social and technological change. His texts became increasingly repetitious as time passed, but those reproduced here from the 1920s and 1930s exemplify his new priorities, and for that reason are included.

It also turned out, unexpectedly for the editor, that including later texts made it possible to organize this volume by theme, as well as chronology, which may be helpful for readers.

The final text is Wright's 1949 acceptance speech for the American Institute of Architects Gold Medal for lifetime achievement, an award he felt was long overdue, as he told the AIA in no uncertain terms, an appropriate conclusion to a book about a man constitutionally unable to let sleeping dogs lie. Or so it seems to me.

Readers will note that all material in this volume is reproduced as initially published. Since Wright sometimes rewrote speeches for a second audience or for later insertion in books, it seemed best to include only originals, to better capture his thinking as it emerged and not as reformulated with hindsight. There are no excerpts here from his many books as these are available in stores and libraries. (*The Japanese Print* [Document 7] was published as a book but is in fact an essay.) There is a certain economy to the essay form to which of necessity Wright had to conform, even in his later years when on numerous occasions his prose was less than concise.

The editor has corrected without indication the few instances of misspelling and incorrect punctuation in the original texts, and has also inserted in brackets what context suggests were Wright's intended words misread by journal editors.

A number of people were instrumental in assembling this collection. Special thanks to Mary Woolever, archivist, the Libraries, the Art Institute, Chicago, who, no matter my project, always makes it easier, and to her assistant, Kim Krueger. To Judy Connorton, librarian, School of Architecture, the City College of New York, and to her assistant, Nilda Sanchez. To William Whitaker, collections manager, Architectural Archives, University of Pennsylvania. And to Thomas A. Heinz, Chicagoland architect, author, photographer, and all-around talent, who helped me lately in several ways, including on this project.

Thanks also to Frederik Heller, manager, Virtual Library and Archives, National Association of Realtors, Chicago; to Elisabeth Broome, managing editor, the *Architectural Record*, New York; and to Irina Mayakova of Time Inc., New York.

Nancy Green at Norton demonstrated again what anyone who has worked with her knows: that she is an immensely helpful and encouraging editor.

This book is dedicated to my late wife Jeanne Chase, the finest scholar I have ever known, who believed I had become the historian that the late Professor Gunther Barth, years ago my Harvard honors tutor, hoped I would be. This book is dedicated to him as well.

"Truth Against the World"

Frank Lloyd Wright was born in 1867, when Andrew Johnson was president, the United States purchased Alaska, and historical eclecticism dominated the architectural scene. When he died in 1959 at the age of ninety-one, Dwight D. Eisenhower was in the White House, the Soviet spacecraft Luna 1 reached the moon, and architecture meant "modernism." Born in the Victorian era, he lived through the Gay Nineties, the Roaring Twenties, the Great Depression, two world wars, and on into the Atomic Age and the Cold War. In 1867 the Civil War was only two years past, and in 1959 the computer age was just beginning.

His professional life was also exceptionally long and varied. The first building on which he worked was Unity Chapel in Spring Green, Wisconsin, designed in 1886 by Chicago architect Joseph L. Silsbee for the Lloyd Joneses, an enormous extended family from which Wright descended on his mother's side. A week before he died, he was still at it, almost seventy-three years after that first supervisory job. Wright's career lasted longer than the average American's life span at the time.

In the beginning he shunned Victorian eclecticism, and well before the end he was a staunch opponent of "modernism." Despite going against whatever grain was in vogue, he was extraordinarily prolific. Over four hundred of his nearly five hundred executed buildings in numerous genres still stand, a little more than half of all he designed. Detached, single-family residences for middle- and upper-middle-class clients account for approximately three-quarters of his built and unbuilt work, an exceptionally high percentage for world-famous architects, who usually avoid relatively unremunerative but labor-intensive commissions like houses unless for the superrich.

Wright was born in the farming community of Richland Center, Wisconsin, fifty miles west of Madison, where his family settled in 1878 when he was eleven, after living in Iowa, Massachusetts, and Rhode Island. He spent his summers working on Lloyd Jones farms, where he must have been struck by the beauty of the Wisconsin River winding through tree-filled, green rolling hills dotted with buff limestone strata. In Madison he attended grammar school and high school. Despite failing to graduate from the latter, he was admitted in January 1886 to the University of Wisconsin as a "special student" in the "scientific" curriculum. He did not fare especially well, earning "average" grades in descriptive geometry and drawing, the only courses for which there are records during his single year in attendance.

It may be that financial difficulties stemming from his parents' divorce in 1885 prompted him to take a job in Professor Allan D. Conover's architectural office during the spring and fall semesters of 1886, and to work that summer for Silsbee in Spring Green. Perhaps his love for architecture was kindled by those two men. Or it may be that with prosperous relatives, his mother—with whom he lived, his father having left Madison—did not need further assistance, and that Wright sought employment because his love had already blossomed on its own. Whatever the circumstances, he withdrew from the university in December. Early 1887 found him in Chicago working for Silsbee as a renderer and draughtsman.

He changed employers once, and then early in 1888 signed on with Dankmar Adler and Louis Sullivan, whose staff was stretched to its limits designing the enormous 1886–90 Chicago Auditorium Building. During the next five years Wright rose from draughtsman to chief draughtsman to Sullivan's protégée and confidant, primarily responsible for the handful of residential commissions the firm accepted, but also working on an array of other buildings. Perhaps because Sullivan and Wright had grown so intimate—the one finding the "son" he never had, the other acquiring a substitute "father"—it became a matter of personal rejection, at least to Sullivan, when the two disagreed over the terms of Wright's contract and the conditions of his employment. Feeling himself betrayed, Sullivan fired Wright, who immediately opened his own office in 1893.

During the next eight years he produced a body of well-crafted, excellently detailed buildings, mostly houses of somewhat distinctive appearance, that slowly, surely, but only in retrospect inevitably evolved (this was a period of experimentation; he had not yet settled on an architectural language) into "A Home in a Prairie Town," a new kind of dwelling soon to be the basis of his fame, depicted in the February 1901 *Ladies' Home Journal*. It is from the title of this article that terms like "Prairie house," "Prairie school," and "Prairie period" derive.

"I brought the whole house down in scale," he later wrote in *An Autobiography*. "Walls were now started at the ground on a . . . water table that looked like a low platform under the building . . . and stopped at the second-story window-sill to let the bedrooms come through above in a continuous window series below the broad eaves of a gently sloping, overhanging roof." The Upper Midwest climate being "violent in extremes . . . , I gave broad protecting roof-shelter to the whole. . . . The underside of roof-projections was flat and usually light in color to create a glow of reflected light that softly brightened the upper rooms. Overhangs had double value: shelter and preservation for the walls . . . , as well as this diffusion of reflected light. . . . The house began to associate with the ground," he explained, "and become natural to its prairie site."

The exterior, he continued, "was all there, chiefly because of what happened *inside*." Rejecting what he called "boxes beside boxes or inside boxes," he redefined the "whole lower floor as one room, cutting off the kitchen as a laboratory, putting the servants' sleeping and living quarters next to the kitchen but semi-detached.... Then I screened various portions of the big room for certain domestic purposes like dining, reading, receiving callers." (Only upstairs did he retain sleeping "boxes.") "The ceilings," he added, were "brought down . . . by way of horizontal bands of plaster on the walls themselves above the windows and colored the same as the room-ceilings" which had the effect of emphasizing intimacy and integration, further enhanced by strips of continuous molding running around the room at window and door tops tying everything together. Solids and voids, verticals and horizontals, were thus united in a holistic composition that also included furniture, fixtures, art glass, and landscaping.

Over the course of the next eight years, Wright designed some 150 structures of all sorts in the prairie genre. There was no shortage of clients for his work, which was well reviewed and received; he was much in demand as a speaker and essayist; and he established a national reputation. But in September 1909 his life and career took an abrupt turn. In 1904 he had designed a house for Edwin H. and Mamah Borthwick Cheney in Oak Park, Illinois, where Wright himself had lived since 1889 with his wife Catherine, whom he married that year. The four became friends, understood around town to be something of a foursome. The Cheneys had two children, the Wrights six. But in September 1909, Wright and Borthwick, suddenly and unexpectedly to all but a few, met clandestinely in New York en route to Berlin, leaving their friends, Oak Park, and the architectural world in shock. It was then that the proverbial biodegradable substance hit the fan.

A November 1910 editorial in the Minneapolis-based *Western Architect* illustrates professional reaction that in turn reflected public opinion. When something like this affair occurs, it opined, "American and foreign architects have claimed . . . the right to allude to shady intrigue as 'temperament.' [But] baldly and properly viewed, 'temperament' that will send a man flitting about the capitals of Europe with another man's wife cannot be classified as anything but the shoddiest cloak for immorality. Temperament is another name for moral laxness." Little wonder Wright would assert in 1914 (Document 8) that "the spirit of fair play," along with other desirable characteristics, "is unhappily too rare among editors."

After a year on the Continent and another in Oak Park trying unsuccessfully to resolve differences with mates and children—Mamah secured a divorce in August 1911, but Catherine did not consent until 1922—the couple decided in 1911 to live together permanently in Spring Green, Wisconsin, where Wright had been constructing Taliesin as their home and his design studio. Roundly attacked for living "in sin" while being socially ostracized, Wright and Borthwick nevertheless constructed a mutually productive life, including her translations of writings by Swedish feminist Ellen Key and his architectural practice, which, measured against the number of commissions executed between 1905 and 1909, however, declined by more than 50 percent from 1910 to 1914. Still, with community hostility diminishing somewhat by 1914, it appeared the two would ride out the storm, eventually resuming normal lives. Then came the worst blow of Wright's life.

On August 14, 1914, while he was supervising construction of a building in Chicago, Mamah Borthwick was presiding at lunch with her two visiting children, a friend of theirs, and five Taliesin workmen. Unknown to them, another employee set brush and gasoline fires under the dining room windows and stationed himself at the only door, which he had locked, hatcheting to death those attempting to force their way out. Most of Taliesin burned to the ground, and in the ashes Mamah and six others, including her children, lay dead.

Wright was devastated. He eulogized her in the local newspaper and buried her across the road in the Lloyd Jones family graveyard at the same Unity Chapel he had worked on twenty-eight years before. Fortunately for his sanity, he was occupied with two large projects, the Midway Gardens in Chicago (where he had been working on August 14) and preliminary drawings for the Imperial Hotel in Tokyo (see Document 10), but his highest priority was to rebuild Taliesin. "I shall set it all up again for the spirit of the mortal that lived in it and loved it," he wrote, "and will live in it still. My home will still be there."

But hopes for a quiet, productive future were soon dashed. Partly because of his inability to live alone, and his compelling need for a woman in his life, the next decade and a half were tempestuous, to say the least. Shortly after Mamah's death, he invited Miriam Noel, whom he had not met, to visit him at Taliesin on the strength of her moving letter of condolence. Despite obvious incompatibilities, they lived together off and on for the next eight years, fighting all the while. They were nonetheless married in November 1923, then separated in April 1924 and divorced in 1927. Seemingly endless lawsuits and court orders about monetary and property settlements, including ownership of Taliesin—she had helped finance its rebuilding—periodically denied him access to his studio, as did a very destructive 1925 electrical fire requiring him to rebuild yet again. In the meantime, he met Olga Milanoff in November 1924, moved her into Taliesin the following February, and fathered her second child—his seventh—before 1925 was out, prompting Miriam to sue for alienation of affection. Although legal disputes with Miriam Noel dragged on until 1930, Wright married Olgivanna (as she now called herself) in 1928 as soon as the law allowed, at last finding the peace he had sought since 1914. Their marriage lasted until his death.

Every one of these and other events were scrutinized in the press, seriously damaging Wright's career. From 1915 to 1924 he executed only twenty-nine buildings, three a year on average, far fewer than during the Prairie period, fewer even than during his life with Mamah, but from 1925 to 1935 that meager total plummeted to a mere six, two for himself and a third for a relative. It is true that he spent forty months in Japan from 1916 to 1922 working on the Imperial Hotel and that the Great Depression limited architectural production, but it is also true that potential clients shied away from a man whose domestic situation led them perhaps unfairly to question his professional reliability. The upshot is that during the Roaring Twenties, when architects were prospering, Wright had very little work but also, ironically, that during the depths of the Depression, while they suffered, he began an amazing comeback.

Three widely publicized commissions essentially account for that: world-famous Fallingwater (1935–37), the luxury country house for Edgar J. Kaufmann at Bear Run, Pennsylvania; the Johnson Wax Company Administration Building (1936–39) in Racine, Wisconsin; and the Herbert Jacobs residence (1936–37) in Westmoreland (now Madison), Wisconsin, generally considered his first "Usonian" house (see Documents 14a–c). From that time forward, except during World War Two, Wright's career blossomed. His final thirteen or fourteen years were the most productive of his life.

Wright's son John wrote that "something in him died with her, something gentle and loveable . . . in my father" that Mamah Borthwick had nurtured. That "something" is difficult to isolate but its consequences are not. The Lloyd Jones family motto was "Truth Against the World," to which Wright alluded in his eulogy to Mamah when he wrote that, despite condemnation and ostracism, "we lived frankly and sincerely . . . and we have tried to help others live . . . according to their ideals. . . . The 'freedom' in which we joined was infinitely more difficult than any conformity to customs. . . . Few will ever venture it."

"You wives with certificates for loving," he exhorted, "pray that you may love and be loved as well as was Mamah Borthwick! You mothers and fathers with daughters—be satisfied if what life you have invested in them works itself out upon as high a plane as it has done in the life of this lovely woman." Unless we realize that Right Now is the most important moment of our lives, "there will come a bitter time when the thought of how much more potent with love and affection that precious 'Present' might have been, will desolate out hearts."

Mamah Borthwick was the love of Wright's life and remained so throughout his relationships with other women. Together they stood for "truth against the world," and as their situation in Spring Green gradually improved, he came to think that their unconventional life might actually be accepted, possibly admired, and perhaps become a liberating model for other people. But then she was murdered, initiating fourteen exceedingly difficult years, convincing him that his hopes had been misplaced. Even the peace he found with Olgivanna did not prevent him from concluding that only he—he alone—stood for "truth against the world." Had not Mamah's fate proven that two people together, challenging social norms, doubled the chance of retribution?

On one level, that "truth" was architectural. After the Gothic period ended, he repeatedly said (as texts in this volume demonstrate) that only he and Louis Sullivan understood that architecture must be "organic" to be authentic. Anything else was socially and culturally inappropriate. In the United States "organic architecture" was by definition "democratic architecture" because democracy was *au fond* this nation's defining characteristic. So anything not democratic was not organic, equally so the other way around, which by the late 1920s meant in his mind anything he himself had not designed. These notions had been implicit in his thinking all along, but after the trials and tribulations of the 1910s and 1920s they became explicit, repeated constantly (see documents 12a–12d and 15), often tiresomely, to readers and listeners. Those same documents also reveal changes in his writing style, never especially fluent or polished, but now increasingly rambling, with garbled syntax making his prose and his meaning more difficult to fathom, sometimes exceedingly so. It was not that Wright purposefully eschewed clarity; he obviously wanted to spread his message. His idiosyncratic prose suggests, rather, a form of self-centeredness, further revealed when almost completely stripped of the literary and poetic quotations and references with which he had peppered his pre-1914 statements. Gone were Goethe, Schiller, Hugo, Carlyle, and the others who had once graced his pages. One wonders if Wright had stopped reading. Or whether he had decided that he was his own best authority.

Prior to 1914 he had offered his unconventional architecture as a challenge to colleagues to rethink what they were doing for the good of society, but by the late 1920s he used it to assert his own superiority over a profession for which little hope remained. Prior to 1914 his prose had served to explain his work in a reasonably straightforward manner, but by the late 1920s clear explanation gave way to a kind of literary solipsism. There were exceptions, to be sure, among them texts included here on the Usonian House (which suffer in comparison, however, with documents 1–11 but especially 1–9), and his 1954 *The Natural House*, a useful, easily accessible, how-to, what-to-look-for handbook for potential homebuilders. By the late 1920s, in essence, his designs and his prose—as well as an increasingly flamboyant, high-wide-and-handsome in-your-face living style—represented to him, consciously or not, the rule-breaking to which he felt his genius entitled him. To write this is not to condemn, but to propose that in his own mind "Truth Against the World" had become his best refuge, his last defense against a society that for a horrible decade and a half had ostracized and condemned him, a decade and a half that, in his own mind, had become his entire life. Much of the above is speculation, of course. What is not is that Wright ended his career in a blaze of glory, with commissions large and small flowing in from around the world. His conceptual, technical, and compositional innovations are vital contributions to architectural history, but remain especially relevant for today's recognition that environmentally sensitive siting, materials, and form are more necessary now than ever. Not the least important lesson of his work, which these texts show is not limited to environmental considerations, is that the primary responsibility of architects is to society at large.

Nor should we forget his profound commitment to individualism, to everyone's duty to be one's self, regardless of social pressure, while keeping in mind the goal of social harmony. Equally important was his commitment, not to a predatory individualism leading to the accumulation of uncurbed power, but of every person's obligation to oppose it in the name of democratic principle. As a latter-day Jeffersonian democrat, Wright spent a good deal of time criticizing government and corporate hegemony, believing it would inevitably subvert personal freedoms. However poorly he may have expressed himself at times, the very fact that he spoke of such things set him apart from most architects, and still does.

Frank Lloyd Wright

ESSENTIAL TEXTS

ONE

The Architect

(1900)

This is not Wright's first public lecture, but it is the first to be published in full, shortly after its presentation to the second annual convention of the Architectural League of America meeting at the Art Institute, Chicago. In it he laments his profession's commercialization and its persistent use of historical design forms, which he believed to be outcomes of the corporatization of American business and a national feeling of cultural inferiority.

The antidote, he argues, is for the young architect to study the natural world, the nature of his own civilization, and science and industry in order to develop "something of his own," because Wright was convinced that "the very strength of individuality developed in a free nation, and the richness of our own inheritance" would in the end produce a distinctively American architecture.

From The Brickbuilder, *9 (June 1900).*

"Liberal sects do their work not by growing strong, but by making all others more liberal."[1]

A vital point of difference between professional man and man of business is that money-making to the professional man should, by virtue of his assumption, be incidental; to the business man it is primary.

Money has its limitations; while it may buy quantity, there is something beyond it, and that is "quality."

When the practice of a profession touching the arts is assumed, certain obligations to the public concerning quality and beyond money-making are also assumed, and without their faithful discharge the professional man degenerates to the weakest type of social menial in the entire system,—an industrial parasite.

An architect practises a Fine Art as a profession, with the Commercial and the Scientific of his time as his technique. Men are his tools.

In this age of "quantity" there is a growing tendency on the part of the public to disregard the architect in favor of the plan-factory magnate or architectural broker, and there is consequent confusion in the mind of the young architect of to-day and of to-morrow as to the sound constitution of his ideal, if that ideal is to be consistent with the "success" every man of him hopes to achieve. This confusion exists, and naturally enough, because the topography of his field of action has changed. It has changed to such an extent that in the letter, at least, the antique professional standard he may not recognize if he would. But the spirit of practice in the old field is still sound to the core,—the spirit that made of the professional man a champion of finer forces in the lives of his people.

The influence chiefly responsible for this change and most easily recognized is that of Science and its Commercialism.

The tremendous forward march of scientific attainment with attendant new forces and resources, cultivation of the head at cost to the heart, of mind and matter at the expense of the emotions;— which has nevertheless given to him new and masterful tools that demand of him their proper use, and have taken from him temporarily his power to so use them.

Because he has failed to realize and grasp his situation in its new bearings, he is not quite like his brother the artist,—a "thing afraid" of organization and its symbol the machine; but the architect, the master of creative effort whose province it was to make imperishable record of the noblest in the life of his race in his time, for the time being has been caught in the commercial rush and whirl, and hypnotized into trying to be the commercial himself. He has dragged his ancient monuments to the market places, tortured them with ribs of steel, twisted and unstrung them, set them up on pins, and perforated them until he has left them—not a rag!

He has degenerated to a fakir. A fakir who flatters thin business imbecility with "Art architecture shop fronts" worn in the fashion of the old "dickie," or panders to silly women his little artistic sweets. His "Art is upon the 'town' to be chucked beneath the chin by every passing gallant, coaxed within the drawing room of the period, and there betrayed as a proof of culture and refinement." [2]

Do you wonder at the prestige of the plan factory when architecture has become a commodity,—"a thing" to be applied like a poultice or a porous plaster? Do you wonder that architecture becomes of less and less consequence to the public, and that the architect has small standing except as he measures his success by the volume of business he transacts?

Divorced from fine art, the architect is something yet to be classified, though he is tagged with a license in Illinois. So is the banana pedler and the chiropodist.

Do you wonder that his people demand that he be at least a good business man, a good salesman, as something that they can understand and appreciate?—when as for the commodity he is selling, it has been dead to them so long as to be unrecognizable, except by virtue of association with the dim past, and it is not quite respectable even yet to do without something of the sort.

That commodity is as dead to the salesman as to the buyer, and to the fact that the thing is more easily handled dead than alive, the salesman, captain of industry though he be, owes his existence. In business it is in the stock pattern that fortunes are made:— so in architecture it is in the ready-made article that the money lies, altered to fit by any popular "sartorial artist"—the less alteration the greater the profit—and the architect.

The present generation of the successful architect has been submerged, overwhelmed by the commercialism of his time. He has yielded to the confusion and feverish demand of the moment, and has become a high-grade salesman of a high-priced imported article. His duty to the public as professional man laid aside, if it was ever realized, and merely because the public was ignorant of its claim and willing to buy even if the paint came off and the features peeled.

What has been gained by his feverish haste to offer his art on the altar of commercial sacrifice has been quantity at expense to quality,—a general depreciation of architectural values and a corruption of the birthright of the "buyers."

In consequence, architecture to-day has not even commercial integrity; and the architect as he practises his profession is humiliated and craven.

Robbed by his own cowardice and mediocrity of his former commanding position in the arts, he hesitates between stalking his victim outright or working wires—otherwise his friends—for the "job," as his opportunity is now styled.

He joins the club and poses, or hanging to the coattails of his friends he teases for the "jobs" they may carry in their pockets, his mouth sticky and his hands dirty, pulling and working for "more." Then he starves in the lower ranks of a doubtful aristocracy unless he comes by influence in other than architectural ways,—by inheritance, by marriage, or by politics. Does a sale of property appear in a trade journal, immediately the owner is besieged by ten "first-class architects," suing for the privilege of submitting "samples free of charge," assuring the owner, meanwhile, that he would be granting a personal favor in permitting them to do so, and if the samples were not what he wanted they would love each other none the less. Or his friend drops in shortly after the owner decides to build and incidentally mentions so and so as a good fellow and a winning architect. His wife, perhaps, has had influence brought to bear before he gets home, and while against the principles of the architect to work for nothing, yet the combination is of such a friendly nature as to form a special case, and "sketches," in this instance, in place of "samples" are finally submitted to all intents and purposes as before, but a little higher in the social scale, inasmuch as the method is less rude and abrupt.

The latest development is the hiring of a professional promoter by the year to drum up "trade"—mine and counter-mine the social system with pitfalls for the unwary to be ensnared for the practice of his principal. And talk to the best of him concerning "professional" advertising, making capital of himself in subtle telling ways—poor devil, the naiveté of some of him would wring the tear of pity from commerce herself. How many architects would live (and they are just the number that *should* live) if they depended upon the work that came to them because of intelligent, critical appreciation of actual qualifications or work performed? There would be a good many, but probably about 7 per cent of the profession. There is usually the maneuver, the pull, sometimes methods more open, but no more weak and shameful.

Because this matter of architecture itself has become of little moment to the average client, architecture as a Fine Art is really out of it, and for the present architecture as a commodity is a case of friendly favor and interference, or a matter of "fashion."

The fact that all this has become so generally accepted as good form is proof of the architect's danger and the damnable weakness of his position.

Another feature of his present plight is that not wholly respecting himself (how can he?) he is apt to be a hypersensitive individual, and like other unfortunates who depend upon pre-eminence of personality to get in the way of "the choosers" he is interested in pretty much everything as long as he counts one, and at that No. 1; none of his bloom or luster is to be rubbed off by contact. So, concerted effort in matters touching the welfare of his profession is rare among him. Perhaps this is in the nature of the proposition.

There are intelligent architects who argue that only the selfish few give value to art, the high lights only give value to the pattern of the fabric; but I believe it is because of warp and woof, undertone and motive, that he has any value as a "high light," and that type of individualism is one of the superstitions he must shed before he comes to his own.

The architect, so-called to-day, is struggling in a general depression in the level of his art, owing to the unknown character of the country patiently awaiting his exploration, prophesied by the past, but of which no map may yet be made, and of which no chart has been provided by the schools.

He is complacent inanity personified, and counts not at all; or blinded by the baser elements of commerce, choked by greed, goaded by ambition for "success" of the current type, the feverish unrest, common to false ideals, racks his bones and wastes his substance until he finally settles, dazed and empty, in his muddy tracks, which amounts, I suppose, to giving the people what they want.

For the generalization of the situation, then, the architect is rapidly becoming accepted as a middle-man, or broker, with the business instinct and ability, but who can have no business integrity because of the nature of his self-imposed occupation. He sells the public ready-made imported architecture that he himself buys in a "job lot" of unfortunates in a "home" which he establishes to protect them from a condition which he himself has developed and fostered. This architecture is applied to his client's condition as a poultice or porous plaster would be applied to his aching back, and is accepted with a clamor for "more" through lack of acquaintance with the real thing, lack of an ideal and of educational force in the profession itself. Meanwhile the younger aspirant for better things is either assimilated by the winners, plucked and shoved behind the scenes with the unfortunate, or settles down to give the people what they want, which simply means producing more of the type the plan factory fashions.

An example of a once noble profession prostituted by a "commercial knight of untiring industry,"[3] abandoned to her fate by the "architect" (in quotation marks), who shrugs his shoulders, looks aghast, and contributes inocuous expectation of her ability "to pull out" (and pull him out too) to the general blight.

And why this net-work of cross purposes?

Is it because the architect is now confronted with a condition which they say demands a combination of two of him and a corps of trained experts, where before one was absolute?

Is it because he is now in a position that demands that an intricate commercial machine be perfected to carry into effect an idea?

Or is it because architecture is a great thing in small hands, and ideals, noble theories, if you will, "the rails of the track on which the car of Progress runs," have fallen to disrepute?

"Give me a great thought," cried the dying Herder, "that I may refresh myself with it."[4]

He was of the stuff from which an *architect* is made.

The regeneration of architecture does not lie in the hands of classicist, or fashion-monger of the East nor of the West.

Their work is almost written at its length, and no spark of life and but a shroud of artistic respectability will cling to it half a century hence.

It is but archæological dry bones bleaching in the sun!

America will regard it as crude,—Chicago, even now, regards her County Courthouse[5] as something weak and servile, an insult to the people who entrusted to chosen ones the fruit of honest toil and were betrayed to perpetuate the degenerate art of a degenerate people. The American nation has a heart and backbone of its own, and is rapidly forming a mind of its own. It has not yet been taught self-expression except in the matter of dollars and cents, and recently of war. Presently Light, Grace, and Ethics, true to as virile an individuality as history has known, will come as naturally to her as the breath of life that is already hers; and then, oh, ye Stuffed Prophets of Plethoric "Success"! will she look with pride upon the time that you bedizened her with borrowed finery; pierced her ears for borrowed ornaments; taught her to speak with a lisp, and mince in her gait? No! Your very success was your undoing and her disgrace.

In her new code no one man will be entrusted with the amount of work that occasioned the "plan factory." As no Rockefeller may rise to a legitimate point of vantage that would justify the control of such a vast share of the earth's resources, *how unspeakably vulgar and illegitimate will it be for one man to undertake in the Fine Arts more than he can characterize in noble fashion as a work of Art!*

The plan factory is the product of a raw commercial state, perhaps a necessary evil to be passed through as we pass through the dark before day.

Perhaps the epidemic of Renaissance, French, Dutch, and English, that encumbers the land was a contagious malady such as little children bring from school. Soonest over, soonest mended.

It is argued that we are witnessing the same development in architecture that we see is legitimate enough as a means to an end in trade, as the department store and the trust. But it is not in architecture a development, but a *reflection*, or reflex action, that is passing but causing painful confusion. It is making of art a network of cross purposes, but temporarily.

Art will reign as long as life, and greater than ever her prestige, when the harmony between commerce, science, and art is better understood. It is this Harmony, this Commercialism, that the younger architect should strive to understand and appreciate, for it is the measure of his technique in his new field; but he should strive to understand it as a "master," not as a "huckster"; to poetize and deify it as an instrument in his hands.

He should help his lame, halt, and blind profession again to its place by respecting his art and respecting himself; by making the solution of problems that come fairly his way such as will compel the recognition that there is no commercial dignity without that kind of art; that will make the man of business see that a Greek temple made over to trade is an unhallowed joke, and that he is the butt when genuine dignity and beauty might be his for less money; that will make the householder realize that if he would live in a Louis XV environment, he is but a step removed from the savage, with a ring in his nose; and make it felt that architecture is not a matter of the scene painting of periods, nor a mere matter of scene painting in any sense whatever.

Give back the slogan "a good copy is better than a poor original" to those whose desire for "success" out-measured their capacity to perform and who framed it in self-defense.

"A poor thing but mine own" is better stuff for men when coupled with reverence and honesty, and carries the fundamental principle of harmonious independence graven over the gate of the new country promised of old.

The architect should help the people to feel that architecture is a destroyer of vulgarity, sham, and pretense, a benefactor of tired nerves and jaded souls, an educator in the higher ideals and better purposes of yesterday, to-day, and to-morrow.

Such an art only is characteristic of the better phase of commercialism itself, and is true to American independence, America's hatred of cant, hypocrisy, and base imitation. When once Americans are taught in terms of building construction the principles so dear to them at their firesides, the architect will have arrived.

But his own education is a matter of the greatest concern. We all catch a glimpse of the magnificent awaiting him, but how to prepare him is a more difficult matter.

It is for a higher law and more freedom in his architectural school that we plead, not anarchy—a deeper sense of the significance to his Art of Nature, manly independence, and vigorous imagination, a truer reverence for his precedent. He should learn method of attack; have cultivated in him the quality that gets at an architectural proposition from the inside outward, for and by itself. He should be a thinking quantity when he leaves school, standing on his own legs,—such as they are,—with ears and eyes wide open, receptive, eager, and enthusiastic; his faculties sharpened by metaphysical drill, his heart wide open to beauty, whether of a specific brand or no; and a *worker* first, last, and all the time a *worker;* his mind alive to opportunity, knowing the direction in which it lies, gauging his own fitness in relation to it; far-sighted enough to decline the opportunity that he was unfitted to undertake if it should come to him (and many such do come to all architects); courageous enough to decline it and wait for one "his size." And when it came he would make it count without making his client pay too large for a share of his education in the field.

He would gain experience and strength, and build up solidly, if slowly; and the respect and confidence would in time be his that would make his personality a power for the architectural good of his country.

His experience is to be gained only by solving problems for and by themselves.

Advice never built a character worth the name, though advice is good.

So an architect may practise architecture extensively with book and precedent, and die without experience, without a character.

The man who has worked out the salvation of a summer cottage on his merits, held the conditions in rational solution, and expressed them in terms of wood and plaster, with beauty germane to the proposition, has more valuable experience than he who builds a city with the pomp and circumstance of established forms.

The education of the architect should commence when he is two days old—"three days is too much"—and continue until he passes beyond, leaving his experiments by the wayside to serve his profession as warning signs or guide-posts.

The kindergarten circle of sympathetic discernment should be drawn about him when he is born, and he should be brought into contact with Nature by prophet and seer until abiding sympathy with her is his. He should be a true child of hers, in touch with her moods, discerning her principles and harmonics until his soul overflows with love of Nature in the highest, and his mind is stored with a technical knowledge of her forms and processes.

Braced and stayed by that, he should move into the thick of civilization to study man and his methods in the things that are his and the ways thereof, taking his averages and unraveling seeming inconsistencies, shoulder to shoulder with his fellow-men as one with them.

Meanwhile, as his discipline, he should acquire the technical skill of the mill, forge, and try-pit of commerce in the light of science; study the beauty of the world as created by the hand of man, as his birthright and his advantage; finding his passion and delight in various initial steps of composition with the encouraging guidance of a catholic-minded, Nature-wise, and loving master.

In short, a master that would make the distinction between Fine Art and Fine Artisanship plain.

Now he is taught certain architectural phraseology of form and color dubbed "grammar" by his professors, and much foreign technique.

If teaching him that minutes and modules of the architraves and cornice of one type in certain measure make Greek, and of another type in combination make Roman, and when they corrode each other the result is "Renaissance"—there he is taught "grammar."

I imagine it to be a more difficult matter to teach him the "grammar" of Goth and Moore; but architecture has no business primarily with this "grammar," which, at its best, I suppose, might mean putting the architectural together correctly, but as taught means putting the architectural together as predetermined by fashion of previous races and conditions.

So the young student is eternally damned by the dogmas of Vignola and Vitruvius, provided with a fine repertoire of stock phrases as architectural capital and technique enough to make them go if he is let alone and conditions are favorable, which he never is and they never are.

He comes to think these fine phrases and this technique are architecture, and sells both in judicious mixture to the "buyers" as such with the circumstance of the "scholar" and the "classical," and he would be shocked if told that he is a swindler.

He is sent out a callow, complacent fledgling, sure of his precedent, afraid of little but failure to "succeed," puffed up with architectural "Excelsior," and wadded with "deafening," to become soaked and sodden in the field, hopelessly out of shape.

The architect primarily should have something of his own to say, or keep silence.

There are more legitimate fields of action for him than the field of architecture.

If he has that something to say in noble form, gracious line, and living color, each expression will have a "grammar" of its own, using the term in its best sense, and will speak the universal language of Beauty in no circumscribed series of set architectural phrase as used by people in other times, although a language in harmony with elemental laws to be deduced from the beautiful of all peoples in all time.

This elemental law and order of the beautiful is as much more profound than the accepted grammatical of phrase in architecture as Nature is deeper than Fashion.

Let the young student add to his wisdom the strength and wisdom of past ages; that is his advantage. *But let him live his own life, nor mistake for the Spirit the Letter.*

I would see him relieved of the unnatural, educational incubus that sowed the seed of the plan factory and nurtured the false ideals that enable it to exist.

I would see him relieved of architectural lockjaw, not by prying the set teeth of his Art apart with a crowbar, nor by cracking its jaws with a sledge-hammer, but by a realization that life was given the architect that architecture may grow and expand naturally as a noble Fine Art and as becomes a free-hearted, vigorous young people.

It may be that the very cosmopolitan nature of our nation will prevent a narrow confirmation of any one type.

I hope that we are destined to greater variety in unity than has yet existed in the art of a great people.

The very strength of individuality developed in a free nation, and the richness of our inheritance, will find expression in more diverse and splendid ways than could be expected of a more narrowly nurtured race. Yet it will find expression in an art that is indigenous and characteristic as an architecture measured by the laws of Fine Art, the hardy grace of the wild flower, perhaps, rather than the cultivated richness of the rose, but a further contribution to the art of the world,—not a servile extraction!

The architect has a hard road to travel and far to go.

He should know what he is to encounter in the field, and be trained to meet it by men who have faced it in all its ugly significance with unconquerable soul and clear vision.

He should understand that to go into the field penniless with a family to support means the ultimate addition of one more craven to the ranks, unless some chance saves him, or his fortitude is of the stuff that will see his wife and children suffer for ideals that may seem ridiculous, and are to the average mind incomprehensible.

If he goes single-handed he must be content to walk behind, to work and wait.

The work to be done by the young architect entering the lists would better be done by him whose board and lodging is assured for life, and whose communication with his base of supplies is not apt to be cut off.

He is going into a country almost abandoned to the enemy.

Yet the hardy pioneer who takes his architectural life in hand and fares boldly forth in quest of his ideal, not scorning hardtack for food nor a plank for a bed,—

> Withal a soul like the bird,
> Who, pausing in her flight
> A while on boughs too slight,
> Feels them give way beneath her and yet sings,
> Knowing that she hath wings,— [6]

is perhaps the stuff from which the missionary we need is to come. The spirit that conquered Western wilds and turned them to fallow fields transmuted to the realm of Art, a boy with the heart of a king; the scent of the pine woods deep in his nostrils, sweetness and light in his soul—the erudition of the world at his fingers' ends. Will the flickering art spirit of this age produce him? If he is the stuff that architects are made of, he is not to be discouraged by limitations.

The limitations within which an artist works do grind him, and sometimes seem insurmountable; yet without these very limitations there is no art. They are at once his problems and his best friends,—his salvation in disguise.

In the arts every problem carries within, its own solution, and the only way yet discovered to reach it is a very painstaking way—to sympathetically look within the thing itself, to proceed to analyze and sift it, to extract its own consistent and essential beauty, which means its *common sense truthfully idealized.*

That is the heart of the poetry that lives in architecture.

That is what they should teach the young architect in the schools, beginning early. But the schools will have to be taught before they will ever teach him.

His scientific possibilities and demands have outrun his handmade Art as planned for him in the school curriculum. He is without lettered precedent as he stands to-day on the threshold of great development in the industrial direction of the world.

A highly organized, complex condition confronts him.

He will understand it, learn the secret of its correspondencies and their harmonics, and work with them, not against them. For his Art is of Life itself; it will endure.

Life is preparing the stuff to satisfy the coming demand; and the architect will know the capacities of modern methods, processes, and machines, and become their master. He will sense the significance to his art of the new materials that are his, of which steel is but one.

He will show in his work that he has been emancipated from the meager unit established by brick arch and stone lintel, and his imagination will transfigure to new beauty his primitive art.

He will realize that the narrow limitations of structure outlined in his precedents are too mean and small to be longer useful or binding, and that he is comparatively a free man to clothe new structural conditions in the living flesh of virile imagination.

He will write large, in beautiful character, the song of steel and steam:—

> Lord, thou hast made this world below the shadow of a
>   dream,
> And taught by time, I take it so, exceptin' always steam.
>
> Romance! Those first-class passengers, they like it very well,
> Printed and bound in little books, but why don't poets tell?
> I'm sick of all their quirks and turns, the loves and doves
>   they dream.
> Lord! Send a man like Bobbie Burns to sing the song of steam,
> To match with Scotia's noblest speech, yon orchestra sublime,
> Whereto—uplifted like the Just—the tail rods mark the time,
> The crank-throws give the double bass, the feed-pump sobs
>   and heaves;
> And now the main eccentrics start their quarrel on the
>   sheaves,
> Her time—her own appointed time—the rocking link-head
>   bides,
> Till—hear that note—the rods return, whings glimmering
>   through the guides.
> They're all away, true beat, full power, the clanging chorus
>   goes
> Clear to the tunnel where they sit, my purring dynamos.
> Interdependence absolute, foreseen, ordained, decreed,
> To work ye'll note at any tilt, on any rate of speed.
> From skylight lift to furnace bars, backed, bolted, braced,
>   and stayed,
> And singing like the morning stars for joy that they are made;
> While, out o' touch of vanity, the sweating thrust-block says:

Not unto us the praise, or man—not unto us the praise.
Now all together, hear them lift their lessons, theirs and mine:
Law, Order, Duty, and Restraint, Obedience, Discipline.
Mill, forge, and try-pit taught them that when roaring they
    arose,
And th' while I wonder if a soul was gied them wi' the blows.
Oh, for a man to weld it then in one trip-hammer strain,
Till even first-class passengers could tell the meanin' plain.

The architect will weld that strain and build that song in noble
line and form.
He will write that record for all time.
He may not last to "judge her line or take her curve,"[7] but he
may say that he, too, has lived and worked; whether he has done
well or ill, he will have worked as a man and given a shoulder to
his fellows climbing after.

NOTES

1. From "Samuel T. Coleridge" by Elbert Hubbard (1856–1915), American author, editor, and designer, in his *Little Journeys to the Homes of the Great*
   (1895–1909), vol. 5, *Little Journeys to the Homes of English Authors*.
2. From James McNeill Whistler (1834–1903), American painter, the "Ten O'-
   Clock" public lecture at Prince's Hall, London, February 20, 1885, published
   in his *Gentle Art of Making Enemies* (1890). The passage reads: "Art is upon
   the Town!—to be chucked under the chin, by the passing gallant!—to be
   enticed within the gates of the house-holder—to be coaxed into company, as
   a proof of culture and refinement!"
3. From Whistler's booklet, *The Baronet and the Butterfly: A Valentine with a
   Verdict* (1890).
4. Paul Friedrich Richter (aka Jean Paul, 1763–1825), German novelist and
   humorist, reported that Johann Gottfried Herder (1744–1803), German
   philosopher and poet, said this on his deathbed.

5. Wright may have been referring to the Cook County Criminal Courts Building (1892, Chicago) by Otto H. Metz.

6. From Victor Hugo's poem "Dans l'Église de ***" ("In the Church of . . .") in *Les Chants du Crépuscule (Twilight Songs)*, 1835.

7. This line and the lengthy passage above are from Rudyard Kipling's "McAndrew's Hymn," first published in *Scribner's Magazine*, December 1894.

TWO

The Art and Craft of the Machine

(1901)

This is one of Wright's most famous and enduring speeches, largely because of its early recognition that modern machinery would expand architectural possibility. Delivered to the Chicago Arts and Crafts Society at Hull House on March 6, 1901 (then to the Western Society of Engineers meeting in Chicago on March 20), Wright urged his listeners to collaborate with sympathetic manufacturers for the aesthetic and social benefit of the nation.

Founded by Jane Addams and Ellen Gates Starr in 1889, Hull House was a pioneering "settlement house" patterned on East London's Toynbee Hall which offered educational, political, and social assistance to working-class neighbors, many of them recent migrants. The Arts and Crafts Society—part of an Anglo-American "movement" of that name primarily influenced by William Morris and John Ruskin—met there regularly to discuss, and with its own members' artistic endeavors to demonstrate, how the drudgery of factory labor and harsh social consequences of industrialization might be ameliorated.

Perhaps because it was also Wright's objective to harness the machine for humane purposes, he seems to have absorbed some of the antiprivilege, antimaterialistic, even antirationalist aspects of the still vigorous Romantic impulse originating in the eighteenth century, and his prose here reflects that sensibility. When he asserts, for

example, that "the Machine . . . is no more or less than the principle
of organic growth working irresistibly the Will of Life through the
medium of Man," he presupposes the existence of spiritual, natural,
and emotional forces humanity might channel but not control.
His romantic sensibility was such that when he calls Chicago
"the greatest of machines" and the machine the "Forerunner of
Democracy," he may not have noticed, or cared about, the implica-
tion that the city fostered democracy. Later in life he would repeat-
edly insist that nature, not the city, was the preferred setting for
democratic growth (see Document 13).
But that was for the future. Wright's intention here was to con-
vince the public, particularly artists to whom he spoke and architects
in whose journal this speech was published, that thanks to the ma-
chine a new day had dawned.

From the Chicago Architectural Club Catalogue of the 14th Annual Exhibition *(1901).*

As we work along our various ways, there takes shape within us, in
some sort, an ideal—something we are to become—some work to
be done. This, I think, is denied to very few, and we begin really to
live only when the thrill of this ideality moves us in what we will
to accomplish. In the years which have been devoted in my own
life to working out in stubborn materials a feeling for the beautiful, in the vortex of distorted complex conditions, a hope has
grown stronger with the experience of each year, amounting now
to a gradually deepening conviction that in the Machine lies the
only future of art and craft—as I believe, a glorious future; that
the Machine is, in fact, the metamorphosis of ancient art and
craft; that we are at last face to face with the machine—the modern Sphinx—whose riddle the artist must solve if he would that

art live—for his nature holds the key. For one, I promise "whatever gods may be" to lend such energy and purpose as I may possess to help make that meaning plain; to return again and again to the task whenever and wherever need be; for this plain duty is thus relentlessly marked out for the artist in this, the Machine Age, although there is involved an adjustment to cherished gods, perplexing and painful in the extreme; the fire of many long-honored ideals shall go down to ashes to reappear, phœnix like, with new purposes.

The great ethics of the Machine are as yet, in the main, beyond the ken of the artist or student of sociology; but the artist mind may now approach the nature of this thing from experience, which has become the commonplace of his field, to suggest, in time, I hope, to prove, that the machine is capable of carrying to fruition high ideals in art—higher than the world has yet seen!

Disciples of William Morris cling to an opposite view. Yet William Morris himself deeply sensed the danger to art of the transforming force whose sign and symbol is the machine, and though of the new art we eagerly seek he sometimes despaired, he quickly renewed his hope.

He plainly foresaw that a blank in the fine arts would follow the inevitable abuse of new-found power, and threw himself body and soul into the work of bridging it over by bringing into our lives afresh the beauty of art as she had been, that the new art to come might not have dropped too many stitches nor have unraveled what would still be useful to her.

That he had abundant faith in the new art his every essay will testify.

That he miscalculated the machine does not matter. He did sublime work for it when he pleaded so well for the process of elimination its abuse had made necessary; when he fought the innate vulgarity of theocratic impulse in art as opposed to democratic; and when he preached the gospel of simplicity.

All artists love and honor William Morris.

He did the best in his time for art and will live in history as the great socialist, together with Ruskin, the great moralist: a significant fact worth thinking about, that the two great reformers of modern times professed the artist.

The machine these reformers protested, because the sort of luxury which is born of greed had usurped it and made of it a terrible engine of enslavement, deluging the civilized world with a murderous ubiquity, which plainly enough was the damnation of their art and craft.

It had not then advanced to the point which now so plainly indicates that it will surely and swiftly, by its own momentum, undo the mischief it has made, and the usurping vulgarians as well.

Nor was it so grown as to become apparent to William Morris, the grand democrat, that the machine was the great forerunner of democracy.

The ground plan of this thing is now grown to the point where the artist must take it up no longer as a protest: genius must progressively dominate the work of the contrivance it has created; to lend a useful hand in building afresh the "Fairness of the Earth." [1]

That the Machine has dealt Art in the grand old sense a death-blow, none will deny.

The evidence is too substantial.

Art in the grand old sense—meaning Art in the sense of structural tradition, whose craft is fashioned upon the handicraft ideal, ancient or modern; an art wherein this form and that form as structural parts were laboriously joined in such a way as to beautifully emphasize the manner of the joining: the million and one ways of beautifully satisfying bare structural necessities, which have come down to us chiefly through the books as "Art."

For the purpose of suggesting hastily and therefore crudely wherein the machine has sapped the vitality of this art, let us assume Architecture in the old sense as a fitting representative of Traditional-art, and Printing as a fitting representation of the Machine.

What printing—the machine—has done for architecture—the fine art—will have been done in measure of time for all art immediately fashioned upon the early handicraft ideal.

With a masterful hand Victor Hugo, a noble lover and a great student of architecture, traces her fall in "Notre Dame."

The prophecy of Frollo, that "The book will kill the edifice," [2] I remember was to me as a boy one of the grandest sad things of the world.

After seeking the origin and tracing the growth of architecture in superb fashion, showing how in the middle ages all the intellectual forces of the people converged to one point—architecture—he shows how, in the life of that time, whoever was born poet became an architect. All other arts simply obeyed and placed themselves under the discipline of architecture. They were the workmen of the great work. The architect, the poet, the master, summed up in his person the sculpture that carved his façades, painting which illuminated his walls and windows, music which set his bells to pealing and breathed into his organs—there was nothing which was not forced in order to make something of itself in that time, to come and frame itself in the edifice.

Thus down to the time of Gutenberg architecture is the principal writing—the universal writing of humanity.

In the great granite books begun by the Orient, continued by Greek and Roman antiquity, the middle ages wrote the last page.

So to enunciate here only summarily a process it would require volumes to develop, down to the fifteenth century the chief register of humanity is architecture.

In the fifteenth century everything changes.

Human thought discovers a mode of perpetuating itself, not only more resisting than architecture, but still more simple and easy.

Architecture is dethroned.

Gutenberg's letters of lead are about to supersede Orpheus' letters of stone.

The book is about to kill the edifice.

The invention of printing was the greatest event in history.

It was the first great machine, after the great city.

It is human thought stripping off one form and donning another.

Printed, thought is more imperishable than ever—it is volatile, indestructible.

As architecture it was solid; it is now alive; it passes from duration in point of time to immortality.

Cut the primitive bed of a river abruptly, with a canal hollowed out beneath its level, and the river will desert its bed.

See how architecture now withers away, how little by little it becomes lifeless and bare. How one feels the water sinking, the sap departing, the thought of the times and people withdrawing from it. The chill is almost imperceptible in the fifteenth century, the press is yet weak, and at most draws from architecture a super-abundance of life, but with the beginning of the sixteenth century, the malady of architecture is visible. It becomes classic art in a miserable manner; from being indigenous, it becomes Greek and Roman; from being true and modern, it becomes pseudo-classic.

It is this decadence which we call the Renaissance.

It is the setting sun which we mistake for dawn.

It has now no power to hold the other arts; so they emancipate themselves, break the yoke of the architect, and take themselves off, each i[n] its own direction.

One would liken it to an empire dismembered at the death of its Alexander, and whose provinces become kingdoms.

Sculpture becomes statuary, the image trade becomes painting, the canon becomes music. Hence Raphael, Angelo, and those splendors of the dazzling sixteenth century.

Nevertheless, when the sun of the middle ages is completely set, architecture grows dim, becomes more and more effaced. The printed book, the gnawing worm of the edifice, sucks and devours it. It is petty, it is poor, it is nothing.

Reduced to itself, abandoned by other arts because human thought is abandoning it, it summons bunglers in place of artists. It is miserably perishing.

Meanwhile, what becomes of printing?

All the life, leaving architecture, comes to it. In proportion as architecture ebbs and flows, printing swells and grows. That capital of forces which human thought had been expending in building is hereafter to be expended in books; and architecture, as it was, is dead, irretrievably slain by the printed book; slain because it endures for a shorter time; slain because human thought has found a more simple medium of expression, which costs less in human effort; because human thought has been rendered volatile and indestructible, reaching uniformly and irresistibly the four corners of the earth and for all.

Thenceforth, if architecture rise again, reconstruct, as Hugo prophesies she may begin to do in the latter days of the nineteenth century, she will no longer be mistress, she will be one of the arts, never again *the* art; and printing—the Machine—remains the second Tower of Babel of the human race.

So the organic process, of which the majestic decline of Architecture is only one case in point, has steadily gone on down to the present time, and still goes on, weakening the hold of the artist upon the people, drawing off from his rank poets and scientists until architecture is but a little, poor knowledge of archeology, and the average of art is reduced to the gasping poverty of imitative realism; until the whole letter of Tradition, the vast fabric of precedent, in the flesh, which has increasingly confused the art ideal while the machine has been growing to power, is a beautiful corpse from which the spirit has flown. The spirit that has flown is the spirit of the new art, but has failed the modern artist, for he has lost it for hundreds of years in his lust for the *letter*, the beautiful body of art made too available by the machine.

So the artist craft wanes.

Craft that will not see that human thought is stripping off one form and donning another, and artists are everywhere, whether catering to the leisure class of old England or ground beneath the heel of commercial abuse here in the great West, the unwilling symptoms of the inevitable, organic nature of the machine they combat, the hell-smoke of the factories they scorn to understand.

And, invincible, triumphant, the machine goes on, gathering force and knitting the material necessities of mankind ever closer into a universal automatic fabric; the engine, the motor, and the battle-ship, the works of art of the century!

The Machine is Intellect mastering the drudgery of earth that the plastic art may live; that the margin of leisure and strength by which man's life upon the earth can be made beautiful, may immeasurably widen; its function ultimately to emancipate human expression!

It is a universal educator, surely raising the level of human intelligence, so carrying within itself the power to destroy, by its own momentum, the greed which in Morris' time and still in our own time turns it to a deadly engine of enslavement. The only comfort left the poor artist, side-tracked as he is, seemingly is a mean one; the thought that the very selfishness which man's early art idealized, now reduced to its lowest terms, is swiftly and surely destroying itself through the medium of the Machine.

•

The artist's present plight is a sad one, but may he truthfully say that society is less well off because Architecture, or even Art, as it was, is dead, and printing, or the Machine, lives? Every age has done its work, produced its art with the best tools or contrivances it knew, the tools most successful in saving the most precious thing in the world—human effort. Greece used the chattel slave as the essential tool of its art and civilization. This tool we have discarded, and we would refuse the return of Greek art upon the terms of its restoration, because we insist now upon a basis of Democracy.

Is it not more likely that the medium of artistic expression itself has broadened and changed until a new definition and new direction must be given the art activity of the future, and that the Machine has finally made for the artist, whether he will yet own it or not, a splendid distinction between the Art of old and the Art to come? A distinction made by the tool which frees human labor, lengthens and broadens the life of the simplest man, thereby the basis of the Democracy upon which we insist.

To shed some light upon this distinction, let us take an instance in the field naturally ripened first by the machine—the commercial field.

The tall modern office building is the machine pure and simple.

We may here sense an advanced stage of a condition surely entering all art for all time; its already triumphant glare in the deadly struggle taking place here between the machine and the art of structural tradition reveals "art" torn and hung upon the steel frame of commerce, a forlorn head upon a pike, a solemn warning to architects and artists the world over.

We must walk blindfolded not to see that all that this magnificent resource of machine and material has brought us so far is a complete, broadcast degradation of every type and form sacred to the art of old; a pandemonium of tin masks, huddled deformities, and decayed methods; quarreling, lying, and cheating, with hands at each other's throats—or in each other's pockets; and none of the people who do these things, who pay for them or use them, know what they mean, feeling only—when they feel at all—that what is most truly like the past is the safest and therefore the best; as typical Marshall Field, speaking of his new building, has frankly said: "A good copy is the best we can do."[3]

A pitiful insult, art and craft!

With this mine of industrial wealth at our feet we have no power to use it except to the perversion of our natural resources? A confession of shame which the merciful ignorance of the yet material frame of things mistakes for glorious achievement.

We half believe in our artistic greatness ourselves when we toss up a pantheon to the god of money in a night or two, or pile up a mammoth aggregation of Roman monuments, sarcophagi and Greek temples for a postoffice in a year or two—the patient retinue of the machine pitching in with terrible effectiveness to consummate this unhallowed ambition—this insult to ancient gods. The delicate, impressionable facilities of terra cotta becoming imitative blocks and voussoirs of tool-marked stone, badgered into all manner of structural gymnastics, or else ignored in vain endeavor to be honest; and granite blocks, cut in the fashion of the followers of Phidias,[4] cunningly arranged about the steel beams and shafts, to look "real"—leaning heavily upon an inner skeleton of steel for support from floor to floor, which strains beneath the "reality" and would fain, I think, lie down to die of shame.

The "masters"—ergo, the fashionable followers of Phidias— have been trying to make this wily skeleton of steel seem seventeen sorts of "architecture" at once, when all the world knows—except the "masters"—that it is not one of them.

See now, how an element—the vanguard of the new art—has entered here, which the structural-art equation cannot satisfy without downright lying and ignoble cheating.

This element is the structural necessity reduced to a skeleton, complete in itself without the craftsman's touch. At once the million and one little ways of satisfying this necessity beautifully, coming to us chiefly through the books as the traditional art of building, vanish away—become history. The artist is emancipated to work his will with a rational freedom unknown to the laborious art of structural tradition—no longer tied to the meager unit of brick arch and stone lintel, nor hampered by the grammatical phrase of their making—but he cannot use his freedom.

His tradition cannot think.

He will not think.

His scientific brother has put it to him before he is ready.

The modern tall office building problem is one representative problem of the machine. The only rational solutions it has received in the world may be counted upon the fingers of one hand. The fact that a great portion of our "architects" and "artists" are shocked by them to the point of offense is as valid an objection as that of a child refusing wholesome food because his stomach becomes dyspeptic from over-much unwholesome pastry—albeit he be the cook himself.

We may object to the mannerism of these buildings, but we can take no exception to their manner nor hide from their evident truth.

The steel frame has been recognized as a legitimate basis for a simple, sincere clothing of plastic material that idealizes its purpose without structural pretense.

This principle has at last been recognized in architecture, and though the masters refuse to accept it as architecture at all, it is a glimmer in a darkened field—the first sane word that has been said in Art for the Machine.

The Art of old idealized a Structural Necessity—now rendered obsolete and unnatural by the Machine—and accomplished it through man's joy in the labor of his hands.

The new will weave for the necessities of mankind, which his Machine will have mastered, a robe of ideality no less truthful, but more poetical, with a rational freedom made possible by the machine, beside which the art of old will be as the sweet, plaintive wail of the pipe to the outpouring of full orchestra.

It will clothe Necessity with the living flesh of virile imagination, as the living flesh lends living grace to the hard and bony human skeleton.

The new will pass from the possession of kings and classes to the every-day lives of all—from duration in point of time to immortality.

This distinction is one to be felt now rather than clearly defined.

The definition is the poetry of this Machine Age, and will be written large in time; but the more we, as artists, examine into this premonition, the more we will find the utter helplessness of old forms to satisfy new conditions, and the crying need of the machine for plastic treatment—a pliant, sympathetic treatment of its needs that the body of structural precedent cannot yield.

To gain further suggestive evidence of this, let us turn to the Decorative Arts—the immense middle-ground of all art now mortally sickened by the Machine—sickened that it may slough the art ideal of the constructural art for the plasticity of the new art—the Art of Democracy.

Here we find the most deadly perversion of all—the magnificent prowess of the machine bombarding the civilized world with the mangled corpses of strenuous horrors that once stood for cultivated luxury—standing now for a species of fatty degeneration simply vulgar.

Without regard to first principles or common decency, the whole letter of tradition—that is, ways of doing things rendered wholly obsolete and unnatural by the machine—is recklessly fed into its rapacious maw until you may buy reproductions for

ninety-nine cents at "The Fair"[5] that originally cost ages of toil
and cultivation, worth now intrinsically nothing—that are harm-
ful parasites befogging the sensibilities of our natures, belittling
and falsifying any true perception of normal beauty the Creator
may have seen fit to implant in us.

The idea of fitness to purpose, harmony between form and use
with regard to any of these things, is possessed by very few, and utilized by them as a protest chiefly—a protest against the machine!

As well blame Richard Croker for the political iniquity of
America.[6]

As "Croker is the creature and not the creator" of political evil,
so the machine is the creature and not the creator of this iniquity;
and with this difference—that the machine has noble possibilities
unwillingly forced to degradation in the name of the artistic; the
machine, as far as its artistic capacity is concerned, is itself the
crazed victim of the artist who works while he waits, and the artist
who waits while he works.

There is a nice distinction between the two.

Neither class will unlock the secrets of the beauty of this time.

They are clinging sadly to the old order, and would wheedle
the giant frame of things back to its childhood or forward to its
second childhood, while this Machine Age is suffering for the
artist who accepts, works, and sings as he works, with the joy of
the *here* and *now!*

We want the man who eagerly seeks and finds, or blames himself if he fails to find, the beauty of this time; who distinctly accepts as a singer and a prophet; for no man may work while he
waits or wait as he works in the sense that William Morris' great
work was legitimately done—in the sense that most art and craft
of to-day is an echo; the time when such work was useful has gone.

Echoes are by nature decadent.

Artists who feel toward Modernity and the Machine now as
William Morris and Ruskin were justified in feeling then, had best

distinctly wait and work sociologically where great work may still be done by them. In the field of art activity they will do distinct harm. Already they have wrought much miserable mischief.

If the artist will only open his eyes he will see that the machine he dreads has made it possible to wipe out the mass of meaningless torture to which mankind, in the name of the artistic, has been more or less subjected since time began; for that matter, has made possible a cleanly strength, an ideality and a poetic fire that the art of the world has not yet seen; for the machine, the process now smooths away the necessity for petty structural deceits, soothes this wearisome struggle to make things seem what they are not, and can never be; satisfies the simple term of the modern art equation as the ball of clay in the sculptor's hand yields to his desire—comforting forever this realistic, brain-sick masquerade we are wont to suppose art.

William Morris pleaded well for simplicity as the basis of all true art. Let us understand the significance to art of that word—SIMPLICITY—for it is vital to the Art of the Machine.

We may find, in place of the genuine thing we have striven for, an affectation of the naïve, which we should detest as we detest a full-grown woman with baby mannerisms.

English art is saturated with it, from the brand-new imitation of the old house that grew and rambled from period to period to the rain-tub standing beneath the eaves.

In fact, most simplicity following the doctrines of William Morris is a protest; as a protest, well enough; but the highest form of simplicity is not simple in the sense that the infant intelligence is simple—nor, for that matter, the side of a barn.

A natural revulsion of feeling leads us from the meaningless elaboration of to-day to lay too great stress on mere platitudes, quite as a clean sheet of paper is a relief after looking at a series of bad drawings—but simplicity is not merely a neutral or a negative quality.

Simplicity in art, rightly understood, is a synthetic, positive quality, in which we may see evidence of mind, breadth of scheme, wealth of detail, and withal a sense of completeness found in a tree or a flower. A work may have the delicacies of a rare orchid or the stanch fortitude of the oak, and still be simple. A thing to be simple needs only to be true to itself in [the] organic sense.

With this ideal of simplicity, let us glance hastily at a few instances of the machine and see how it has been forced by false ideals to do violence to this simplicity; how it has made possible the highest simplicity, rightly understood and so used. As perhaps wood is most available of all homely materials and therefore, naturally, the most abused—let us glance at wood.

Machinery has been invented for no other purpose than to imitate, as closely as possible, the wood-carving of the early ideal—with the immediate result that no ninety-nine cent piece of furniture is salable without some horrible botchwork meaning nothing unless it means that art and craft have combined to fix in the mind of the masses the old hand-carved chair as the *ne plus ultra* of the ideal.

The miserable, lumpy tribute to this perversion which Grand Rapids[7] alone yields would mar the face of Art beyond repair; to say nothing of the elaborate and fussy joinery of posts, spindles, jig sawed beams and braces, butted and strutted, to outdo the sentimentality of the already over-wrought antique product.

Thus is the wood-working industry glutted, except in rarest instances. The whole sentiment of early craft degenerated to a sentimentality having no longer decent significance nor commercial integrity; in fact all that is fussy, maudlin, and animal, basing its existence chiefly on vanity and ignorance.

Now let us learn from the Machine.

It teaches us that the beauty of wood lies first in its qualities as wood; no treatment that did not bring out these qualities all the time could be plastic, and therefore not appropriate—so not beautiful, the machine teaches us, if we have left it to the machine that certain simple forms and handling are suitable to bring out the beauty of wood and certain forms are not; that all wood-carving is apt to be a forcing of the material, an insult to its finer possibilities as a material having in itself intrinsically artistic properties, of which its beautiful markings is one, its texture another, its color a third.

The machine, by its wonderful cutting, shaping, smoothing, and repetitive capacity, has made it possible to so use it without waste that the poor as well as the rich may enjoy to-day beautiful surface treatments of clean, strong forms that the branch veneers of Sheraton and Chippendale only hinted at, with dire extravagance, and which the middle ages utterly ignored.

The machine has emancipated these beauties of nature in wood; made it possible to wipe out the mass of meaningless torture to which wood has been subjected since the world began, for it has been universally abused and maltreated by all peoples but the Japanese.

Rightly appreciated, is not this the very process of elimination for which Morris pleaded?

Not alone a protest, moreover, for the machine, considered only technically, if you please, has placed in artist hands the means of idealizing the true nature of wood harmoniously with man's spiritual and material needs, without waste, within reach of all.

And how fares the troop of old materials galvanized into new life by the Machine?

Our modern materials are these old materials in more plastic guise, rendered so by the Machine, itself creating the very quality needed in material to satisfy its own art equation.

We have seen in glancing at modern architecture how they fare at the hands of Art and Craft; divided and sub-divided in orderly sequence with rank and file of obedient retainers awaiting the master's behest.

Steel and iron, plastic cement and terra-cotta.

Who can sound the possibilities of this old material, burned clay, which the modern machine has rendered as sensitive to the creative brain as a dry plate to the lens—a marvelous simplifier? And this plastic covering material, cement, another simplifier, enabling the artist to clothe the structural frame with a simple, modestly beautiful robe where before he dragged in, as he does still drag, five different kinds of material to compose one little cottage, pettily arranging it in an aggregation supposed to be picturesque—as a matter of fact, millinery, to be warped and beaten by sun, wind, and rain into a variegated heap of trash.

There is the process of modern casting in metal—one of the perfected modern machines, capable of any form to which fluid will flow, to perpetuate the imagery of the most delicately poetic mind without let or hindrance—within reach of everyone, therefore insulted and outraged by the bungler forcing it to a degraded seat at his degenerate festival.

Multitudes of processes are expectantly awaiting the sympathetic interpretation of the master mind; the galvano-plastic and its electrical brethren, a prolific horde, now cheap fakirs imitating real bronzes and all manner of the antique, secretly damning it in their vitals.

Electro-glazing, a machine shunned because too cleanly and delicate for the clumsy hand of the traditional designer, who depends upon the mass and blur of leading to conceal his lack of touch.

That delicate thing, the lithograph—the prince of a whole reproductive province of processes—see what this process becomes in the hands of a master like Whistler. He has sounded but one note in the gamut of its possibilities, but that product is intrinsically true to the process, and as delicate as the butterfly's wing. Yet the most this particular machine did for us, until then in the hands of Art and Craft, was to give us a cheap, imitative effect of painting.

So spins beyond our ability to follow to-night, a rough, feeble thread of the evidence at large to the effect that the machine has weakened the artist; all but destroyed his hand-made art, if not its ideals, although he has made enough miserable mischief meanwhile.

These evident instances should serve to hint, at least to the thinking mind, that the Machine is a marvelous simplifier; the emancipator of the creative mind, and in time the regenerator of the creative conscience. We may see that this destructive process has begun and is taking place that Art might awaken to the power of fully developed senses promised by dreams of its childhood, even though that power may not come the way it was pictured in those dreams.

Now, let us ask ourselves whether the fear of the higher artistic expression demanded by the Machine, so thoroughly grounded in the arts and crafts, is founded upon a finely guarded reticence, a recognition of inherent weakness or plain ignorance?

Let us, to be just, assume that it is equal parts of all three, and try to imagine an Arts and Crafts Society that may educate itself to prepare to make some good impression upon the Machine, the destroyer of their present ideals and tendencies, their salvation in disguise.

Such a society will, of course, be a society for mutual education.

Exhibitions will not be a feature of its programme for years, for there will be nothing to exhibit except the short-comings of the society, and they will hardly prove either instructive or amusing at this stage of proceedings. This society must, from the very nature of the proposition, be made up of the people who are in the work—that is, the manufacturers—coming into touch with such of those who assume the practice of the fine arts as profess a fair sense of the obligation to the public such assumption carries with it, and sociological workers whose interests are ever closely allied with art, as their prophets Morris, Ruskin, and Tolstoy evince, and all those who have as personal graces and accomplishment perfected handicraft, whether fashion old or fashion new.

Without the interest and co-operation of the manufacturers, the society cannot begin to do its work, for this is the corner-stone of its organization.

All these elements should be brought together on a common ground of confessed ignorance, with a desire to be instructed, freely encouraging talk and opinion, and reaching out desperately for any one who has special experience in any way connected, to address them.

I suppose, first of all, the thing would resemble a debating society, or something even less dignified, until some one should suggest that it was time to quit talking and proceed to do something, which in this case would not mean giving an exhibition, but rather excursions to factories and a study of processes in place—that is, the machine in processes too numerous to mention, at the factories with the men who organize and direct them, but not in the spirit of the idea that these things are all gone wrong, looking for that in them which would most nearly approximate the handicraft ideal; not looking into them with even the thought of handicraft, and not particularly looking for craftsmen, but getting a scientific ground-plan of the process in mind, if possible, with a view to its natural bent and possibilities.

Some processes and machines would naturally appeal to some, and some to others; there would undoubtedly be among us those who would find little joy in any of them.

This is, naturally, not child's play, but neither is the work expected of the modern artist.

I will venture to say, from personal observation and some experience, that not one artist in one hundred has taken pains to thus educate himself. I will go further and say what I believe to be true, that not one educational institution in America has as yet attempted to forge the connecting link between Science and Art by training the artist to his actual tools, or, by a process of nature-study that develops in him the power of independent thought, fitting him to use them properly.

Let us call these preliminaries then a process by which artists receive information nine-tenths of them lack concerning the tools they have to work with to-day—for tools to-day are processes and machines where they were once a hammer and a gouge.

The artist to-day is the leader of an orchestra, where he once was a star performer.

Once the manufacturers are convinced of due respect and appreciation on the part of the artist, they will welcome him and his counsel gladly and make any experiments having a grain of apparent sense in them.

They have little patience with a bothering about in endeavor to see what might be done to make their particular machine mediæval and restore man's joy in the mere work of his hands—for this once lovely attribute is far behind.

This proceeding doubtless would be of far more educational value to the artist than to the manufacturer, at least for some time to come, for there would be a difficult adjustment to make on the part of the artist and an attitude to change. So many artists are chiefly "attitude" that some would undoubtedly disappear with the attitude.

But if out of twenty determined students a ray of light should come to one, to light up a single operation, it would have been worth while, for that would be fairly something; while joy in mere handicraft is like that of the man who played the piano for his own amusement—a pleasurable personal accomplishment without real relation to the grim condition confronting us.

Granting that a determined, dauntless body of artist material could be brought together with sufficient persistent enthusiasm to grapple with the Machine, would not some one be found who would provide the suitable experimental station (which is what the modern Arts and Crafts shop should be)—an experimental station that would represent in miniature the elements of this great pulsating web of the machine, where each pregnant process or significant tool in printing, lithography, galvano-electro processes, wood and steel working machinery, muffles and kilns would have its place and where the best young scientific blood could mingle with the best and truest artistic inspiration, to sound the depths of these things, to accord them the patient, sympathetic treatment that is their due?

Surely a thing like this would be worth while—to alleviate the insensate numbness of the poor fellows out in the cold, hard shops, who know not why nor understand, whose dutiful obedience is chained to botch work and bungler's ambition; surely this would be a practical means to make their dutiful obedience give us something we can all understand, and that will be as normal to the best of this machine age as a ray of light to the healthy eye; a real help in adjusting the *Man* to a true sense of his importance as a factor in society, though he does tend a machine.

Teach him that that machine is his best friend—will have widened the margin of his leisure until enlightenment shall bring him a further sense of the magnificent ground plan of progress in which he too justly plays his significant part.

If the art of the Greek, produced at such cost of human life, was so noble and enduring, what limit dare we now imagine to an Art based upon an adequate life for the individual?

The machine is his!

In due time it will come to him!

Meanwhile, who shall count the slain?

From where are the trained nurses in this industrial hospital to come if not from the modern arts and crafts?

Shelley says a man cannot say—"I will compose poetry." "The greatest poet even cannot say it, for the mind in creation is as a fading coal which some invisible influence, like an inconstant wind, awakens to transitory brightness; this power arises from within like the color of a flower which fades and changes as it is developed, and the conscious portions of our nature are unprophetic either of its approach or its departure;" and yet in the arts and crafts the problem is presented as a more or less fixed quantity, highly involved, requiring a surer touch, a more highly disciplined artistic nature to organize it as a work of art.

The original impulses may reach as far inward as those of Shelley's poet, be quite as wayward a matter of pure sentiment, and yet after the thing is done, showing its rational qualities, is limited in completeness only by the capacity of whoever would show them or by the imperfection of the thing itself.

This does not mean that Art may be shown to be an exact Science.

"It is not pure reason, but it is always reasonable."[8]

It is a matter of perceiving and portraying the harmony of organic tendencies; is originally intuitive because the artist nature is a prophetic gift that may sense these qualities afar.

To me, the artist is he who can truthfully idealize the common sense of these tendencies in his chosen way.

So I feel conception and composition to be simply the essence of refinement in organization, the original impulse of which may be registered by the artistic nature as unconsciously as the magnetic needle vibrates to the magnetic law, but which is, in synthesis or analysis, organically consistent, given the power to see it or not.

And I have come to believe that the world of Art, which we are so fond of calling the world outside of Science, is not so much outside as it is the very heart quality of this great material growth—as religion is its conscience.

A foolish heart and a small conscience.

A foolish heart, palpitating in alarm, mistaking the growing pains of its giant frame for approaching dissolution, whose sentimentality the lusty body of modern things has outgrown.

Upon this faith in Art as the organic heart quality of the scientific frame of things, I base a belief that we must look to the artist brain, of all brains, to grasp the significance to society of this thing we call the Machine, if that brain be not blinded, gagged, and bound by false tradition, the letter of precedent. For this thing we call Art is it not as prophetic as a primrose or an oak? Therefore, of the essence of this thing we call the Machine, which is no more or less than the principle of organic growth working irresistibly the Will of Life through the medium of Man.

Be gently lifted at nightfall to the top of a great down-town office building, and you may see how in the image of material man, at once his glory and menace, is this thing we call a city.

There beneath, grown up in a night, is the monster leviathan, stretching acre upon acre into the far distance. High overhead hangs the stagnant pall of its fetid breath, reddened with the light from its myriad eyes endlessly everywhere blinking. Ten thousand acres of cellular tissue, layer upon layer, the city's flesh, outspreads enmeshed by intricate network of veins and arteries, radiating into the gloom, and there with muffled, persistent roar, pulses and circulates as the blood in your veins, the ceaseless beat of the activity to whose necessities it all conforms.

Like to the sanitation of the human body is the drawing off of poisonous waste from the system of this enormous creature; absorbed first by the infinitely ramifying, thread-like ducts gathering at their sensitive terminals matter destructive to its life, hurrying it to millions of small intestines, to be collected in turn by larger, flowing to the great sewer, on to the drainage canal, and finally to the ocean.

This ten thousand acres of flesh-like tissue is again knit and inter-knit with a nervous system marvelously complete, delicate filaments for hearing, knowing, almost feeling the pulse of its organism, acting upon the ligaments and tendons for motive impulse, in all flowing the impelling fluid of man's own life.

Its nerve ganglia!—The peerless Corliss tandems whirling their hundred ton fly-wheels, fed by gigantic rows of water tube boilers burning oil, a solitary man slowly pacing backward and forward, regulating here and there the little feed valves controlling the deafening roar of the flaming gas, while beyond, the incessant clicking, dropping, waiting—lifting, waiting, shifting of the governor gear controlling these modern Goliaths seems a visible brain in intelligent action, registered infallibly in the enormous magnets, purring in the giant embrace of great induction coils, generating the vital current meeting with instant response in the rolling cars on elevated tracks ten miles away, where the glare of the Bessemer steel converter makes a conflagration of the clouds.[9]

More quietly still, whispering down the long, low rooms of factory buildings buried in the gloom beyond, range on range of stanch, beautifully perfected automations, murmur contentedly with occasional click-clack, that would have the American manufacturing industry of five years ago by the throat to-day; manipulating steel as delicately as a mystical shuttle of the modern loom manipulates a silk thread in the shimmering pattern of a dainty gown.

And the heavy breathing, the murmuring, the clangor, and the roar!—how the voice of this monstrous thing, this greatest of machines, a great city, rises to proclaim the marvel of the units of its structure, the ghastly warning boom from the deep throats of vessels heavily seeking inlet to the water-way below, answered by the echoing clangor of the bridge bells growing nearer and more ominous as the vessel cuts momentarily the flow of the nearer artery, warning the current from the swinging bridge now closing on its stately passage, just in time to receive in a rush of steam, as a streak of light, the avalanche of blood and metal hurled across it and gone, roaring into the night on its glittering bands of steel, ever faithfully encircled by the slender magic lines tick-tapping its invincible protection.

Nearer, in the building ablaze with midnight activity, the wide white band streams into the marvel of the multiple press, receiving unerringly the indelible impression of the human hopes, joys, and fears throbbing in the pulse of this great activity, as infallibly as the gray matter of the human brain receives the impression of the senses, to come forth millions of neatly folded, perfected news sheets, teeming with vivid appeals to passions, good or evil; weaving a web of intercommunication so far reaching that distance becomes as nothing, the thought of one man in one corner of the earth one day visible to the naked eye of all men the next; the doings of all the world reflected as in a glass, so marvelously sensitive this wide white band streaming endlessly from day to day becomes in the grasp of the multiple press.

If the pulse of activity in this great city, to which the tremor of the mammoth skeleton beneath our feet is but an awe-inspiring response, is thrilling, what of this prolific, silent obedience?

And the texture of the tissue of this great thing, this Forerunner of Democracy, the Machine, has been deposited particle by particle, in blind obedience to organic law, the law to which the great solar universe is but an obedient machine.

Thus is the thing into which the forces of Art are to breathe the thrill of ideality! A SOUL!

NOTES

1. From William Morris, "Makeshift," an November 18, 1894 address in Manchester, England: "Another makeshift which really cannot be dissociated from the makeshift of building . . . is that we must needs turn the fairness of the earth in the very countryside itself into a makeshift of what it should be."

2. Claude Frollo is the title character of Victor Hugo's *The Hunchback of Notre Dame* (1831).

3. Wright refers either to the 1892–93 Annex to Marshall Field & Company's department store by Charles B. Atwood of D. H. Burnham & Company or to an expansion of the original building located at another address.

4. Phidias (c. 500–c. 432 BCE), possibly the greatest of Greek sculptors.

5. The Fair was a popular, somewhat middlebrow Chicago department store.

6. Richard Croker (1841–1922) was from 1886 to 1902 the leader of Tammany Hall, New York City's Democratic Party political organization.

7. Grand Rapids, Michigan, was a center of mass-produced furniture.

8. These and the lines quoted above are from Percy Bysshe Shelley, "A Defence of Poetry" (1821), published posthumously by his wife, Mary Shelley, in *A Defence of Poetry and Other Essays* (1840).

9. In 1848, American George H. Corliss (1817–88) invented the most powerful steam engine then known; in 1855 Englishman Harry Bessemer (1813–98) patented a process for converting molten pig iron into steel.

THREE

The New Larkin Administration Building (1906)

Wright infrequently wrote at length about a particular building of his own or anyone else's design (see Document 10, however), although as an older man he loved to drop sarcastic one-liners: Le Corbusier's 1945–52 Unité d'habitation in Marseilles was a "massacre on the waterfront"; he "wouldn't walk on the same side of the street" as "those [1950s] skinny glass boxes" for fear the "fool things might explode." An essay like this, therefore, indicates a larger agenda.

The Larkin Soap Company, founded in 1875 by John D. Larkin, Darwin D. Martin, and Elbert Hubbard (see Document 1, n. 1), among others, expanded rapidly to sell a variety of household goods by mail order and in branch stores as far west as Chicago, so that by the time Wright designed and executed its new administrative headquarters (c. 1903–6, demolished 1950) its reported $4,000,000 price tag was entirely acceptable to the ownership.

In this essay for the company's in-house publication, Wright comments on the innovations and other features of which he felt most proud—climate control, lighting, fireproofing, furniture, employee amenities, service and utility zones, and more—but also stresses his struggle to keep costs down, perhaps anticipating criticism. His real point, however, was something else.

In "The Architect" of 1900 (Document 1) he had intimated that only when Americans fully understood who they were and of what their defining values consisted would they be able to develop their own architecture. In Document 4, published eight years later, he will reflect upon what he had accomplished toward that end during his extraordinarily fruitful Prairie period, the first decade of the twentieth century. Stylistically and programmatically, the Larkin Building was one of his boldest of that period. So when he writes here that it "is wholly American in its directness and freshness of treatment . . . [wearing] no badge of servitude to foreign 'styles,'" he was not only anticipating his 1908 essay but also saying in effect that his hopes in "The Architect" were well on their way to fruition.

The Larkin Company must have agreed, because some of its officers, as well as the company itself, commissioned Wright to design at least a half dozen projects during his Prairie years.

From The Larkin Idea *(November 1906)*

The architect has been asked to tell the "Larkin Family" why the big pile of brick across the street from the Larkin factories is an economical head-piece to house the intellectuals of a great industry.

Before the office building was begun the physical side of the plant was well developed in the extensive fire-proof buildings devoted to manufacture; but the brains and nervous system to make its corporeal bulk count for something hadn't developed the proper "forehead" with the sort of working-room behind it that would make its nervous energy and intelligence effective to the utmost and, what is good also, to let the light of the Ideal outwardly shine in the countenance of an institution that has in reality become "a great business of the people."

What the "Larkin Family" ought to know, I am told, is wherein all this expenditure of thousands upon mere brains and countenance, *pays*, particularly as some of the money has been spent to reach the heart, too.

Has the Larkin Company in this instance been true to its traditions and "saved all cost which adds no value?" Perhaps not, if all values are to be reckoned in money. Real values are subjective and more difficult to estimate than the more obvious ones of the balance-sheet.

And yet, if, over-and-above the mere house-room required by 1800 workers, clean, pure, properly-tempered air for them to breathe whatever the season or weather or however enervating the environment may be is worth "money" to young lungs and old ones, we have that,—the best in the world.

If ideal sanitary conditions and toilet facilities are worth "money," we have those,—perfect.

If the positive security insured by the use of permanent fire-proof materials throughout an isolated building and its fittings and furnishing is valuable,—we have that.

If a restful, harmonious environment, with none of the restless, distracting discords common to the eye and ear in the usual commercial environment, promoting the efficiency of the 1800 or more young lives whose business home the building now is can be counted an asset, why we have that too, together with total immunity from conditions outside the building which are entirely the reverse. If the frame of mind of the worker reacts on his work we have paved the way for a favorable reaction by providing in detail and in ensemble a harmonious unity as complete as it is rare.

If law and order put into close touch with all the facilities for instantaneous inter–communication and easy systematic operation that clever people have yet invented saves time therefore money,—we have that.

In short, if the incentive that results from the family–gathering under conditions ideal for body and mind counts for lessened errors, cheerful alacrity and quickened and sustained intelligence in duties to be performed, we have created some very real values.

There are other things beside, calculated to make this family home helpful and uplifting still more difficult to estimate in money but the men who shape the destiny and determine the character of the work to be done by this family believe in them.

By the shrewd heads of many commercial enterprises these other things are considered to "*pay*" and are ceaselessly exploited as material for advertising, but I think the belief in them in this case lies deeper than that, for I have felt the spirit of the men behind this work and I know that they believe they pay, as the sunshine and the trees, and as the flowers and a clear conscience pay: their love of their work and their pride in it would permit them to do no less.

Let us see whether the means chosen for the purpose of attaining all these things were economical and true or not as there are many unusual features in the construction of the building not easily comprehended without some study. To begin with, the site, for an office building, necessarily was unattractive. Smoke, noise and dirt of railroads were round about, which made it seem wise to depend upon pleasantness within, shutting out the environment completely so far as requirements of light and air would permit. The design of the building derives its outward character from this circumstance perhaps more than from any other. So the structure is hermetically sealed with double glass at all window openings. By mechanical means the fresh air is taken in at the roof levels, drawn to the basement, washed by passing through a sheet of water sprays (which in summer reduces its temperature two or three degrees), heated (in winter), circulated and finally exhausted from beneath the great skylight where the winter's snow will melt as it falls.

Outside the building is an enormous pile of impervious brick with splendid deep reveals. The stair chambers, air intakes and exhausts with their necessary machinery, pipe shafts and plumbing are grouped at all the outer corners of the main rectangle where light is least obstructed from the interior. The resultant walls of solid masonry at the corners where wall surfaces usually are slight give a noble cliff-like mass to the structure. Moreover this insulates the stairways where they serve as practical fire escapes so that all the 1800 occupants of the entire building could safely and com fortably escape to the outside grounds in something like three minutes, if such a need in such a building can be supposed. These chambers also establish a ready means of continuous communication between stories at four points on each floor.

By this means the main building is systematically quartered in arrangement and is wired, heated and ventilated in quadruple insuring easy distribution and positive operation throughout the appurtenance systems with easy inter-communications between floors. Then the superimposed stories necessary to accommodate the required number of clerks are all aired, lighted and unified by a long, open, skylighted central court preserving in the occupation of the interior the character of the family gathering, making the interior as a whole light, airy and beautiful altogether.

The floor areas surrounding this court have all been kept intact for business; the toilet accommodations, entrance and exit features being clustered in the four storied convenience-annex which is reached directly from Seneca or Swan Streets, at the ends. This entrance annex has been semi-attached to the side of the main structure so as to obstruct the light from it as little as possible.

The top floor of the annex and of the main building with its mezzanine and outlying roof surfaces are the family recreation grounds where the clerks and their guests may be fed and entertained. Here are completely appointed kitchen, bakery and commodious dining rooms, lecture rooms and library, class rooms, rest rooms and roof gardens, and conservatories that will furnish a gay note to the interior summer and winter.

It can honestly be said that there are no flimsy makeshifts out-side or inside the building. Simplicity, straightforwardness, good materials and dignified proportion of the various parts are all that give it architectural effect; the sole ornaments of the exterior are the stone groups surmounting the piers advertising and accenting the terminals of the longitudinal central aisle of the interior court, together with the stone bas-reliefs over the water-basins flanking and accenting the entrances.

The exterior is dark in color and durable. The interior light in color and no less durable. The interior walls are lined with a semi-vitreous, hard cream-colored brick. The floors and the interior trimmings of this brick lining have been worked out in magnesite, a new building material consistently used for the first time in this structure. Stairs, floors, doors, window sills, coping, capitals, par-titions, desk tops, plumbing slabs, all are of this material and are worked "in situ" without seams or joints with sanitary curves at all wall surfaces, finishing hard and durable as iron, as light in color as the brick work and, not the least valuable of its properties, light in weight also. The solid concrete floors are cushioned with this magnesite and wood fibre permeated and made fireproof with magnesite, deafening the floors throughout the building and ren-dering them less cold and hard to the foot than masonry would be. They are then finished with a hard, durable surfacing of the magnesite.

The interior represents a full score of old building-problems in a new phase. Many experiments have been made in order that all the various appurtenance systems, filing systems and furnish-ings might make a time-saving, consistent, cleanly and easily-cleanable whole. To this end also a vacuum cleaning system has been installed with pneumatic motors to do the sweeping and scrubbing; and everything, where possible, has been designed free of the floor. The water-closets and their enclosures are all hung free of the floor with few horizontal joints anywhere in which dirt may lodge and instead of the usual dusty, banging doors, cleanable sliding screens are used. The metal lockers likewise and the metal desks are all designed with metal bases that at intervals only, touch the floor. The seats themselves are swung free of the floor onto the desk legs, never to scrape noisily about or be lifted by the janitor for cleaning purposes; think of the labor that would be required each night to pile 1800 chairs on top of 1800 desks and then to pile them down again! The desk tops are adjustable to various heights and the cabinets beneath them are interchangeable so that type-writer- and graphophone-desks may be introduced in the rows anywhere at will. The desk tops are of the same material as the floors, as are all the panels in the sides of the desks. The general scheme of arrangement of the desks and filing system is as orderly and systematically complete as a well disciplined army drawn up for review might be and all is threaded together with a system of electric wiring so that the mere pressure of a button puts any official of the organization in instant communication with any other member.

In the interior all matters of heating, ventilating, lighting, plumbing, refrigeration, mechanical carriers, pneumatic cleaning and inter-communication and electrical control have been assimilated into the structure and in such a way that a failure in any point may readily be reached and remedied.

Within the circular Information Desk, a prominent feature of the entrance lobby, are located the telephone switchboards, with a capacity of 300 connections, the electrical Master Clock controlling the numerous secondary clocks and register clocks and automatically ringing the signal gongs throughout the building; the switchboard by which the electric time system is operated, and private telegraph wires of both the Western Union and Postal Companies. From the visitors' gallery surrounding the lobby, furnished appropriately with steel chairs and writing tables, the operation of all of these devices is in plain sight. Wires extend from the switchboards to all parts of the building, accessible through metal outlet boxes sunk in the floors, permitting at any desk a direct and invisible connection with telephone, phonograph, light or power, or all of them.

Little disorder and no confusion arose from the inauguration of the building, for the building is its own furnishing—or its furnishings a part of the building. Finished, it is complete and ready for use. I know of no building in the country so complete in this respect. This means that patience and study were required in the work; and effort to eliminate all crudities and conflicting parts in order that the result might be simplicity itself.

It has taken a longer time to build the building than would have been necessary if the market had contained all the materials, ready at hand, as it does for ordinary buildings.

Unfortunately there is no ready-made market wherein to let contracts for architectural work of this nature. Work like this is not a matter of stock patterns or stock methods: Established processes dislike interruption; workmen do not like to think; contractors are afraid of the new thing for which they have no gauge; so in this instance the Larkin Company through the medium of an intelligent, experienced contractor,[1] has gone beyond the middleman in many cases. "From Factory-to-Family" was still the rule in the building of the Office Building; in this instance, however, the family in question is the Larkin Co. itself.

The stone came from Lake Superior quarries direct to the building and was cut on the ground by days' labor at a cost $20,000.00 less than the work could have been let for by contract to Buffalo.

The magnesite interior trimming throughout the structure was another [example] of,—from the magnesite mines of Greece direct to the building,—to be manufactured there by days' labor into the various features of the interior, at a cost less than any permanent masonry-material known, and with a lightness and a sanitary and artistic perfection very difficult if not impossible to achieve in either stone or terra cotta.

Extreme care has been exercised in searching what market there was for the special thing, in almost every case, wanted. For instance, the iron fence enclosure was put out for bids in Buffalo and Cleveland and the lowest bids received were approximately $8000.00. Many concerns in Chicago were tried with slightly better results until a man was found who had new machinery capable of punching as though it were mere tin, the heavy iron we proposed to use in its construction. This man[2] made the fence for Jackson Park in Chicago and was accustomed to contract for heavy fence by the mile and he was not afraid to undertake to furnish our fence for $4100.00.

The glass in the ceiling lights cannot be bought again for double the price paid,—another case of finding the right thing after long search. The inside brick will never be sold again at the price the Larkin Company paid for it. The reinforced concrete floor-construction was finally let for half the Buffalo bids and it was found impossible to sublet the plain concrete work of the building for the price which the Larkin Company paid for it. A sub-contract was twice let for the interior trim in magnesite but each concern got into trouble before the time came to "make good" and then the architect and the contractor had to stump the country for means to carry out the work; many men and firms were consulted, in Chicago, in Buffalo, in Dayton, in Pittsburgh and finally in New York they found the man whose experience and ingenuity has aided the contractor in overcoming obstacles which seemed at the outset almost insurmountable. And I might recite in detail most structural items of the features going to make up the construction. All the items—and their name it seems to me is legion—have been threshed out to the limit of endurance, with, in almost every case, a gratifying result.

Besides, this building is a better building in many respects than the one we began to build, for the best in appliances and materials were considered to be economical and some search was necessary to uncover the cheapest and best; moreover, the scope of the building broadened as it progressed; in fact the business grew so fast that new requirements had constantly to be met. The one question the directors were determined to have satisfactorily answered when matters of betterment were under consideration was whether the betterments to be made were real and if they were the answer was always "yes."

But perhaps the final proof, on account of the balance sheet at least, of the care and ingenuity exercised in behalf of the structure is the fact that this thoroughbred, fireproof building, by no means impoverished architecturally, including possibly the most complete heating and ventilating system in the country, with much plumbing and elaborate systems of electric wiring, together with its impressive and extensive fence-enclosure, was erected for approximately 17 cents per cubic foot whereas fireproof buildings by no means superior usually run from 23 cents to 30 cents per cubic foot.

The fact remains, for what it is worth, that in this case the Larkin Company has not fattened the middleman nor paid the high price attached usually to high specialties but comes into possession of a sound, modern, wholesome building scientifically adapted to facilitate the transaction of its business and insure the permanence of its records and continuity of its service to its customers as well as to promote the health and cheerfulness of its official family at comparatively a very low cost.

The ease with which the interior may be cared for, the relatively low cost of janitors' service and of repairs for many years to come will contribute toward a profitable operation.

Finally—it seems to me—that the American flag is the only flag that would look well on or in this building; the only flag with its simple stars and bars that wouldn't look incongruous and out of place with the simple rectangular masses of the exterior and the straightforward rectilinear treatment of the interior. I think our building is wholly American in its directness and freshness of treatment. It wears no badge of servitude to foreign "styles" yet it avails itself gratefully of the treasures and the wisdom bequeathed to it by its ancestors.

There may be some to question whether it is beautiful or not; there always will be the usual two opinions about that, for it has "*character*" and when character is pronounced in buildings or in people there is always a "for" and an "against,"—even when one's artistic instincts have not been perverted as ours have been by too much borrowed architectural finery. But in-so-far as it is simple and true it will live, a blessing to its occupants, fulfilling in a measure on behalf of the men who planted it there their two great reciprocal duties, duty to the Past and duty to the Future—duties self imposed upon all right thinking men.

NOTES

1. The general contractor was Paul F. P. Mueller (1864–1934) of Chicago, who worked with Wright on several projects.
2. Not even Jack Quinan in his excellent, thoroughly researched *Frank Lloyd Wright's Larkin Building: Myth and Fact* (Cambridge, MA: MIT Press, 1987), 143, was able to identify the fence builder.

FOUR

In the Cause of Architecture
(1908)

Seven years after Wright proclaimed the dawning of a new day for architecture (in Document 2) he discusses here the ways in which he applies "the art and craft of the machine" to his work. Referring in the instance to windows but equally applicable to furnishings, room arrangement, indeed, to entire buildings conceived holistically, his "simple rhythmic arrangement of straight lines and squares" are intended, he writes, to "make the best of the technical contrivances that produce them." So in a sense this essay is a report card on how theory was put into practice.

But it is also his lengthiest discussion to date about nature—not its externalities, but about how the essence of its forms and functions influence the plan, massing, and grammar of his designs. Using the word "organic" more than ever now, Wright is well on his way to articulating a fully developed concept of "organic architecture," the label by which his work is known to history.

In notably unvarnished prose he lists six "propositions" central to his thinking, describes his buildings' defining characteristics, and explains his modus operandi within the context of the social and professional atmosphere affecting it.

In short, "In the Cause of Architecture" is Wright's most concise statement of design philosophy to this point in his career, making it every bit, if not more essential than "The Art and Craft of the Ma-chine" for understanding his work.

From The Architectural Record, *23 (March 1908).*

Radical though it be, the work here illustrated is dedicated to a cause conservative in the best sense of the word. At no point does it involve denial of the elemental law and order inherent in all great architecture; rather, is it a declaration of love for the spirit of that law and order, and a reverential recognition of the elements that made its ancient letter in its time vital and beautiful.

Primarily, Nature furnished the materials for architectural motifs out of which the architectural forms as we know them to-day have been developed, and, although our practice for centuries has been for the most part to turn from her, seeking inspiration in books and adhering slavishly to dead formulae, her wealth of sug-gestion is inexhaustible; her riches greater than any man's desire. I know with what suspicion the man is regarded who refers matters of fine art back to Nature. I know that it is usually an ill-advised return that is attempted, for Nature in external, obvious aspect is the usually accepted sense of the term and the nature that is reached. But given inherent vision there is no source so fertile, so suggestive, so helpful aesthetically for the architect as a compre-hension of natural law. As Nature is never right for a picture so is she never right for the architect—that is, not ready-made. Never-theless, she has a practical school beneath her more obvious forms in which a sense of proportion may be cultivated, when Vignola and Vitruvius fail as they must always fail. It is there that he may develop that sense of reality that translated to his own field in terms of his own work will lift him far above the realistic in his art; there he will be inspired by sentiment that will never degenerate to sentimentality and he will learn to draw with a surer hand the every-perplexing line between the curious and the beautiful.

A sense of the organic is indispensable to an architect; where can he develop it so surely as in this school? A knowledge of the relations of form and function lies at the root of his practice; where else can he find the pertinent object lessons Nature so readily furnishes? Where can he study the differentiations of form that go to determine character as he can study them in the trees? Where can that sense of inevitableness characteristic of a work of art be quickened as it may be by intercourse with nature in this sense?

Japanese art knows this school more intimately than that of any people. In common use in their language there are many words like the word "edaburi," which, translated as near as may be, means the formative arrangement of the branches of a tree. We have no such word in English, we are not yet sufficiently civilized to think in such terms, but the architect must not only learn to think in such terms but he must learn in this school to fashion his vocabulary for himself and furnish it in a comprehensive way with useful words as significant as this one.

For seven years it was my good fortune to be the understudy of a great teacher and a great architect, to my mind the greatest of his time—Mr. Louis H. Sullivan.[1]

Principles are not invented, they are not evolved by one man or one age, but Mr. Sullivan's perception and practice of them amounted to a revelation at a time when they were commercially inexpedient and all but lost to sight in current practice. The fine art sense of the profession was at that time practically dead; only glimmerings were perceptible in the work of Richardson and of Root.

Adler and Sullivan had little time to design residences. The few that were unavoidable fell to my lot outside of office hours. So largely, it remained for me to carry into the field of domestic architecture the battle they had begun in commercial building.

During the early years of my own practice I found this lonesome work. Sympathizers of any kind were then few and they were not found among the architects. I well remember how "the message" burned within me, how I longed for comradeship until I began to know the younger men and how welcome was Robert Spencer, and then Myron Hunt, and Dwight Perkins, Arthur Heun, George Dean and Hugh Garden. Inspiring days they were, I am sure, for us all. Of late we have been too busy to see one another often, but the "New School of the Middle West" is beginning to be talked about and perhaps some day it is to be. For why not the same "Life" and blood in architecture that is the essence of all true art?

In 1894, with this text from Carlyle at the top of the page— "The Ideal is within thyself, thy condition is but the stuff thou art to shape that same Ideal out of"[2]—I formulated the following "propositions." I set them down here much as they were written then, although in the light of experience they might be stated more completely and succinctly.

I.—Simplicity and Repose are qualities that measure the true value of any work of art.

But simplicity is not in itself an end nor is it a matter of the side of a barn but rather an entity with a graceful beauty in its integrity from which discord, and all that is meaningless, has been eliminated. A wild flower is truly simple. Therefore:

1. A building should contain as few rooms as will meet the conditions which give it rise and under which we live, and which the architect should strive continually to simplify; then the ensemble of the rooms should be carefully considered that comfort and utility may go hand in hand with beauty. Beside the entry and necessary work rooms there need be but three rooms on the ground floor of any house, living room, dining room

and kitchen, with the possible addition of a "social office"; really there need be but one room, the living room with requirements otherwise sequestered from it or screened within it by means of architectural contrivances.

2. Openings should occur as integral features of the structure and form, if possible, its natural ornamentation.

3. An excessive love of detail has ruined more fine things from the standpoint of fine art or fine living than any one human shortcoming—it is hopelessly vulgar. Too many houses, when they are not little stage settings or scene paintings, are mere notion stores, bazaars or junk-shops. Decoration is dangerous unless you understand it thoroughly and are satisfied that it means something good in the scheme as a whole; for the present you are usually better off without it. Merely that it "looks rich" is no justification for the use of ornament.

4. Appliances or fixtures as such are undesirable. Assimilate them together with all appurtenances into the design of the structure.

5. Pictures deface walls oftener than they decorate them. Pictures should be decorative and incorporated in the general scheme as decoration.

6. The most truly satisfactory apartments are those in which most or all of the furniture is built in as a part of the original scheme considering the whole as an integral unit.

II.—There should be as many kinds (styles) of houses as there are kinds (styles) of people and as many differentiations as there are different individuals. A man who has individuality (and what man lacks it?) has a right to its expression in his own environment.

III.—A building should appear to grow easily from its site and be shaped to harmonize with its surroundings if Nature is manifest there, and if not try to make it as quiet, substantial and organic as She would have been were the opportunity Hers.*

　　We of the Middle West are living on the prairie. The prairie has a beauty of its own and we should recognize and accentuate this natural beauty, its quiet level. Hence, gently sloping roofs, low proportions, quiet sky lines, suppressed heavyset chimneys and sheltering overhangs, low terraces and out-reaching walls sequestering private gardens.

IV.— Colors require the same conventionalizing process to make them fit to live with that natural forms do; so go to the woods and fields for color schemes. Use the soft, warm, optimistic tones of earths and autumn leaves in preference to the pessimistic blues, purples or cold greens and grays of the ribbon counter; they are more wholesome and better adapted in most cases to good decoration.

V.—Bring out the nature of the materials, let their nature intimately into your scheme. Strip the wood of varnish and let it alone—stain it. Develop the natural texture of the plastering and stain it. Reveal the nature of the wood, plaster, brick or stone in your designs; they are all by nature friendly and beautiful. No treatment can be really a matter of fine art when these natural characteristics are, or their nature is, outraged or neglected.

VI.—A house that has character stands a good chance of growing more valuable as it grows older while a house in the prevailing mode, whatever that mode may be, is soon out of fashion, stale and unprofitable.

---

*In this I had in mind the barren town lots devoid of tree or natural incident, town houses and board walks only in evidence.

Buildings like people must first be sincere, must be true and then withal as gracious and lovable as may be.

Above all, integrity. The machine is the normal tool of our civilization, give it work that it can do well—nothing is of greater importance. To do this will be to formulate new industrial ideals, sadly needed.

These propositions are chiefly interesting because for some strange reason they were novel when formulated in the face of conditions hostile to them and because the ideals they phrase have been practically embodied in the buildings that were built to live up to them. The buildings of recent years have not only been true to them, but are in many cases a further development of the simple propositions so positively stated then.

Happily, these ideals are more commonplace now. Then the sky lines of our domestic architecture were fantastic abortions, tortured by features that disrupted the distorted roof surfaces from which attenuated chimneys like lean fingers threatened the sky; the invariably tall interiors were cut up into box-like compartments, the more boxes the finer the house; and "Architecture" chiefly consisted in healing over the edges of the curious collection of holes that had to be cut in the walls for light and air and to permit the occupant to get in or out. These interiors were always slaughtered with the butt and slash of the old plinth and corner block trim, of dubious origin, and finally smothered with horrible millinery.

That individuality in a building was possible for each home maker, or desirable, seemed at that time to rise to the dignity of an idea. Even cultured men and women care so little for the spiritual integrity of their environment; except in rare cases they are not touched, they simply do not care for the matter so long as their dwellings are fashionable or as good as those of their neighbors and keep them dry and warm. A structure has no more meaning to them aesthetically than has the stable to the horse. And this came to me in the early years as a definite discouragement. There are exceptions, and I found them chiefly among American men of business with unspoiled instincts and untainted ideals. A man of this type usually has the faculty of judging for himself. He has rather liked the "idea" and much of the encouragement this work receives comes straight from him because the "common sense" of the thing appeals to him. While the "cultured" are still content with their small châteaux, Colonial wedding cakes, English affectations or French millinery, he prefers a poor thing but his own. He errs on the side of character, at least, and when the test of time has tried his country's development architecturally, he will have contributed his quota, small enough in the final outcome though it be; he will be regarded as a true conservator.

In the hope that some day America may live her own life in her own buildings, in her own way, that is, that we may make the best of what we have for what it honestly is or may become, I have endeavored in this work to establish a harmonious relationship between ground plan and elevation of these buildings, considering the one as a solution and the other an expression of the conditions of a problem of which the whole is a project. I have tried to establish an organic integrity to begin with, forming the basis for the subsequent working out of a significant grammatical expression and making the whole, as nearly as I could, consistent.

What quality of style the buildings may possess is due to the artistry with which the conventionalization as a solution and an artistic expression of a specific problem within these limitations has been handled. The types are largely a matter of personal taste and may have much or little to do with the American architecture for which we hope.

From the beginning of my practice the question uppermost in my mind has been not "what style" but "what is style?" and it is my belief that the chief value of the work illustrated here will be found in the fact that if in the face of our present day conditions any given type may be treated independently and imbued with the quality of style, then a truly noble architecture is a definite possibility, so soon as Americans really demand it of the architects of the rising generation.

I do not believe we will ever again have the uniformity of type which has characterized the so-called great "styles." Conditions have changed; our ideal is Democracy, the highest possible expression of the individual as a unit not inconsistent with a harmonious whole. The average of human intelligence rises steadily, and as the individual unit grows more and more to be trusted we will have an architecture with richer variety in unity than has ever arisen before; but the forms must be born out of our changed conditions, they must be *true* forms, otherwise the best that tradition has to offer is only an inglorious masquerade, devoid of vital significance or true spiritual value. . . .

The trials of the early days were many and at this distance picturesque. Workmen seldom like to think, especially if there is financial risk entailed; at your peril do you disturb their established processes mental or technical. To do anything in an unusual, even if in a better and simpler way, is to complicate the situation at once. Simple things at that time in any industrial field were nowhere at hand. A piece of wood without a moulding was an anomaly; a plain wooden slat instead of a turned baluster a joke; the omission of the merchantable "grille" a crime; plain fabrics for hangings or floor covering were nowhere to be found in stock.

To become the recognized enemy of the established industrial order was no light matter, for soon whenever a set of my drawings was presented to a Chicago mill-man for figures he would willingly enough unroll it, read the architect's name, shake his head and return it with the remark that he was "not hunting for trouble"; sagacious owners and general contractors tried cutting out the name, but in vain, his perspicacity was rat-like, he had come to know "the look of the thing." So, in addition to the special preparation in any case necessary for every little matter of construction and finishing, special detail drawings were necessary merely to show the things to be left off or not done, and not only studied designs for every part had to be made but quantity surveys and schedules of mill work furnished the contractors beside. This, in a year or two, brought the architect face to face with the fact that the fee for his service "established" by the American Institute of Architects was intended for something stock and shop, for it would not even pay for the bare drawings necessary for conscientious work.

The relation of the architect to the economic and industrial movement of his time, in any fine art sense, is still an affair so sadly out of joint that no one may easily reconcile it. All agree that something has gone wrong and except the architect be a [plan] factory magnate, who has reduced his art to a philosophy of old clothes and sells misfit or made-over-ready-to-wear garments with commercial aplomb and social distinction, he cannot succeed on the present basis established by common practice. So, in addition to a situation already complicated for them, a necessarily increased fee stared in the face the clients who dared. But some did dare, as the illustrations prove.

The struggle then was and still is to make "good architecture," "good business." It is perhaps significant that in the beginning it was very difficult to secure a building loan on any terms upon one of these houses, now it is easy to secure a better loan than ordinary; but how far success has attended this ambition the owners of these buildings alone can testify. Their trials have been many, but each, I think, feels that he has as much house for his money as any of his neighbors, with something in the home intrinsically valuable besides, which will not be out of fashion in one lifetime, and which contributes steadily to his dignity and his pleasure as an individual.

It would not be useful to dwell further upon difficulties encountered, for it is the common story of simple progression everywhere in any field; I merely wish to trace here the "motif" behind the types. A study of the illustrations will show that the buildings presented fall readily into three groups having a family resemblance; the low-pitched hip roofs, heaped together in pyramidal fashion, or presenting quiet, unbroken skylines; the low roofs with simple pediments countering on long ridges; and those topped with a simple slab. Of the first type, the Winslow, Henderson, Willits, Thomas, Heurtley, Heath, Cheney, Martin, Little, Gridley, Millard, Tomek, Coonley and Westcott houses, the Hillside Home School and the Pettit Memorial Chapel are typical. Of the second type the Bradley, Hickox, Davenport and Dana houses are typical. Of the third, Atelier for Richard Bock, Unity Church, the concrete house of the Ladies' Home Journal and other designs in process of execution. The Larkin Building is a simple, dignified utterance of a plain, utilitarian type with sheer brick walls and simple stone copings. The studio is merely an early experiment in "articulation."[3]

Photographs do not adequately present these subjects. A building has a presence as has a person that defies the photographer, and the color so necessary to the complete expression of the form is necessarily lacking, but it will be noticed that all the structures stand upon their foundations to the eye as well as physically. There is good, substantial preparation at the ground for all the buildings and it is the first grammatical expression of all the types. This preparation, or watertable, is to these buildings what the stylobate was to the ancient Greek temple. To gain it, it was necessary to reverse the established practice of setting the supports of the building to the outside of the wall and to set them to the inside, so as to leave the necessary support for the outer base. This was natural enough and good enough construction but many an owner was disturbed by private information from the practical contractor to the effect that he would have his whole house in the cellar if he submitted to it. This was at the time a marked innovation though the most natural thing in the world and to me, to this day, indispensable.

With this innovation established, one horizontal stripe of raw material, the foundation wall above ground, was eliminated and the complete grammar of type one made possible. A simple, un-broken wall surface from foot to level of second story sill was thus secured, a change of material occuring at that point to form the simple frieze that characterizes the earlier buildings. Even this was frequently omitted as in the Francis apartments and many other buildings and the wall was let alone from base to cornice or eaves.

"Dress reform houses" they were called, I remember, by the charitably disposed. What others called them will hardly bear rep-etition.

As the wall surfaces were thus simplified and emphasized, the matter of fenestration became exceedingly difficult and more than ever important, and often I used to gloat over the beautiful build-ings I could build if only it were unnecessary to cut holes in them; but the holes were managed at first frankly as in the Winslow house and later as elementary constituents of the structure grouped in rhythmical fashion, so that all the light and air and prospect the most rabid client could wish would not be too much from an artistic standpoint; and of this achievement I am proud. The groups are managed, too, whenever required, so that overhanging eaves do not shade them, although the walls are still protected from the weather. Soon the poetry-crushing characteristics of the guillotine window, which was then firmly rooted, became appar-ent and, single-handed I waged a determined battle for casements swinging out, although it was necessary to have special hardware made for them as there was none to be had this side of England. Clients would come ready to accept any innovation but "those swinging windows," and when told that they were in the nature of the proposition and that they must take them or leave the rest,

they frequently employed "the other fellow" to give them something "near," with the "practical" windows dear to their hearts.

With the grammar so far established, came an expression pure
and simple, even classic in atmosphere, using that much-abused
word in its best sense; implying, that is, a certain sweet reasonableness of form and outline naturally dignified.

I have observed that Nature usually perfects her forms; the individuality of the attribute is seldom sacrificed; that is, deformed or
mutilated by co-operative parts. She rarely says a thing and tries to
take it back at the same time. She would not sanction the "classic"
proceeding of, say, establishing an "order," a colonnade, then
building walls between the columns of the order reducing them to
pilasters, thereafter cutting holes in the wall and pasting on cornices with more pilasters around them, with the result that every
form is outraged, the whole an abominable mutilation, as is most
of the the architecture of the Renaissance wherein style corrodes
style and all the forms are stultified.

In laying out the ground plans for even the more insignificant
of these buildings, a simple axial law and order and the ordered
spacing upon a system of certain structural units definitely established for each structure in accord with its scheme of practical
construction and æsthetic proportion, is practiced as an expedient
to simplify the technical difficulties of execution, and, although
the symmetry may not be obvious always, the balance is usually
maintained. The plans are as a rule much more articulate than is
the school product of the Beaux Arts. The individuality of the various functions of the various features is more highly developed; all
the forms are complete in themselves and frequently do duty at
the same time from within and without as decorative attributes of
the whole. This tendency to greater individuality of the parts emphasized by more and more complete articulation will be seen in
the plans for Unity Church, the cottage for Elizabeth Stone at
Glencoe and the Avery Coonley house in process of construction

at Riverside, Illinois. Moreover, these ground plans are merely the actual projection of a carefully considered whole. The "architecture" is not "thrown up" as an artistic exercise, a matter of elevation from a preconceived ground plan. The schemes are conceived in three dimensions as organic entities, let the picturesque perspective fall how it will. While a sense of the incidental perspectives the design will develop is always present, I have great faith that if the thing is rightly put together in true organic sense with proportions actually right the picturesque will take care of itself. No man ever built a building worthy the name of architecture who fashioned it in perspective sketch to his taste and then fudged the plan to suit. Such methods produce mere scene-painting. A perspective may be a proof but it is no nurture.

As to the mass values of the buildings the æsthetic principles outlined in proposition III will account in a measure for their character.

In the matter of decoration the tendency has been to indulge it less and less, in many cases merely providing certain architectural preparation for natural foliage or flowers, as it is managed in say, the entrance to the Lawrence house at Springfield. This use of natural foliage and flowers for decoration is carried to quite an extent in all the designs and, although the buildings are complete without this effloresence, they may be said to blossom with the season. What architectural decoration the buildings carry is not only conventionalized to the point where it is quiet and stays as a sure foil for the nature forms from which it is derived and with which it must intimately associate, but it is always *of* the surface, never *on* it.

The windows usually are provided with characteristic straight line patterns absolutely in the flat and usually severe. The nature of the glass is taken into account in these designs as is also the metal bar used in their construction, and most of them are treated as metal "grilles" with glass inserted forming a simple rhythmic arrangement of straight lines and squares made as cunning as possible so long as the result is quiet. The aim is that the designs shall make the best of the technical contrivances that produce them.

In the main the ornamentation is wrought in the warp and woof of the structure. It is constitutional in the best sense and is felt in the conception of the ground plan. To elucidate this element in composition would mean a long story and perhaps a tedious one though to me it is the most fascinating phase of the work, involving the true poetry of conception.

The differentiation of a single, certain simple form characterizes the expression of one building. Quite a different form may serve for another, but from one basic idea all the formal elements of design are in each case derived and held well together in scale and character. The form chosen may flare outward, opening flower-like to the sky as in the Thomas house; another, droop to accentuate artistically the weight of the masses; another be noncommittal or abruptly emphatic, or its grammar may be deduced from some plant form that has appealed to me, as certain properties in line and form of the sumach were used in the Lawrence house at Springfield; but in every case the motif is adhered to throughout so that it is not too much to say that each building æsthetically is cut from one piece of goods and consistently hangs together with an integrity impossible otherwise.

In a fine art sense these designs have grown as natural plants grow, the individuality of each is integral and as complete as skill, time, strength and circumstances would permit.

The method in itself does not of necessity produce a beautiful building, but it does provide a framework as a basis which has an organic integrity, susceptible to the architect's imagination and at once opening to him Nature's wealth of artistic suggestion, ensuring him a guiding principle within which he can never be wholly false, out of tune, or lacking in rational motif. The subtleties, the shifting blending harmonies, the cadences, the nuances are a matter of his own nature, his own susceptibilities and faculties.

But self denial is imposed upon the architect to a far greater extent than upon any other member of the fine art family. The temptation to sweeten work, to make each detail in itself lovable and expressive is always great; but that the whole may be truly eloquent of its ultimate function restraint is imperative. To let individual elements arise and shine at the expense of final repose is for the architect a betrayal of trust, for buildings are the background or framework for the human life within their walls and a foil for the nature efflorescence without. So architecture is the most complete of conventionalizations and of all the arts the most subjective except music.

Music may be for the architect ever and always a sympathetic friend whose counsels, precepts and patterns even are available to him and from which he need not fear to draw. But the arts are to-day all cursed by literature; artists attempt to make literature even of music, usually of painting and sculpture and doubtless would of architecture also, were the art not moribund; but whenever it is done the soul of the thing dies and we have not art but something far less for which the true artist can have neither affection nor respect. . . .

Contrary to the usual supposition this manner of working out a theme is more flexible than any working out in a fixed, historic style can ever be, and the individuality of those concerned may receive more adequate treatment within legitimate limitations. This matter of individuality puzzles many; they suspect that the individuality of the owner and occupant of a building is sacrificed to that of the architect who imposes his own upon Jones, Brown and Smith alike. An architect worthy of the name has an individuality, it is true; his work will and should reflect it, and his buildings will all bear a family resemblance one to another. The individuality of an owner is first manifest in his choice of his architect, the individual to whom he entrusts his characterization. He sympathizes with his work; its expression suits him and this furnishes the common ground upon which client and architect may come together.

Then, if the architect is what he ought to be, with his ready technique he conscientiously works for the client, idealizes his client's character and his client's tastes and makes him feel that the building is his as it really is to such an extent that he can truly say that he would rather have his own house than any other he has ever seen. Is a portrait, say by Sargent, any less a revelation of the character of the subject because it bears his stamp and is easily recognized by any one as a Sargent? Does one lose his individuality when it is interpreted sympathetically by one of his own race and time who can know him and his needs intimately and idealize them; or does he gain it only by having adopted or adapted to his condition a ready-made historic style which is the fruit of a seed-time other than his, whatever that style may be?

The present industrial condition is constantly studied in the practical application of these architectural ideals and the treatment simplified and arranged to fit modern processes and to utilize to the best advantage the work of the machine. The furniture takes the clean cut, straight-line forms that the machine can render far better than would be possible by hand. Certain facilities, too, of the machine, which it would be interesting to enlarge upon, are taken advantage of and the nature of the materials is usually revealed in the process.

Nor is the atmosphere of the result in its completeness new and hard. In most of the interiors there will be found a quiet, a simple dignity that we imagine is only to be found in the "old" and it is due to the underlying organic harmony, to the each in all and the all in each throughout. This is the modern opportunity—to make of a building, together with its equipment, appurtenances and environment, an entity which shall constitute a complete work of art, and a work of art more valuable to society as a whole than has before existed because discordant conditions endured for centuries are smoothed away; everyday life here finds an expression germane to its daily existence; an idealization of the common need sure to be uplifting and helpful in the same sense that pure air to breathe is better than air poisoned with noxious gases.

An artist's limitations are his best friends. The machine is here to stay. It is the forerunner of the democracy that is our dearest hope. There is no more important work before the architect now than to use this normal tool of civilization to the best advantage instead of prostituting it as he has hitherto done in reproducing with murderous ubiquity forms born of other times and other conditions and which it can only serve to destroy.

The exteriors of these structures will receive less ready recognition perhaps than the interiors and because they are the result of a radically different conception as to what should constitute a building. We have formed a habit of mind concerning architecture to which the expression of most of these exteriors must be a shock, at first more or less disagreeable, and the more so as the habit of mind is more narrowly fixed by so called classic training. Simplicity is not in itself an end; it is a means to an end. Our æsthetics are dyspeptic from incontinent indulgence in "Frenchite" pastry. We crave ornament for the sake of ornament; cover up our faults of design with ornamental sensualities that were a long time ago sensuous ornament. We will do well to distrust this unwholesome and unholy craving and look to the simple line; to the clean though living form and quiet color for a time, until the true significance of these things has dawned for us once more. The old structural forms which up to the present time have spelled "architecture" are decayed. Their life went from them long ago and new conditions industrially, steel and concrete and terra cotta in particular, are prophesying a more plastic art wherein as the flesh is to our bones so will the covering be to the structure, but more truly and beautifully expressive than ever. But that is a long story. This reticence in the matter of ornamentation is characteristic of these structures and for at least two reasons: first, they are the expression of an idea that the ornamentation of a building should be constitutional, a matter of the nature of the structure beginning with the ground plan. In the buildings themselves, in the sense of the whole, there is lacking neither richness nor incident but their qualities are secured not by applied decoration, they are found in the fashioning of the whole, in which color, too, plays as significant a part as it does in an old Japanese wood block print. Second; because, as before stated, buildings perform their highest function in relation to human life within and the natural efflorescence without; and to develop and maintain the harmony of a true chord between them making of the building in this sense a sure foil for life, broad simple surfaces and highly conventionalized forms are inevitable. These ideals take the buildings out of school and marry them to the ground; make them intimate expressions or revelations of the exteriors; individualize them regardless of preconceived notions of style. I have tried to make their grammar perfect in its way and to give their forms and proportions an integrity that will bear study, although few of them can be intelligently studied apart from their environment. So, what might be termed the democratic character of the exteriors is their first undefined offence—the lack, wholly, of what the professional critic would deem architecture; in fact, most of the critic's architecture has been left out.

There is always a synthetic basis for the features of the various structures, and consequently a constantly accumulating residue of formulae, which becomes more and more useful; but I do not pretend to say that the perception or conception of them was not at first intuitive, or that those that lie yet beyond will not be grasped in the same intuitive way; but, after all, architecture is a scientific art, and the thinking basis will ever be for the architect his surety, the final court in which his imagination sifts his feelings. . . .

The few draughtsmen so far associated with this work have been taken into the draughting room, in every case almost wholly unformed, many of them with no particular previous training, and patiently nursed for years in the atmosphere of the work itself, until, saturated by intimate association, at an impressionable age, with its motifs and phases, they have become helpful. To develop the sympathetic grasp of detail that is necessary before this point is reached has proved usually a matter of years, with little advantage on the side of the college-trained understudy. These young people have found their way to me through natural sympathy with the work, and have become loyal assistants. The members, so far, all told here and elsewhere, of our little university of fourteen years' standing are: Marion Mahony, a capable assistant for eleven years; William Drummond, for seven years; Francis Byrne,[4] five years; Isabel Roberts, five years; George Willis, four years; Walter Griffin, four years; Andrew Willatzen, three years; Harry Robinson, two years; Charles E. White, Jr., one year; Erwin Barglebaugh and Robert Hardin, each one year; Albert McArthur entering.

Others have been attracted by what seemed to them to be the novelty of the work, staying only long enough to acquire a smattering of form, then departing to sell a superficial proficiency elsewhere. Still others shortly develop a mastery of the subject, discovering that it is all just as they would have done it, anyway, and, chafing at the unkind fate that forestalled them in its practice, resolve to blaze a trail for themselves without further loss of time. It is urged against the more loyal that they are sacrificing their individuality to that which has dominated this work; but it is too soon to impeach a single understudy on this basis, for, although they will inevitably repeat for years the methods, forms and habit of thought, even the mannerisms of the present work, if there is virtue in the principles behind it that virtue will stay with them through the preliminary stages of their own practice until their own individualities truly develop independently. I have noticed that those who have made the most fuss about their "individuality" in early stages, those who took themselves most seriously in that regard, were inevitably those who had least.

Many elements of Mr. Sullivan's personality in his art—what might be called his mannerisms—naturally enough clung to my work in the early years, and may be readily traced by the casual observer; but for me one real proof of the virtue inherent in this work will lie in the fact that some of the young men and women who have given themselves up to me so faithfully these past years will some day contribute rounded individualities of their own, and forms of their own devising to the new school.

This year I assign to each a project that has been carefully conceived in my own mind, which he accepts as a specific work. He follows its subsequent development through all its phases in drawing room and field, meeting with the client himself on occasion, gaining an all-round development impossible otherwise, and insuring an enthusiasm and a grasp of detail decidedly to the best interest of the client. These privileges in the hands of selfishly ambitious or overconfident assistants would soon wreck such a system; but I can say that among my own boys it has already proved a moderate success, with every prospect of being continued as a settled policy in future.

Nevertheless, I believe that only when one individual forms the concept of the various projects and also determines the character of every detail in the sum total, even to the size and shape of the pieces of glass in the windows, the arrangement and profile of the most insignificant of the architectural members, will that unity be secured which is the soul of the individual work of art. This means that fewer buildings should be entrusted to one architect. His output will of necessity be relatively small—small, that is, as compared to the volume of work turned out in any one of fifty "successful offices" in America. I believe there is no middle course worth considering in the light of the best future of American architecture. With no more propriety can an architect leave the details touching the form of his concept to assistants, no matter how sympathetic and capable they may be, than can a painter entrust the painting in of the details of his picture to a pupil; for an architect who would do individual work must have a technique well developed and peculiar to himself, which, if he is fertile, is still growing with his growth. To keep everything "in place" requires constant care and study in maters that the old-school practitioner would scorn to touch. . . .

As for the future—the work shall grow more truly simple; more expressive with fewer lines, fewer forms; more articulate with less labor; more plastic; more fluent, although more coherent; more organic. It shall grow not only to fit more perfectly the methods and processes that are called upon to produce it, but shall further find whatever is lovely or of good repute in method or process, and idealize it with the cleanest, most virile stroke I can imagine. As understanding and appreciation of life matures and deepens, this work shall prophesy and idealize the character of the individual it is fashioned to serve more intimately, no matter how inexpensive the result must finally be. It shall become in its atmosphere as pure and elevating in its humble way as the trees and flowers are in their perfectly appointed way, for only so can architecture be worthy its high rank as a fine art, or the architect discharge the obligation he assumes to the public—imposed upon him by the nature of his own profession.

NOTES
1. Wright worked roughly five years for Sullivan, from early 1888 to early 1893.
2. Slightly altered from Thomas Carlyle, *Sartor Resartus: The Life and Opinions of Herr Teufelsdrockh*, published in *Fraser's Magazine* (London, 1833–34) and as a book in 1838.
3. Less readily identifiable are "A Fireproof House for $5,000," *Ladies' Home Journal*, 24 (April 1907) and his own 1895 Oak Park, Illinois, studio.
4. Wright misidentifies Barry Byrne.

FIVE

Ethics of Ornament
(1909)

Brief though it is, this speech excerpt requires a comparatively lengthy introduction because it addresses an issue many early-twentieth-century architects faced, including Wright: given the archaic quality of ornament in the machine age, what role, if any, should it play and of what should it consist?

In 1892 during Wright's tenure in his office, Louis Sullivan argued that "there exists a peculiar sympathy between the ornament and the structure," as if ornament "had come forth from the very substance of the [building] material . . . by the same right that a flower appears amid the leaves of its parent plant." Representing another point of view entirely, Viennese architect Alfred Loos wrote in a 1908 essay that "since ornament is no longer organically linked with our culture, it is no longer the expression of our culture." Wright agreed with each of these seemingly contradictory statements.

Loos's essay compared ornament with "crime" while Wright said it "is a burlesque of the beautiful," encrusting "dead things." Loos wrote that "ornament generally increases the cost of an article" but Wright upped the ante by saying it "is consuming at least two-thirds of our economic resources." Whether under- or overstating, each condemned ornament, yet along with Sullivan used it consistently (Loos in interiors especially).

This is not a contradiction because the three conceived ornament "organically," as did Louis Kahn, who in 1969 said that "the joint is the beginning of ornament,"[1] *acknowledging it was integral to his work since he always emphasized joinery. So it is that four so-called modern architects, whose overlapping careers spanned a century, welcomed ornament despite the vocal opposition of most of their colleagues.*

Wright's speech divides into two parts. The first criticizes the ways in which ornament is ordinarily developed and deployed; the second suggests what "true ornament" could and should be. Wright had touched on the subject before but only in passing, and in coming years would rarely concentrate on it (not until 1932 would he again use "ornament" in the title of a publication), making this short document especially important.

Key to his thinking is the word "conventional," as in the phrase "conventional representations," here used twice (but see Document 7). "Conventional" to Wright did not mean "ordinary," "habitual," or anything similar. Conventional representation referred to the intellectual process of isolating the essence of the object—perhaps a sumac leaf—and depicting it orthogonally as an abstraction, idealization, or representation; that is, as a conventionalization of its literal form, then integrating it seamlessly with grammar and materials to produce an harmonious whole.

When Kahn said "the joint is the beginning of ornament," he meant that buildings were invariably self-decorated, which is to say that construction always left its markings, to which Wright adds— and Kahn would have agreed—that the innate color, texture, and graining of materials, the placement of doors and windows, the composition resulting from contrasting solids and voids, in short, "the nature of that which is ornamented" generates its own decoration, which is not applied to, but the inevitable outcome of, the process of executing a design.

The following is an excerpt from a lecture to the Nineteenth Century Club, Oak Park, Illinois, January 11, 1909, published in Oak Leaves, *the local newspaper, January 16, 1909.*

The desire for works of ornament is co existent with the earliest attempts of civilization of every people, and today this desire is consuming at least two-thirds of our economic resources.

Understanding is essential to a real sense of loveliness, but this we have lost; exaggeration serves us now instead of interpretation; imitation and prettifying externals combine in a masquerade of flimsy finery and affection that outrages sensibility.

Modern ornamentation is a burlesque of the beautiful, as pitiful as it is costly. We never will be civilized to any extent until we know what ornament means and use it sparingly and significantly. Possession without understanding and appreciation means either waste or corruption. With us almost all these things which ought to be proofs of spiritual culture go by default and are, so far as our real life is concerned, an ill-fitting garment. The environment reflects unerringly the society.

If the environment is stupid and ugly, or borrowed and false, one may assume that the substratum of its society is the same. The measure of man's culture is the measure of his appreciation. We are ourselves what we appreciate and no more.

The matter of ornament is primarily a spiritual matter, a proof of culture, an expression of the quality of the soul in us, easily read and enjoyed by the enlightened when it is a real expression of ourselves. The greater the riches, it seems, the less poetry and less healthful significance.

Many homes are the product of lust for possession, and in no sense an expression of a sympathetic love for the beautiful. This is as true of the New York millionaire as of his more clumsy Chicago imitator.

He who meddles with the aesthetic owes a duty to others as well as to himself. This is true not only where the result is to stand conspicuous before the public eye but also in regard to the personal belongings of the individual. Back of all our manners, customs, dogmas and morals there is something preserved for its aesthetic worth, and that is the soul of the thing.

We are living today encrusted with dead things, forms from which the soul is gone, and we are devoted to them, trying to get joy out of them, trying to believe them still potent.

It behooves us, as partially civilized beings, to find out what ornament means, and the first wholesome effects of this attitude of inquiry is to make us do away with most of it; to make us feel safer and more comfortable with plain things.

Simple things are not necessarily plain, but plain things are all that most of us are really entitled to, in any spiritual reckoning, at present.

True ornament is not a matter of prettifying externals. It is organic with the structure it adorns, whether a person, a building or a park. At its best it is an emphasis of structure, a realization in graceful terms of the nature of that which is ornamented. Above all, it should possess fitness, proportion, harmony; the result of all of which is repose. So it is that structure should be decorated.

Decoration should never be purposely constructed. True beauty results from that repose which the mind feels when the eye, the intellect, the affections, are satisfied from the absence of any want—in other words, when we take joy in the thing.

Now to make application, I would impress upon you one law, concerning which all great artists are agreed, and that has been universally observed in the best periods of the world's art, and equally violated when art declined; it is fundamental, therefore inviolable.

Flowers or other natural objects should not be used as ornaments, but conventional representations founded upon them, sufficiently suggestive to convey the intended image to the mind without destroying the unity of the object decorated. With birds and flowers on hats, fruit pieces on the walls, imitation or realism in any form, ornamentation in art goes to the ground.

This conventional representation must always be worked out in harmony with the nature of the materials used, to develop, if possible, some beauty peculiar to this material. Hence one must know materials and apprehend their nature before one can judge an ornament.

Fitness to use and form adapted to function is part of the rule.

Construction should be decorated. Decoration never should be purposely constructed, which would finally dispose of almost every ornamental thing one possesses.

The principles discoverable in the works of the past belong to us. To take the results is taking the end for the means.

NOTES

1. Louis Sullivan, "Ornament in Architecture," *Engineering Magazine*, 3 (August 1892); Adolf Loos, "Ornament and Crime" (1908), reprinted in Ulrich Conrads, ed., *Programs and Manifestoes on 20th-century Architecture* (Cambridge, MA: MIT Press, 1964); Louis Kahn, "Silence and Light," lecture at Eidgenossiche Technische Hochschule, Zurich, February 12, 1969, reprinted in Robert Twombly, ed., *Louis Kahn: Essential Texts* (New York: W. W. Norton & Co., 2003).

SIX

Studies and Executed Buildings
(1910)

Wright arrived in Berlin in the autumn of 1909 to oversee two 1910 publications by Ernst Wasmuth: Frank Lloyd Wright: Ausgeführte Bauten, *a book of plans and photographs of "executed buildings" from roughly the mid-1890s to 1909, and* Ausgeführte Bauten und Entwürfe von Frank Lloyd Wright, *a drawing portfolio of "executed buildings and studies" of the same period, for which this essay is the introduction. During his year on the Continent—he returned home in the fall of 1910—he traveled widely, residing for a time in Fiesole, Italy, on the outskirts of Florence.*

Having immersed himself in the study of vernacular and artist-designed buildings, he elaborates here on assertions made in Document 2, concluding that Renaissance architecture was "a polyglot tangle of borrowed [historical] forms" applied inorganically to contemporary conditions for which they were inappropriate. The Gothic, on the other hand, was an organic expression of life and work in its own time and place. It is not Gothic forms from which twentieth-century architects might benefit, however, but the Gothic spirit: the "simplifying process" of creating indigenous architecture true to the culture from which it arose.

The American ideal, he writes, is individualism, the foundation of democracy, which he defines as "the highest possible development of the individual consistent with a harmonious [social] whole."

Democracy, accepting the machine (which also means believing in progress), individualism, common sense—these are the national characteristics that Wright says present "a new architectural proposition," which is, that an American architecture, an organic architecture, based on a renewed Gothic spirit is about to emerge, most likely in western and midwestern regions least damaged by eastern revivalism, more attuned to the beneficial influence of nature.

"Studies and Executed Buildings" is a more comprehensive statement than "In the Cause of Architecture," which in turn was more comprehensive than "The Art and Craft of the Machine." But the three concisely capture Wright's evolving design philosophy that in 1910 reached its maturity, all major aspects now in place.

And, because of his Berlin publications, his ideas began to penetrate the Continent, especially Germany and the Netherlands, inspiring a younger generation that during the 1910s and 1920s pioneered what came to be called "the International Style." (More on this in the introduction to Documents 12a–d.) Because of its overseas circulation, this essay may very well be the most influential of Wright's career.

Introduction to Ausgeführte Bauten und Entwürfe von Frank Lloyd Wright *(Berlin: Ernst Wasmuth, 1910).*

Florence Italy, June, 1910.

Since a previous article,[1] written in an endeavor to state the nature of the faith and practice fashioning this work, I have had the privilege of studying the work of that splendid group of Florentine sculptors and painters and architects, and the sculptor-painters and painter-sculptors, who were also architects: Giotto, Masaccio, Mantegna, Arnolfo, Pisano, Brunelleschi, and Bramante, Sansovino and Angelo.

No line was drawn between the arts and their epoch. Some of the sculpture is good painting; most of the painting is good sculpture; and in both lie the patterns of architecture. Where this confusion is not a blending of these arts, it is as amazing as it is unfortunate. To attempt to classify the works severely as pure painting, pure sculpture, or pure architecture would be quite impossible, if it were desirable for educational purposes. But be this as it may, what these men of Florence absorbed from their Greek, Byzantine and Roman forbears, they bequeathed to Europe as the kernel of the Renaissance; and this, if we deduct the Gothic influence of the Middle Ages, has constituted the soul of the Academic fine arts on the Continent.

From these Italian flames were lighted myriads of French, German and English lights that flourished, flickered feebly for a time, and soon smouldered in the sensuality and extravagance of later periods, until they were extinguished in banal architecture like the Rococo, or in nondescript structures such as the Louvre.

This applies to those buildings which were more or less "professional" embodiments of a striving for the beautiful, those buildings which were "good school" performances, which sought consciously to be beautiful. Nevertheless, here as elsewhere, the true basis for any serious study of the art of architecture is in those indigenous structures, the more humble buildings everywhere, which are to architecture what folk-lore is to literature or folk-songs are to music, and with which architects were seldom concerned. In the aggregate of these lie the traits that make them characteristically German or Italian, French, Dutch, English or Spanish in nature, as the case may be. The traits of these structures are national, of the soil; and, though often slight, their virtue is intimately interrelated with environment and with the habits of life of the people. Their functions are truthfully conceived, and rendered directly with natural feeling. They are always instructive and often beautiful. So, underlying the ambitious and self-conscious blossoms of the human soul, the expressions of "Maryolatry," or adoration of divinity, or cringing to temporal power, there is the love of life which quietly and inevitably finds the right way, and in lovely color, gracious line and harmonious arrangement imparts it untroubled by any burden,—as little concerned with literature or indebted to it as the flower by the wayside that turns its petals upward to the sun is concerned with the farmer who passes in the road or is indebted to him for the geometry of its petals or the mathematics of its structure.

Of this joy in living, there is greater proof in Italy than elsewhere. Buildings, pictures and sculpture seem to be born, like the flowers by the roadside, to sing themselves into being. Approached in the spirit of their conception, they inspire us with the very music of life.

No really Italian building seems ill at ease in Italy. All are happily content with what ornament and color they carry, as naturally as the rocks and trees and garden slopes which are one with them. Wherever the cypress rises, like the touch of a magician's wand, it resolves all into a composition harmonious and complete.

The secret of this ineffable charm would be sought in vain in the rarefied air of scholasticism or pedantic fine art. It lies close to the earth. Like a handful of the moist, sweet earth itself, it is so simple that, to modern minds, trained in intellectual gymnastics, it would seem unrelated to great purposes. It is so close that almost universally it is overlooked.

Along the wayside some blossom, with unusually glowing color or prettiness of form, attracts us: held by it, we accept gratefully its perfect loveliness; but, seeking to discover the secret of its charm, we find the blossom, whose more obvious claim first arrests our attention, intimately related to the texture and shape of its foliage; we discover a strange sympathy between the form of the flower and the system upon which the leaves are arranged about the stalk. From this we are led to observe a characteristic habit of growth, and resultant nature of structure, having its first direction and form in the roots hidden in the warm earth, kept moist by the conservative covering of leaf mould. This structure proceeds from the general to the particular in a most inevitable way, arriving at the blossom to proclaim in its lines and form the nature of the structure that bore it. It is an organic thing. Law and order are the basis of its finished grace and beauty: its beauty is the expression of fundamental conditions in line, form and color, true to them, and existing to fulfill them according to design.

We can in no wise prove beauty to be the result of these harmonious internal conditions. That which through the ages appeals to us as beautiful does not ignore in its fibre the elements of law and order. Nor does it take long to establish the fact that no lasting beauty ignores these elements ever present as conditions of its existence. It will appear, from study of the forms or styles which mankind has considered beautiful, that those which live longest are those which in greatest measure fulfill these conditions. That a thing grows is no concern of ours, because the quality of life is beyond us and we are not necessarily concerned with it. Beauty, in its essence, is for us as mysterious as life. All attempts to say what it is, are as foolish as cutting out the head of a drum to find whence comes the sound. But we may study with profit these truths of form and structure, facts of form as related to function, material traits of line determining character, laws of structure inherent in all natural growth. We ourselves are only a product of natural law. These truths, therefore, are in harmony with the essence of our own being, and are perceived by us to be good. We instinctively feel the good, true and beautiful to be essentially one in the last analysis. Within us there is a divine principle of growth to some end; accordingly we select as good whatever is in harmony with this law.

We reach for the light spiritually, as the plant does physically, if we are sound of heart and not sophisticated by our education.

When we perceive a thing to be beautiful, it is because we instinctively recognize the rightness of the thing. This means that we have revealed to us a glimpse of something essentially of the fibre of our own nature. The artist makes this revelation to us through his deeper insight. His power to visualize his conceptions being greater than our own, a flash of truth stimulates us, and we have a vision of harmonies not understood to-day, though perhaps to be to-morrow.

This being so, whence came corrupt styles like the Renaissance? From false education, from confusion of the curious with the beautiful. Confounding the sensations awakened by the beautiful with those evoked by things merely curious is a fatal tendency which increases as civilization moves away from nature and founds conventions in ignorance of or defiance of natural law.

The appreciation of beauty on the part of primitive peoples; Mongolian, Indian, Arab, Egyptian, Greek and Goth, was unerring. Because of this their work is coming home to us to-day in another and truer Renaissance, to open our eyes that we may cut away the dead wood and brush aside the accumulated rubbish of centuries of false education. This Renaissance means a return to simple conventions in harmony with nature. Primarily it is a simplifying process. Then, having learned the spiritual lesson that the East has power to teach the West, we may build upon this basis the more highly developed forms our more highly developed life will need.

Nature sought in this way can alone save us from the hopeless confusion of ideas that has resulted in the view that beauty is a matter of caprice, that it is merely a freak of imagination,—to one man divine, to another hideous, to another meaningless. We are familiar with the assertion, that, should a man put eleven stove-pipe hats on top of the cornice of his building and find them beautiful, why then they are beautiful. Yes, perhaps to him; but the only possible conclusion is, that, like the eleven hats on the cornice, he is not beautiful, because beauty to him is utter violation of all the harmonies of any sequence or consequence of his own nature. To find inorganic things of no truth of relation beautiful is but to demonstrate the lack of beauty in oneself and one's unfitness for any office in administering the beautiful, and to provide another example of the stultification that comes from the confusion of the curious with the beautiful.

Education seems to leave modern man less able than the savage to draw the line between these qualities.

A knowledge of cause and effect in line, color and form, as found in organic nature, furnishes guide lines within which an artist may sift materials, test motives and direct aims, thus roughly blocking out, at least, the rational basis of his ideas and ideals. Great artists do this by instinct. The thing is felt or divined, by inspiration perhaps, as synthetic analysis of their works will show. The poetry which is prophecy is not a matter to be demonstrated. But what is of great value to the artist in research of this nature is knowledge of those facts of relation, those qualities of line, form and color which are themselves a language of sentiment, and characterize the pine as a pine as distinguished from those determining the willow as a willow; those characteristic traits which the Japanese seize graphically and unerringly reduce to simple geometry; the graphic soul of the thing, as seen in the geometrical analyses of Holkusai. Korin was the conscious master of the essential in whatever he rendered, and his work stands as a convincing revelation of the soul of the thing he portrayed.[2] So it will be found with all great work,—with the paintings of Velasquez and Frans Hals; with Gothic architecture: organic character in all.

By knowledge of nature in this sense alone are these guiding principles to be established. Ideals gained within these limitations are never lost, and an artist may defy his "education." If he is really for nature in this sense, he may be "a rebel against his time and its laws, but never lawless."

The debased periods of the world's art are far removed from any conception of these principles. The Renaissance, Barok, Rococo, the styles of the Louis, are not developed from within. There is little or nothing organic in their nature; they are put on from without. The freedom from the yoke of authority which the Renaissance gave to men was seemingly a great gain; but it served only to bind them senselessly to tradition, and to mar the art of the Middle Ages past repair. One cannot go into the beautiful edifices of this great period without hatred of the Renaissance growing in his soul. It proves itself a most wantonly destructive thing in its hideous perversity. In every land where the Gothic or Byzantine, or the Romanesque, that was close to Byzantine, grew, it is a soulless blight, a warning, a veritable damnation of the beautiful. What lovely things remain, it left to us in spite of its nature or when it was least itself. It was not a development;—it was a disease.

This is why buildings growing in response to actual needs, fitted into environment by people who knew no better than to fit them to it with native feeling,—buildings that grew as folk-lore and folk-song grew,—are better worth study than highly self-conscious academic attempts at the beautiful; academic attempts which the nations seem to possess in common as a gift from Italy, after acknowledging her source of inspiration.

All architecture worthy the name is a growth in accord with natural feeling and industrial means to serve actual needs. It cannot be put on from without. There is little beyond sympathy with the spirit creating it and an understanding of the ideals that shaped it that can legitimately be utilized. Any attempt to use forms borrowed from other times and conditions must end as the Renaissance ends,—with total loss of inherent relation to the soul life of the people. It can give us only an extraneous thing in the hands of professors that means little more than a mask for circumstance or a mark of temporal power to those whose lives are burdened, not expressed, by it; the result is a terrible loss to life for which literature can never compensate. Buildings will always remain the most valuable asset in a people's environment, the one most capable of cultural reaction. But until the people have the joy again in architecture as a living art that one sees recorded in buildings of all the truly great periods, so long will architecture remain a dead thing. It will not live again until we break away entirely from adherence to the false ideals of the Renaissance. In that whole movement art was reduced to the level of an expedient. What future has a people content with that? Only that of parasites, feeding on past greatness, and on the road to extinction by some barbarian race with ideals and hungering for their realization in noble concrete form.

In America we are more betrayed by this condition than the people of older countries, for we have no traditional forms except the accumulated ones of all peoples that do not without sacrifice fit new conditions, and there is in consequence no true reverence for tradition. As some sort of architecture is a necessity, American architects take their pick from the world's stock of "ready-made" architecture, and are most successful when transplanting form for form, line for line, enlarging details by means of lantern slides from photographs of the originals.

This works well. The people are architecturally clothed and sheltered. The modern comforts are smuggled in cleverly, we must admit. But is this architecture? Is it thus tradition that molded great styles? In this polyglot tangle of borrowed forms, is there a great spirit that will bring order out of chaos? vitality, unity and greatness out of emptiness and discord?

The ideals of the Renaissance will not, for the Renaissance was inorganic.

A conception of what constitutes an organic architecture will lead to better things once it is planted in the hearts and minds of men whose resource and skill, whose real power, are unquestioned, and who are not obsessed by expedients and forms, the nature and origin of which they have not studied in relation to the spirit that produced them. The nature of these forms in not taught in any vital sense in any of the schools in which architects are trained.

A revival of the Gothic spirit is needed in the art and architecture of modern life; an interpretation of the best traditions we have in the world made with our own methods, not a stupid attempt to fasten their forms upon a life that has outgrown them. Reviving the Gothic spirit does not mean using the forms of Gothic architecture handed down from the Middle Ages. It necessarily means something quite different. The conditions and ideals that fixed the forms of the twelfth are not the conditions and ideals that can truthfully fix the forms of the twentieth century. The spirit that fixed those forms is the spirit that will fix the new forms. Classicists and schools will deny the new forms, and find no "Gothic" in them. It will not much matter. They will be living, doing their work quietly and effectively, until the borrowed garments, cut over to fit by the academies, are cast off, having served only to hide the nakedness of a moment when art became detached, academic, alien to the lives of the people.

America, more than any other nation, presents a new architectural proposition. Her ideal is democracy, and in democratic spirit her institutions are professedly conceived. This means that she places a life premium upon individuality,—the highest possible development of the individual consistent with a harmonious whole,—believing that a whole benefited by sacrifice of that quality in the individual rightly considered his "individuality" is undeveloped; believing that the whole, to be worthy as a whole, must consist of individual units, great and strong in themselves, not yoked from without in bondage, but united within, with the right to move in unity, each in its own sphere, yet preserving this right to the highest possible degree for all. This means greater individual life and more privacy in life,—concerns which are peculiarly one's own. It means lives lived in greater independence and seclusion, with all toward which an English nobleman aspires, but with absolute unwillingness to pay the price in paternalism and patronage asked of him for the privilege. This dream of freedom, as voiced by the Declaration of Independence, is dear to the heart of every man who has caught the spirit of American institutions; therefore the ideal of every man American in feeling and spirit. Individuality is a national ideal. Where this degenerates into petty individualism, it is but a manifestation of weakness in the human nature, and not a fatal flaw in the ideal.

In America each man has a peculiar, inalienable right to live in his own house in his own way. He is a pioneer in every right sense of the word. His home environment may face forward, may portray his character, tastes and ideas, if he has any, and every man here has some somewhere about him.

This is a condition at which Englishmen or Europeans, facing toward traditional forms which they are in duty bound to preserve, may well stand aghast. An American is in duty bound to establish traditions in harmony with his ideals, his still unspoiled sites, his industrial opportunities, and industrially he is more completely committed to the machine than any living man. It has given him the things which mean mastery over an uncivilized land,—comfort and resources.

His machine, the tool in which his opportunity lies, can only murder the traditional forms of other peoples and earlier times. He must find new forms, new industrial ideals, or stultify both opportunity and forms. But underneath forms in all ages were certain conditions which determined them. In them all was a human spirit in accord with which they came to be; and where the forms were true forms, they will be found to be organic forms,—an outgrowth, in other words, of conditions of life and work they arose to express. They are beautiful and significant, studied in this relation. They are dead to us, borrowed as they stand.

I have called this feeling for the organic character of form and treatment the Gothic spirit, for it was more completely realized in the forms of that architecture, perhaps, than any other. At least the infinitely varied forms of that architecture are more obviously and literally organic than any other, and the spirit in which they were conceived and wrought was one of absolute integrity of means to ends. In this spirit America will find the forms best suited to her opportunities, her aims and her life.

All the great styles, approached from within, are spiritual treasure houses to architects. Transplanted as forms, they are tombs of a life that has been lived.

This ideal of individuality has already ruthlessly worked its way with the lifeless carcasses of the foreign forms it has hawked and flung about in reckless revel that in East, as well as West, amounts to positive riot.

Brown calls loudly for Renaissance, Smith for a French chateau, Jones for an English manor house, McCarthy for an Italian villa, Robinson for Hanseatic, and Hammerstein for Rococo, while the sedately conservative families cling to "old colonial" wedding cakes with demurely conscious superiority. In all this is found the last word of the *inorganic*. The Renaissance ended in this,—a thing absolutely removed from time, place or people; borrowed finery put on hastily, with no more conception of its meaning or character than Titania had of the donkey she caressed.[3] "All a matter of taste," like the hats on the cornice.

A reaction was inevitable.

•

It is of this reaction that I feel qualified to speak; for the work illustrated in this volume, with the exception of the work of Louis Sullivan, is the first consistent protest in bricks and mortar against this pitiful waste. It is a serious attempt to formulate some industrial and aesthetic ideals that in a quiet, rational way will help to make a lovely thing of an American's home environment, produced without abuse by his own tools, and dedicated in spirit and letter to him.

The ideals of Ruskin and Morris and the teaching of the Beaux Arts have hitherto prevailed in America, steadily confusing, as well as in some respects revealing to us our opportunities. The American, too, of some old-world culture, disgusted by this state of affairs, and having the beautiful harmony in the architecture of an English village, European rural community, or the grandiloquent planning of Paris in view, has been easily persuaded that the best thing we could do was to adopt some style least foreign to us, stick to it and plant it continually; a parasitic proceeding, and in any case futile. New York is a tribute to the Beaux Arts so far as surface decoration goes, and underneath a tribute to the American engineer.

Other cities have followed her lead.

Our better-class residences are chiefly tributes to English architecture, cut open inside and embellished to suit; porches and "conveniences" added: the result in most cases a pitiful mongrel. Painfully conscious of their lack of traditions, our get-rich-quick citizens attempt to buy Tradition ready made, and are dragged forward, facing backwards, in attitudes most absurd to those they would emulate, characteristic examples of conspicuous waste.

The point in all this is the fact that revival of the ideals of an organic architecture will have to contend with this rapidly increasing sweep of imported folly. Even the American with some little culture, going contrary to his usual course in other matters, is becoming painfully aware of his inferiority in matters of dress and architecture, and goes abroad for both, to be sure they are correct. Thus assured, he is no longer concerned, and forgets both. That is more characteristic of the Eastern than the Western man. The real American spirit, capable of judging an issue for itself upon its merits, lies in the West and Middle West, where breadth of view, independent thought and a tendency to take common sense into the realm of art, as in life, are more characteristic. It is alone in an atmosphere of this nature that the Gothic spirit in building can be revived. In this atmosphere, among clients of this type, I have lived and worked.

Taking common sense into the holy realm of art is a shocking thing and most unpopular in academic circles. It is a species of vulgarity; but some of these questions have become so perplexed, so encrusted, by the savants and academies, with layer upon layer of "good school," that their very nature is hidden; approached with common sense, they become childishly simple.

I believe that every matter of artistic import which concerns a building may be put to the common sense of a business man on the right side every time, and thus given a chance at it, he rarely gives a wrong decision. The difficulty found by this man with the Renaissance, when he tries to get inside,—that is, if he does more than merely give the order to "go ahead,"—arises from the fact that the thing has no organic basis to give; there is no good reason for doing anything any particular way rather than another way which can be grasped by him or anybody else; it is all largely a matter of taste. In an organic scheme there are excellent reasons why the thing is as it is, what it is there for, and where it is going. If not, it ought not to go, and as a general thing it doesn't. The people themselves are part and parcel and helpful in producing the organic thing. They can comprehend it and make it theirs, and it is thus the only form of art expression to be considered for a democracy, and, I will go so far as to say, the truest of all forms.

•

So I submit that the buildings here illustrated have for the great-est part been conceived and worked in their conclusion in the Gothic spirit in this respect as well as in respect to the tools that produced them, the methods of work behind them, and, finally, in their organic nature considered in themselves. These are limita-tions, unattractive limitations; but there is no project in the fine arts that is not a problem.

With this idea as a basis, comes another conception of what constitutes a building.

The question then arises as to what is style. The problem no longer remains a matter of working in a prescribed style with what variation it may bear without absurdity if the owner happens to be a restless individualist: so this question is not easily answered.

What is style? Every flower has it; every animal has it; every indi-vidual worthy the name has it in some degree, no matter how much sandpaper may have done for him. It is a free product,—a by-product, the result of an organic working out of a project in character and in one state of feeling.

An harmonious entity of whatever sort in its entirety cannot fail of style in the best sense.

In matters of art the individual feeling of the creative artist can but give the color of his own likes and dislikes, his own soul to the thing he shapes. He gives his individuality, but will not prevent the building from being characteristic of those it was built to serve, because it necessarily is a solution of conditions they make, and it is made to serve their ends in their own way. In so far as these conditions are peculiar in themselves, or sympathy exists be-tween the clients and the architect, the building will be their build-ing. It will be theirs much more truly than though in ignorant selfhood they had stupidly sought to use means they had not con-quered to an end imperfectly foreseen. The architect, then, is their means, their technique and interpreter; the building, an interpretation if he is a true architect in the Gothic sense. If he is chiefly concerned with some marvelous result that shall stand as architecture in good form to his credit, the client be damned, why that is a misfortune which is only another species of the unwisdom of his client. This architect is a dangerous man, and there are lots of his kind outside, and some temptations to him inside, the ranks of the Gothic architects. But the man who loves the beautiful, with ideals of organic nature if an artist, is too keenly sensible of the nature of his client as a fundamental condition in his problem to cast him off, although he may give him something to grow to, something in which he may be a little ill at ease at the outset.

In this lies temptation to abuses. Where ignorance of the nature of the thing exists or where there is a particular character or preference, it is to a certain extent the duty of an architect to give his client something dated ahead; for he is entrusted by his client with his interests in matters in which, more frequently than not, the client is ignorant. A commission therefore becomes a trust to the architect. Any architect is bound to educate his client to the extent of his true skill and capacity in what he as a professional adviser believes to be fundamentally right. In this there is plenty of leeway for abuse of the client; temptations to sacrifice him in the interest of personal idiosyncrasies, to work along lines instinctively his preference, and therefore easy to him. But in any trust there is chance of failure. This educational relationship between client and architect is more or less to be expected, and of value artistically for the reason that, while the architect is educating the client, the client is educating him. And a certain determining factor in this quality of style is this matter growing out of this relation of architect and client to the work in hand, as well as the more definite elements of construction. This quality of style is a subtle thing, and should remain so, and not to be defined in itself so much as to be regarded as a result of *artistic integrity*.

•

Style, then, if the conditions are consistently and artistically cared for little by little will care for itself. As for working in a nominated style beyond a natural predilection for certain forms, it is unthinkable by the author of any true creative effort.

Given similar conditions, similar tools, similar people, I believe that architects will, with a proper regard for the organic nature of the thing produced, arrive at various results sufficiently harmonious with each other and with great individuality. One might swoop all the Gothic architecture of the world together in a single nation, and mingle it with buildings treated horizontally as they were treated vertically or treated diagonally, buildings and towers with flat roofs, long, low buildings with square openings, mingled with tall buildings with pointed ones, in the bewildering variety of that marvelous architectural manifestation, and harmony in the general ensemble inevitably result: the common chord in all being sufficient to bring them unconsciously into harmonious relation.

It is this ideal of an organic working out with normal means to a consistent end that is the salvation of the architect entrusted with liberty. He is really more severely disciplined by this ideal than his brothers of the styles, and less likely to falsify his issue.

So to the schools looking askance at the mixed material entrusted to their charge, thinking to save the nation a terrible infliction of the wayward dreams of mere idiosyncrasies by teaching "the safe course of a good copy," we owe thanks for a conservative attitude, but censure for failure to give to material needed by the nation, constructive ideals that would from *within* discipline sufficiently, at the same time leaving a chance to work out a real thing in touch with reality with such souls as they have. In other words, they are to be blamed for not inculcating in students the conception of architecture as an organic expression of the nature of a problem, for not teaching them to look to this nature for the elements of its working out in accordance with principles found in natural organisms. Study of the great architecture of the world solely in regard to the spirit that found expression in the forms should go with this. But before all should come the study of the nature of materials, the *nature* of the tools and processes at command, and the *nature* of the thing they are to be called upon to do.

A training of this sort was accorded the great artists of Japan. Although it was not intellectually self-conscious, I have no doubt the apprenticeship of the Middle Ages wrought like results.

German and Austrian art schools are getting back to these ideas. Until the student is taught to approach the beautiful from within, there will be no great living buildings which in the aggregate show the spirit of true architecture.

An architect, then, in this revived sense, is a man disciplined from within by a conception of the organic nature of his task, knowing his tools and his opportunity, working out his problems with what sense of beauty the gods gave him.

He, disciplined by the very nature of his undertakings, is the only safe man.

To work with him is to find him master of means to a certain end. He acquires a technique in the use of his tools and materials which may be as complete and in every sense as remarkable as a musician's mastery of the resources of his instrument. In no other spirit is this to be acquired in any vital sense, and without it— well—a good copy is the safest thing. If one cannot live an independent life, one may at least become a modest parasite.

It is with the courage that a conviction of the truth of this point of view has given that the problems in this work have been attempted. In that spirit they have been worked out, with what degree of failure or success no one can know better than I. To be of value to the student they must be approached from within, and not from the viewpoint of the man looking largely at the matter from the depths of the Renaissance. In so far as they are grasped as organic solutions of conditions they exist but to serve, with respect for the limitations imposed by our industrial conditions, and having in themselves a harmony of idea in form and treatment that makes something fairly beautiful of them in relation to life, they will be helpful. Approached from the point of view that seeks characteristic beauty of form and feature as great as that of the Greeks, the Goths or the Japanese, they will be disappointing; and I can only add, it is a little too soon yet to look for such attainment. But the quality of style, in the indefinable sense that it is possessed by any organic thing, that they have. Repose and quiet attitudes they have. Unity of idea, resourceful adaptation of means, will not be found wanting, nor that simplicity of rendering which the machine makes not only imperative but opportune. Although complete, highly developed in detail, they are not.

Self-imposed limitations are in part responsible for this lack of intricate enrichment, and partly the imperfectly developed resources of our industrial system. I believe, too, that much ornament in the old sense is not for us yet: we have lost its significance, and I do not believe in adding enrichment merely for the sake of enrichment. Unless it adds clearness to the enunciation of the theme, it is undesirable, for it is very little understood.

I wish to say, also, what is more to the point,—that, in a structure conceived in the organic sense, the ornamentation is conceived in the very ground plan, and is of the very constitution of the structure. What ornamentation may be found added purely as such in this structure is thus a makeshift or a confession of weakness or failure.

Where the warp and woof of the fabric do not yield sufficient incident or variety, it is seldom patched on. Tenderness has often to be sacrificed to integrity.

It is fair to explain the point, also, which seems to be missed in studies of the work, that in the conception of these structures they are regarded as severe conventions whose chief office is a background or frame for the life within them and about them. They are considered as foils for the foliage and bloom which they are arranged to carry, as well as a distinct chord or contrast, in their severely conventionalized nature, to the profusion of trees and foliage with which their sites abound.

So the forms and the supervisions and refinements of the forms are, perhaps, more elemental in character than has hitherto been the case in highly developed architecture. To be lived with, the ornamental forms of one's environment should be designed to wear well, which means they must have absolute repose and make no especial claim upon attention; to be removed as far from realistic tendencies as a sense of reality can take them. Good colors, soft textures, living materials, the beauty of the materials revealed and utilized in the scheme, these are the means of decoration considered purely as such.

And it is quite impossible to consider the building one thing and its furnishings another, its setting and environment still another. In the spirit in which these buildings are conceived, these are all one thing, to be foreseen and provided for in the nature of the structure. They are all mere structural details of its character and completeness. Heating apparatus, lighting fixtures, the very chairs and tables, cabinets and musical instruments, where practicable, are of the building itself. Nothing of appliances or fixtures is admitted purely as such where circumstances permit the full development of the building scheme.

Floor coverings and hangings are as much a part of the house as the plaster on the walls or the tiles on the roof. This feature of development has given most trouble, and so far is the least satisfactory to myself, because of difficulties inherent in the completeness of conception and execution necessary. To make these elements sufficiently light and graceful and flexible features of an informal use of an abode requires much more time and thought and money than are usually forthcoming. But it is approached by some later structures more nearly, and in time it will be accomplished. It is still in a comparatively primitive stage of development; yet radiators have disappeared, lighting fixtures are incorporated, floor coverings and hangings are easily made to conform. But chairs and tables and informal articles of use are still at large in most cases, although designed in feeling with the building.

There are no decorations, nor is there place for them as such. The easel picture has no place on the walls. It is regarded as music might be, suited to a mood, and provided for in a recess of the wall if desired, where a door like the cover of a portfolio might be dropped and the particular thing desired studied for a time; left exposed for days, perhaps, to give place to another, or entirely put away by simply closing the wooden portfolio. Great pictures should have their gallery. Oratorio is not performed in a drawing-room. The piano, where possible, should and does disappear in the structure, its key-board or open-work or tracery necessary for sound its only visible feature. The dining table and chairs are easily managed in the architecture of the building. So far this development has progressed.

Alternative extremes of heat and cold, of sun and storm, have also to be considered. The frost goes four feet into the ground in winter; the sun beats fiercely on the roof with almost tropical heat in summer: an umbrageous architecture is almost a necessity, both to shade the building from the sun and protect the walls from freezing and thawing moisture, the most rapidly destructive to buildings of all natural causes. The overhanging eaves, however, leave the house in winter without necessary sun, and this is overcome by the way in which the window groups in certain rooms and exposures are pushed out to the gutter line. The gently sloping roofs grateful to the prairie do not leave large air spaces above the rooms; and so the chimney has grown in dimensions and importance, and in hot weather ventilates at the high parts the circulating-air spaces beneath the roofs, fresh air entering beneath the eaves through openings easily closed in winter.

Conductor pipes, disfiguring down-spouts, particularly where eaves overhang, in this climate freeze and become useless in winter, or burst with results disastrous to the walls; so concrete rain basins are built in the ground beneath the angles of the eaves, and the water drops through open spouts into their concave surfaces, to be conducted to the cistern by underground drain tiles.

Another modern opportunity is afforded by our effective system of hot water heating. By this means the forms of buildings may be more completely articulated, with light and air on several sides. By keeping the ceilings low, the walls may be opened with series of windows to the outer air, the flowers and trees, the prospects, and one may live as comfortably as formerly, less shut in. Many of the structures carry this principle of articulation of various arts to the point where each has its own individuality completely recognized in plan. The dining-room and kitchen and sleeping-rooms thus become in themselves small buildings, and are grouped together as a whole, as in the Coonley house. It is also possible to spread the buildings, which once in our climate of extremes were a compact box cut into compartments, into a more organic expression, making a house in a garden or in the country the delightful thing in relation to either or both that imagination would have it.

The horizontal line is the line of domesticity.

The virtue of the horizontal lines is respectfully invoked in these buildings. The inches in height gain tremendous force compared with any practicable spread upon the ground.

To Europeans these buildings on paper seem uninhabitable; but they derive height and air by quite other means, and respect an ancient tradition, the only one here worthy of respect,—the prairie.

In considering the forms and types of these structures, the fact that they are nearly buildings for the prairie should be borne in mind; the gently rolling or level prairies of the Middle West; the great levels where every detail of elevation becomes exaggerated; every tree a tower above the great calm plains of its flowered surfaces as they lie serene beneath a wonderful sweep of sky. The natural tendency of every ill-considered thing is to detach itself and stick out like a sore thumb in surroundings by nature perfectly quiet. All unnecessary heights have for that reason and for other reasons economic been eliminated, and more intimate relation with out-door environment sought to compensate for loss of height.

The differentiation of a single, certain simple form characterizes the expression of one building. Quite a different form may serve for another; but from one basic idea all the formal elements of design are in each case derived and held together in scale and character. The form chosen may flare outward, opening flower-like to the sky, as in the Thomas house; another, droop to accentuate artistically the weight of the masses; another be non-committal or abruptly emphatic, or its grammar may be deduced from some plant form that has appealed to me, as certain properties in line and form of the sumach were used in the Lawrence house at Springfield; but in every case the motif is adhered to throughout.[4]

In the buildings themselves, in the sense of the whole, there is lacking neither richness nor incident; but these qualities are secured not by applied decoration, they are found in the fashioning of the whole, in which color, too, plays as significant a part as it does in an old Japanese wood block print.

These ideals take the buildings out of school and marry them to the ground; make them intimate expressions or revelations of the interiors; individualize them, regardless of preconceived notions of style. I have tried to make their grammar perfect in its way, and to give their forms and proportions an integrity that will bear study, although few of them can be intelligently studied apart from their environment.

A study of the drawings will show that the buildings presented fall readily into three groups having a family resemblance; the low-pitched hip roofs, heaped together in pyramidal fashion, or presenting quiet, unbroken sky lines; the low roofs with simple pediments countering on long ridges; and those topped with a simple slab. Of the first type, the Winslow, Henderson, Willits, Thomas, Heurtley, Heath, Cheney, Martin, Little, Gridley, Millard, Tomek, Coonley and Westcott houses, the Hillside Home School and the Pettit Memorial Chapel are typical. Of the second type, the Bradley, Hickox, Davenport and Dana houses are typical. Of the third, Atelier for Richard Bock, Unity Church, the concrete house of the *Ladies' Home Journal*, and other designs in process of execution. The Larkin Building is a simple, dignified utterance of a plain, utilitarian type, with sheer brick walls and simple stone copings. The studio is merely an early experiment in "articulation."

A type of structure especially suited to the prairie will be found in the Coonley, Thomas, Heurtley, Tomek and Robie houses, which are virtually one floor arrangements, raised a low story height above the level of the ground. Sleeping-rooms are added where necessary in another story.

There is no excavation for this type except for heating purposes. The ground floor provides all necessary room of this nature, and billiard-rooms, or play-rooms for the children. This plan raises the living-rooms well off the ground, which is often damp, avoids the ordinary damp basement, which, if made a feature of the house, sets it so high above the surface, if it is to be made dry, that, in proportion to the ordinary building operation, it rises like a menace to the peace of the prairie.

It is of course necessary that mural decoration and sculpture in these structures should again take their places as architectural developments conceived to conform to their fabric.

To thus make of a dwelling place a complete work of art, in itself as expressive and beautiful and more intimately related to life than anything of detached sculpture or painting, lending itself freely and suitably to the individual needs of the dwellers, an harmonious entity, fitting in color, pattern and nature the utilities, and in itself really an expression of them in character,—this is the modern American opportunity. Once founded, this will become a tradition, a vast step in advance of the day when a dwelling was an arrangement of separate rooms, mere chambers to contain aggregations of furniture, the utility comforts not present. An organic entity this, as contrasted with that aggregation: surely a higher ideal of unity, a higher and more intimate working out of the expression of one's life in one's environment. One thing instead of many things; a great thing instead of a collection of smaller ones.

The drawings, by means of which these buildings are presented here, have been made expressly for this work from colored drawings which were made from time to time as the projects were presented for solution. They merely aim to render the composition in outline and form, and suggest the sentiment of the environment. They are in no sense attempts to treat the subject pictorially, and in some cases fail to convey the idea of the actual building. A certain quality of familiar homelikeness is thus sacrificed in these presentments to a graceful decorative rendering of an idea of an arrangement suggesting, in the originals, a color scheme. Their debt to Japanese ideals, these renderings themselves sufficiently acknowledge.

CHARLES E. ROBERTS, FRANCIS W. LITTLE AND DARWIN D. MARTIN—THREE AMERICAN MEN OF AFFAIRS,—WHO HAVE BELIEVED IN AND BEFRIENDED THIS WORK WHEN NATURAL OPPOSITION FROM WITHOUT AND INHERENT FAULTS WITHIN THREATENED TO MAKE AN END OF IT. WITHOUT THEIR FAITH AND HELP THIS WORK WOULD NEVER HAVE REACHED ITS PRESENT DEVELOPMENT.[5]

FRANK LLOYD WRIGHT

NOTES

1. "In the Cause of Architecture" (1908), Document 4.

2. Wright misspells Katsushika Hokusai (1760–1849), painter and printmaker best known for his *Thirty-Six Views of Mount Fuji* (c. 1831); Ogata Korin (1658–1716), painter and decorator known for his lacquerwork. Both artists went by more than one name.

3. Oberon, King of the Fairies in Shakespeare's *A Midsummer's Night's Dream*, instructs his minion Puck to bring him a flower from Cupid to place on Titania, Queen of the Fairies, while she sleeps so that she will fall in love with the first person she sees upon waking. That turns out to be Nick Bottom, a human, to whom Puck gives the head of a donkey and with whom Titania falls passionately in love.

4. This paragraph and, skipping two, the paragraph beginning "A study of the drawings" are lifted with minimal change from "In the Cause of Architecture" (Document 4).

5. These Wright clients helped finance the publications mentioned in the head-note above.

SEVEN

The Japanese Print: An Interpretation
(1912)

*It has often been suggested that Wright's lifelong interest in Japan be-
gan while visiting its craft exhibits and pavilion at the 1893 World's
Columbian Exposition in Chicago when he was twenty-six. Whatever its origin it is clear that he had devoted enough attention to the
country and its art to make Japan the destination of his first overseas
excursion, for three months in 1905, when most Americans if able to
travel abroad went to Europe.*

*He had also acquired enough expertise to know what to pur-
chase, for he returned with prints sufficient in quality and quantity
to stage a 1906 exhibition at Chicago's Art Institute, the catalogue of
which, entitled* Hiroshige, *was published with an introduction that
served as the basis for this text.*

*By 1912, Wright had become a nationally known expert on
Japanese printmaking, well on his way to assembling what Clay Lan-
caster, a scholar of Japan's influence in the United States, called "one
of the most important collections . . . in the world." Had he somehow
failed as an architect, he might have ended up an internationally
known authority on his avocation.*

The Japanese Print *is a thirty-four page, small format, unillus-
trated booklet—essentially an essay—analyzing the art form in its
cultural milieu. Even a casual reading reveals how thoroughly Wright*

knew his subject, so thoroughly in fact that even today The Japanese Print *remains an important contribution to art history, and not just because a world-famous architect wrote it.*

Its significance here, however, is indeed architectural, especially its concept of "conventionalizing" (see Document 5), which is explained more fully at essay's end than anywhere else in Wright's literary oeuvre. *"Conventionalizing" is so crucial for understanding his* modus operandi *that this essay can be read as a metaphor—or as an autobiographical statement once removed—for the way he thought and worked, for what he intended his buildings to mean and to be at their very core. So it is not without benefit to imagine that Wright himself was once a Japanese printmaker who in his next incarnation became an American architect.*

This comparatively overlooked essay warrants careful inspection not only the better to appreciate Japanese art, itself rewarding, but also and perhaps more importantly to better understand the art of Frank Lloyd Wright.

This is the full text of The Japanese Print: An Interpretation *(Chicago: Ralph Fletcher Seymour Co., 1912).*

The unpretentious colored woodcut of Japan, a thing of significant graven lines on delicate paper which has kissed the color from carved and variously tinted wooden blocks, is helpful in the practice of the fine arts and may be construed with profit in other life concerns as great.

It is a lesson especially valuable to the West, because, in order to comprehend it at all, we must take a viewpoint unfamiliar to us as a people, and in particular to our artists—the purely aesthetic viewpoint. It is a safe means of inspiration for our artists because, while the methods are true methods, the resultant forms are utterly alien to such artistic tradition as we acknowledge and endeavor to make effective.

So, I will neglect the smattering of information as to artists and periods easily obtained from any one of several available works on the subject and try to tell what these colored engravings are in themselves, and more particularly of their cultural use to us in awakening the artistic conscience or at least in making us feel the disgrace of not realizing the fact that we have none.

Go deep enough into your experience to find that beauty is in itself the finest kind of morality—ethical, purely—the essential fact. I mean, of all morals and manners—and you may personally feel in these aesthetic abstractions of the Japanese mind the innocent and vivid joy which, by reason of obviously established sentiment, is yours in the flowers of field or garden.

A flower is beautiful, we say—but why? Because in its geometry and its sensuous qualities it is an embodiment and significant expression of that precious something in ourselves which we instinctively know to be Life. "An eye looking out upon us from the great inner sea of beauty," [1] a proof of the eternal harmony in the nature of a universe too vast and intimate and real for mere intellect to seize. Intuitively we grasp something of it when we affirm that "the flower is beautiful." And when we say, "It is beautiful," we mean that the quality in us which is our very life recognizes itself there or at least what is its very own: so there vibrates in us a sympathetic chord struck mystically by the flower. Now, as it is with the flower, so is it with any work of art and to greater degree: because a work of fine art is a blossom of the human soul, and so more humanly intimate. In it we find the lineaments of man's thought and the exciting traces of man's feeling—so to say, the very human touch, offered to us in terms of the same qualities that make us exclaim that the flower is beautiful; and it is this quality of absolute and essential beauty in the result of the artist's creative efforts that is the Life of the work of art, more truly than any literal import or adventitious significance it may possess. But it is the quick, immediate perception of this subjective quality, or rather, perhaps, the ability to perceive it instinctively in the work of art, that is lacking in us—as a people. Failing in this perception we are untouched by the true vitalizing power of art and remain outside the precincts of the temple, in a realm, literal, objective, realistic, therefore unreal. In art that which is really essential escapes us for lack of a "disciplined power to see."

The most important fact to realize in a study of this subject is that, with all its informal grace, Japanese art is a thoroughly structural art: fundamentally so in any and every medium. It is always, whatever else it is or is not, structural. The realization of the primary importance of this element of "structure" is also at the very beginning of any real knowledge of design. And at the beginning of structure lies always and everywhere geometry. But, in this art, mathematics begins and ends here, as the mathematical begins and ends in music, however organically inherent here as there in the result.

But we have used the word structure, taking for granted that we agreed upon its meaning. The word structure is here used to designate an organic form, an organization in a very definite manner of parts or elements into a larger unity—a vital whole. So, in design, that element which we call its structure is primarily the pure form, an organization in a very definite manner of parts or elements into a larger unity—a vital whole as arranged or fashioned and grouped to "build" the Idea: an idea which must always persuade us of its reasonableness. Geometry is the grammar, so to speak, of the form. It is its architectural principle. But there is a psychic correlation between the geometry of form and our associated ideas, which constitutes its symbolic value. There resides always a certain "spell-power" in any geometric form which seems more or less a mystery, and is, as we say, the soul of the thing. It would carry us far from our subject if we should endeavor to render an accurate, convincing account of the reason why certain geometric forms have come to symbolize for us and potently to suggest certain human ideas, moods, and sentiments—as for instance; the circle, infinity; the triangle, structural unity; the spire, aspiration; the spiral, organic progress; the square, integrity. It is nevertheless a fact that more or less clearly in the subtle differentiations of these elemental geometric forms, we do sense a certain psychic quality which we may call the "spell-power" of the form, and with which the artist freely plays, as much at home with it as the musician at his keyboard with his notes. A Japanese artist grasps form always by reaching underneath for its geometry. No matter how informal, vague, evanescent, the subject he is treating may seem to be, he recognizes and acknowledges geometry as its aesthetic skeleton; that is to say—not its structural skeleton alone, but by virtue of what we have termed the symbolic "spell-power"—it is also the suggestive soul of his work. A Japanese artist's power of geometrical analysis seems little short of miraculous. An essential geometry he sees in everything, only, perhaps, to let it vanish in mystery for the beholder of his finished work. But even so, escaping as it does at first the critical eye, its influence is the more felt. By this grasp of geometric form and sense of its symbol-value, he has the secret of getting to the hidden core of reality. However fantastic his imaginative world may be, it competes with the actual and subdues it by superior loveliness and human meaning. The forms, for instance, in the pine tree (as of every natural object on earth), the geometry that underlies and constitutes the peculiar pine character of the tree—what Plato meant by the eternal idea—he knows familiarly. The unseen is to him visible. A circle and a straight line or two, rhythmically repeated, prescribe for him its essentials perfectly. He knows its textures and color qualities as thoroughly. Having these by heart, he is master of the pine and builds trees to suit his purpose and feeling, each as truly a pine and a pine only as the one from which he wrung the secret.

So, from flying bird to breaking wave, from Fujiyama[2] to a petal of the blossoming cherry afloat upon the stream, he is master, free to create at will. Nor are these forms to him mere specters or flimsy guesses—not fictitious semblances to which he can with impunity do violence. To him they are fundamental verities of structure, pre-existing and surviving particular embodiments in his material world.

What is true of the pine tree, for and by itself, is no less true in the relation of the tree to its environment. The Japanese artist studies pine-tree nature not only in its import and bearing but lovingly understands it in its habitat and natural element as well—which, if the geometry be called the grammar, may by equal privilege of figurative speech be termed the syntax. To acquire this knowledge, he devotes himself to the tree, observes analytically yet sympathetically, then leaves it, and with his brush begins to feel for its attitude and intimate relations as he remembers them. He proceeds from visualized generals to definite particulars in this contemplative study, and as soon as he has recognized really the first elements constituting the skeleton of the structure, which you may see laid bare in the analysis by Hokusai,[3] his progress in its grammar and syntax is rapid. The Japanese artist, by virtue of the shades of his ancestors, is born a trained observer, but only after a long series of patient studies does he consider that he knows his subject. However, he has naturally the ready ability to seize upon essentials, which is the prime condition of the artist's creative insight. Were all pine trees, then, to vanish suddenly from the earth, he could, from this knowledge, furnish plan and specification for the varied portrayal of a true species—because what he has learned and mastered and made his own is the specific and distinguishing nature of the pine tree. Using this word "Nature" in the Japanese sense I do not of course mean that outward aspect which strikes the eye as a visual image of a scene or strikes the ground glass of a camera, but that inner harmony which penetrates the outward form or letter and is its determining character: that quality in the thing (to repeat what we have said before) that is its significance and its Life for us—what Plato called (with reason, we see, psychological if not metaphysical) the "eternal idea of the thing."

We may refer, then, to the nature of a "proposition" as we do to the nature of an animal, of a plant, of an atmosphere, or a building material. Nature, in this sense, is not to be studied much in books. They are little more than the by-product of other men's ideas of the thing, which in order to distill from it his own particular sense of its intrinsic poetry the artist must know at firsthand. This poetry he must find in the thing for himself, the poetry it holds in reserve for him and him alone, and find it by patient, sympathetic study. This brings us to the aesthetics of Japanese art.

Ideas exist for us alone by virtue of form. The form can never be detached from the idea; the means must be perfectly adapted to the end. So in this art the problem of form and style is an organic problem solved easily and finally. Always we find the one line, the one arrangement that will exactly serve. It is a facile art, incapable of adequate analysis, for it is the felicity of an intuitive state of mind and must, on the part of the student, be similarly recognized by intuition.

These simple colored engravings are a language whose purpose is absolute beauty, inspired by the Japanese need of that precise expression of the beautiful, which is to him reality immeasurably more than the natural objects from which he wrested the secret of their being. This expression of the beautiful is inevitable and there inheres in the result that inevitableness which we feel in all things lovely. This process of woodblock printing is but one modest medium by means of which he may express his sense of the universal nature of things, and which he justifies in his characteristic, highly expressive fashion.

So, these prints are designs, patterns, in themselves beautiful as such; and what other meanings they may have are merely incidental, interesting, or curious by-products.

Broadly stated then, the first and supreme principle of Japanese aesthetics consists in stringent simplification by elimination of the insignificant and a consequent emphasis of reality. The first prerequisite for the successful study of this strange art is to fix the fact in mind at the beginning that it is the sentiment of Nature alone which concerns the Japanese artist; the sentiment of Nature as beheld by him in those vital meanings which he alone seems to see and alone therefore endeavors to portray.

The Japanese, by means of this process—to him by this habit of study almost instinctive—casts a glamour over everything. He is a poet. Surely life in old Japan must have been a perpetual communion with the divine heart of Nature. For Nippon drew its racial inspiration from, and framed its civilization in accord with, a native perception of Nature-law. Nippon made its body of morals and customs a strict conventionalization of her nature forms and processes; and therefore as a whole her civilization became a true work of Art. No more valuable object lesson was ever afforded civilization than this instance of a people who have made of their land and the buildings upon it, of their gardens, their manners and garb, their utensils, adornments, and their very gods, a single consistent whole, inspired by a living sympathy with Nature as spontaneous as it was inevitable. To the smallest fraction of Japanese lives what was divorced from Nature was reclaimed by Art and so redeemed. And what was the rule thus established progressively in individual and social life, making of it in itself an art—a thing of strange and poignant beauty—dominated all popular art production also and furnished the criterion.

This process of elimination of the insignificant we find to be the first and most important consideration for artists, after establishing the fundamental mathematics of structure. A Japanese may tell you what he knows in a single drawing, but never will he attempt to tell you all he knows. He is quite content to lay stress upon a simple element, insignificant enough perhaps until he has handled it, then (as we find again and again in the works of Korin and his school)[4] the very slight means employed touches the soul of the subject so surely and intimately that while less would have failed of the intended effect, more would have been profane. This process of simplification is in a sense a dramatization of the subject, just as all Japanese ceremonials are the common offices and functions of their daily life delicately dramatized in little. The tea ceremony is an instance. Nothing more than the most gracefully perfect way of making and serving a cup of tea! Yet, often a more elegant and impressive ceremonial than a modern religious service. To dramatize is always to conventionalize; to conventionalize is, in a sense, to simplify; and so these drawings are all conventional patterns subtly geometrical, imbued at the same time with symbolic value, this symbolism honestly built upon a mathematical basis, as the woof of the weave is built upon the warp. It has little in common with the literal. It is more akin to a delicate musical instrument that needs no dampers or loud pedals. Fleshly shade and materialistic shadow are unnecessary to it, for in itself it is no more than pure living sentiment.

Were we to contrast the spiritual grace of simple wildflowers, with the material richness of doubled varieties under cultivation, we would institute a suggestive comparison of this unpretentious art of the East with the more pretentious art of the West. Where the art of Japan is a poetic symbol, much of ours is attempted realism, that succeeds only in being rather pitifully literal. Where the one is delicately sensuous, the other is only too apt to be stupidly sensual.

This intuition of the Japanese artist for dramatizing his subject is no finer than his touch and tact are unerring. He knows materials and never falsifies them. He knows his tools and never abuses them. And this, too, just because he apprehends the secret of character at every chance contact with the actual. In the slight wash drawings of the kakemono,[5] we find a more sheer and delicate manifestation of reserve than in this more popular, and in a sense therefore, more vulgar form of expression. Always latent, however, in the slightest and seemingly most informal designs, in the least of these works as through the greatest, the geometric structure effects a potent spell. No composition can we find not affected by it and that does not bear this psychic spell meanwhile, as if unconscious of its precious burden, its efficient causes enwoven and subtly hid between the lines of its geometric forms. As the poor saint was believed to bear his mystic nimbus, so each humble masterpiece asserts its magic of invisible perfection. Yet, this mystery is conclusively reduced by Japanese masters to its scientific elements, as exemplified by certain pages of textbooks by Hokusai, wherein the structural diagrams are clearly given and transformation to material objects shown progressively step by step.

This primitive graphic art, like all true art, has limitations firmly fixed; in this case more narrowly fixed than in any art we know. Strictly within these limitations, however, the fertility and resource of the Japanese mind produced a range of aesthetic inventions that runs the whole gamut of sentiment, besides reproducing with faithfulness the costumes, manners, and customs of a unique and remarkable civilization, constituting its most valuable real record—and without violating a single aesthetic tradition.

The faces in these drawings repel the novice and chill the student accustomed to less pure aesthetic abstractions; and the use of the human form in unrealistic fashion has often been explained on the ground of religious scruples. Nothing more than the aesthetic consideration involved is necessary to justify it. The faces in these drawings are "in place," harmonious with the rest, and one may actually satisfy himself on the subject by observing how the tendency toward realism in the faces portrayed by Kiyonaga and Toyokuni[6] vulgarized results artistically, introducing as they did, this element—no doubt, for the same reason that actors some-times play to the applauding gallery. The faces as found in the prints of the great period were the Japanese countenance drama-tized, to use the term once more. They were masks, conventions, the visual image of the ethnic character of a people varied by each artist for himself. A close student may identify the work of any particular artist by merely ascertaining his particular variation, the print being otherwise totally concealed. And although an ac-tor was portrayed in many different roles, the individuality of the countenance, its character, was held throughout in the mask.

You may never fail to recognize Danjuro in all the various drawings by Shunsho and other artists that he inspired,[7] and you may recognize others when you have made their acquaintance. But the means by which this was accomplished are so slight that the convention is scarcely disturbed, and no realism taints the re-sult. A countenance drawn to please us would vulgarize the whole, for its realism would violate the aesthetic law of the structure. You find something like this typical face in the work of the Pre-Raphaelites, Burne-Jones, and Rossetti. These are often inanities as distressing as the more legitimate conventions of the Japanese are satisfying, because they were made in a more or less literal set-ting: the whole being inorganic and inconsistent. You will find something of this conventionalizing tendency employed more con-sistently and artistically in a Morris prose epic or verse tale, or in Spenser's *Faerie Queene*, where raging knightly battles and fright-ful episodes move quietly remote and sedate across the enchanted reader's field of mental vision, affecting him simply by their pic-turesque outlines and charm of color, as might an old arras.

The use of color, always in the flat—that is, without chiaro-scuro—plays a wonderful but natural part in the production of this art and is responsible largely for its charm. It is a means grasped and understood as perfectly as the rhythm of form and line, and it is made in its way as significant. It affords a means of emphasizing and differentiating the forms themselves, at the same time that it is itself an element of the pattern. The blacks are always placed flat in the pattern, as pattern for its own sake—a design within a design. Comments are often made on the wonderfully successful use of masses of deep black, but the other colors at their command are used as successfully, according to the same method, to an identical, if less emphatic effect.

As we see the prints today, it must be confessed that time has imbued the color with added charm. Old vegetable dyes, saturating and qualified by the soft texture of wonderful silken paper, soften and change with the sunlight of the moist climate, much as the colors in oriental rugs. Blues become beautiful yellows: purples soft brown; *beni*, or bright red, fades to luminous pink; while a certain cool green together with the translucent grays and the brilliant red lead are unchangeable. The tenderness of tone found in fine prints is indescribable. This is in great part due to the action of time on the nature of the dye stuffs or pigments employed. When first printed, they were comparatively crude, and much of the credit formerly given by connoisseurs to the printer should be accredited to age. When first printed, also, there was a certain conventionalized symbolism in the use of color, which time confuses. The sky was then usually gray or blue, sometimes yellow; the water blue; grass green; garments polychromatic; woodwork red lead, pink, or yellow. Owing to the manner in which the color was brushed upon the block, few prints are exactly alike, and sometimes great liberty was taken with the color by the printer, most interesting differentiations of color occurring in different prints from the same block. In itself, the color element in the Japanese print is delight—an absolute felicity, unrivaled in charm by the larger means employed in more pretentious mediums. The prints afford a liberal education in color values, especially related to composition. A perfect color balance is rarely wanting in the final result, and although certain qualities in this result are in a sense adventitious, yet it should be strongly insisted, after all, that the foundation for the miracles of harmonious permutation was properly laid by the artist himself.

In this wedding of color and gracious form, we have finally what we call a good decoration. The ultimate value of a Japanese print will be measured by the extent to which it distills, or rather exhales, this precious quality called "decorative." We as a people do not quite understand what that means and are apt to use the term slightingly as compared with art; which has supposedly some other and greater mission. I—speaking for myself—do not know exactly what other mission it legitimately could have, but I am sure of this, at least—that the rhythmic play of parts, the poise and balance, the respect the forms pay to the surface treated, and the repose these qualities attain to and impart and which together constitute what we call good decoration, are really the very life of all true graphic art whatsoever. In the degree that the print possesses this quality, it is abidingly precious: this quality determines—constitutes, its intrinsic value.

As to the subject matter of the figure pieces, it is true that the stories they tell are mainly of the Yoshiwara,[8] or celebrate the lover and the geisha, but with an innocence incomprehensible to us; for Japan at that time—although the family was the unit of her civilization—had not made monopoly of the sex relation the shameless essence of this institution, and the Yoshiwara was the center of the literary and artistic life of the common people. Their fashions were set by the Yoshiwara. The geisha, whose place in Japanese society was the same as that of the Greek Hetaira, or her ancient Hindu equivalent, as for instance she appears in the Hindu comedy, the "*Little Clay Cart*," was not less in her ideal perfection than Aspasia, beloved of Pericles.[9] The geisha was perhaps the most exquisite product, scandalous as the fact may appear, of an exquisite civilization. She was in society the living Japanese work of art: thoroughly trained in music, literature, and the rarest and fairest amenities of life, she was herself the crowning amenity and poetic refinement of their life. This, all must recognize and comprehend; else we shall be tempted by false shames and Puritan prejudices to resent the theme of so many of the loveliest among the prints, and by a quite stupid dogmatism disallow our aesthetic delight in their charm. But we have very likely said enough of the print itself; let us pass on to consider what it has already done for us and what it may yet do. We have seen that this art exists—in itself a thing of beauty—inspired by need of expressing the common life in organic terms, having itself the same integrity, considered in its own nature, as the flower. Caught and bodied forth there by human touch is a measure of that inner harmony which we perceive as a proof of goodness and excellence.

It exists, a material means for us to a spiritual end, perhaps more essentially prophetic in function than it was to the people for whom it came into candid and gracious being. It has already spoken to us a message of aesthetic and ethical import. Indeed, its spirit has already entered and possessed the soul and craft of many men of our race and spoken again through them more intimately and convincingly than ever. That message we recognize in more familiar accents uttered by Whistler, Manet, Monet, the "Plein-air" school of France—Puvis de Chavannes, M. Boutet de Monvel—and through them it has further spread its civilizing, because [of] its conventionalizing, simplifying, clarifying influence to the arts and crafts of the occident on both sides of the Atlantic.[10] Every dead wall in the land bears witness to the direct or indirect influence of this humble Japanese art of the people; for it has given us what we some time ago called "poster art." Because of it, in England Aubrey Beardsley and his kith lived and wrought. Modern France, the first to discover its charm, has fallen under its spell completely; French art and Parisian fashions feel its influence more from year to year. The German and Austrian Secessionist movement owes it a large debt of gratitude. Yet the influence of this art is still young. The German mind has only recently awakened to its significance and proceeds now with characteristic thoroughness to ends only half discerned. It has spread abroad the gospel of simplification as no other modern agency has preached it and has taught that organic integrity within the work of art itself is the fundamental law of beauty. Without it, work may be a meretricious mask with literal suggestion or sensual effect, not true art. That quality in the work which is "real" escapes and the would-be artist remains where he belongs—outside the sanctuary. The print has shown us that no more than a sandbank and the sea, or a foreground, a telegraph pole, and a weed in proper arrangement, may yield a higher message of love and beauty, a surer proof of life than the sentimentality of Raphael or Angelo's magnificent pictorial sculpture. Chaste and delicate, it has taught that healthy and wholesome sentiment has nothing in common with sentimentality, nor sensuous feeling with banal sensuality; that integrity of means to ends is in art indispensable to the poetry of so-called inspired results: and that the inspiring life of the work of art consists and inheres, has its very breath and creative being within the work itself; an integrity, in fine, as organic as anything that grows in the great out-of-doors.

Owing to its marked ethnic eccentricity, this art is a particularly safe means of cultivation for us, because the individual initiative of the artist is not paralyzed by forms which he can use as he finds them, ready-made. It may become most useful on this very account, as a corrector of the fatal tendency to imitation—be the antidote to the very poison it might administer to the weak and unwary—to that corrupting, stultifying, mechanical parasitism that besets and betrays so often to his ruin, in these days of hustle and drive, the eager and ambitious artist. For the architect, particularly, it is a quickening inspiration, without attendant perils, owing to its essentially structural character and diverse materials and methods. To any and all artists it must offer great encouragement, because it is so striking a proof of the fact readily overlooked—that to the true artist his limitations are always, if but understood and rightly wooed, his most faithful and serviceable friends.

If, then, there is a culture we might acquire whereby the beautiful may be apprehended as such and help restore to us the fine instinctive perception of and worship for the beautiful, which should be our universal birthright instead of the distorted ideas, the materialistic perversions of which we are victims, we assuredly want to know what it is and just how it may be had. Nothing at this moment can be of greater importance to us educationally. For the laws of the beautiful are immutable as those of elementary physics. No work sifted by them and found wanting can be a work of art. The laws of the beautiful are like the laws of physics, not derived from external authority, nor have they regard to any ulterior utility. They preexist any perception of them; inhere, latent, and effective, in man's nature and his world. They are not made by any genius, they are perceived first by the great artist and then revealed to mankind in his works. All varieties of form, line, or color, all tendencies in any direction have, besides what value they may have acquired by virtue of the long cultural tradition recounting back to prehistoric man, a natural significance and inevitably express something. As these properties are combined, arranged, and harmonized, expression is gained and modified. Even a discord is in a sense an expression—an expression of the devil or of decay. But the expression we seek and need is that of harmony or of the good; known otherwise as the true, often spoken of as the beautiful, and personified as God. It is folly to say that if the ear can distinguish a harmonious combination of sounds, the eye cannot distinguish a harmonious combination of tones or shapes or lines. For in the degree that the ear is sensitive to sound—to the extent that it can appreciate the harmony of tones—in even a larger degree the eye will see and appreciate, if duly trained to attend them, the expression of harmonies in form, line, and color purely as such; and it is exactly harmonies of this kind, merely, which we find exemplified and exquisitely elucidated in Japanese prints.

Rhythmical and melodious combinations of tone otherwise only "noise" have portrayed the individualities of great souls to us—a Bach, Beethoven, or a Mozart; and while the practice of no musical rule of three could compass their art or sound the depths of their genius, there are definite laws of harmony and structure common to their art which are well known and systematically taught and imparted. So the mysterious impress of personality is revealed in certain qualities of this unpretentious art, as any even cursory observer must note, in the works of Harunobu, Shunsho, Kiyonaga, Hokusai, and Hiroshige.[11]

The principles underlying and in a sense governing the expression of personal feeling and the feeling of personality as expressed in these prints, or for the matter of that in any veritable work of art, have now been clearly formulated anew for many of us by assiduous study of their works. Questions of aesthetics may no longer be so readily referred to with flippancy, as mere negligible "matters of taste." Aside from their ethnic character—the fact that the individuality of these expressions may be but the color, so to say, of some Japanese artist's soul—such expressions do convey an ideal of the conditions they seek to satisfy, for the simple reason that the expression was the sought and wrought response to spiritual need, which nothing less or else could satisfy. Just as Beethoven at his keyboard imposed upon tone the character of his soul, so by these simple colored drawings a similar revelation is achieved by the Japanese artist through the medium of dye stuffs and graven lines applied to sensitive paper, putting together its elements of expression in accord with brain and heart, attaining to beauty as a result insofar as the artist was true to the limitations imposed upon him by the nature of the means he employed. He might merely characterize his subject and possess little more than the eye of the great craftsman; or he might idealize it according to the realizing insight of the great artist; but in either case to the degree that the colors and lines were true to material and means delightfully significant of the idea, the result would be a creative work of art.

Now, all the while, just as in any musical composition, a conventionalizing process would be going on. To imitate that natural modeling of the subject in shade and shadow—to render realistically its appearance and position—would require certain dexterity of hand and a mechanic's eye certainly. But in the artist's mind there was a living conception at work—the idea: the revelation of the vision by means of the brush and dye stuffs and paper applied to engraved wooden blocks, with strict regard and devout respect for the limitations of materials, and active sympathy making all eloquent together; eloquent, however, in their own peculiar fashion as graven lines on sensitive paper, which has received color from the variously tinted blocks and wherein this process is frankly confessed—the confession itself becoming a delightful poetic circumstance. There results from all this a peculiar, exquisite language, not literature, telling a story regardless of the conditions of its structure. For a picture should be no imitation of anything, no pretended hole in the wall through which you glimpse a story about something or behold winter in summer or summer in winter. *Breaking Home Ties*, for instance, or any of its numerous kith and kin cannot be dignified as art. There are many degrees of kinship to *Breaking Home Ties* not so easy to detect, yet all of which bear the marks of vulgar pretense.[12] The message of the Japanese print is to educate us spiritually for all time beyond such banality.

Not alone in the realm of the painter is the message being heeded, but also in that of the musician, the sculptor, and the architect.

In sculpture the antithesis of the lesson is found in the "Rogers Groups," [13] literal replicas of incidents that as sculpture are only pitiful. Sculpture has three dimensions, possibilities of mass and silhouette, as well as definite limitations peculiar to itself. To disregard them is death to art. The Venus, the Victory, [14] classics living in our hearts today, and a long list of noble peers, are true sculpture. But the slavish making of literature has cursed both painter and sculptor. They have been tempted to make their work accomplish what literary art may achieve so much better—forcing their medium beyond its limits to its utter degradation. And this is as true of decorative art and in a sense true of architecture. General principles deduced from this popular art of the Japanese apply readily to these problems of right aesthetic conventionalization of natural things, revealing the potential poetry of nature as it may be required to make them live in the arts. This culture of the East therefore brings to us of the West invaluable aid in the process of our civilization. We marvel, with a tinge of envy, at the simple inevitableness with which the life-principle in so slight a thing as a willow wand will find fullness of expression as a willow tree—a glorious sort of completeness—with that absolute repose which is as of a destiny fulfilled. Inevitably the secret of the acorn is the glory of the oak. The fretted cone arises as the stately pine, finding the fullness of a destined life in untrammeled expression of its life-principle simply, naturally, and beautifully. Then we go to Nature that we may learn her secret, to find out that there has been laid upon us an artificiality that often conceals and blights our very selves, and in mere course of time and the false education of our mistaken efforts, deforms past recognition the life-principle originally implanted in us for our personal growth as men and our expressive function as artists.

We find and feel always in Nature herself from zero to infinity, an accord of form and function with life-principle that seems to halt only with our attempted domestication of the infinite.

Society seems to lose or at least set aside some rare and precious quality in domestication or civilizing—no—that is, in this conventionalizing process of ours which we choose to call civilization. Striving for freedom we gain friction and discord for our pains. The wisest savants and noblest poets have therefore gone direct to Nature for the secret. There they hoped against hope to find the solution of this maddening, perplexing problem; the right ordering of human life. But however much we may love oak or pine in a state of Nature their freedom is not for us. It belongs to us no longer, however much the afterglow of barbarism within us may yearn for it. Real civilization means for us a right conventionalizing of our original state of Nature. Just such conventionalizing as the true artist imposes on natural forms. The lawgiver and reformer of social customs must have, however, the artist soul, the artist eye, in directing this process, if the light of the race is not to go out. So, art is not alone the expression, but in turn must be the great conservator and transmitter of the finer sensibilities of a people. More still: it is to show those who may understand just where and how we shall bring coercion to bear upon the material of human conduct. So the indigenous art of a people is their only prophecy and their true artists, their school of anointed prophets and kings. It is so now more than ever before because we are further removed from Nature as an original source of inspiration. Our own art is the only light by which this conventionalizing process we call "civilization" may eventually make its institutions harmonious with the fairest conditions of our individual and social life.

I wish I might use another word than "conventionalizing" to convey the notion of this magic of the artist mind, which is the constant haunting reference of this paper, because it is the perpetual insistent suggestion of this particular art we have discussed. Only an artist, or one with genuine artistic training, is likely, I fear, to realize precisely what the word means as it is used here. Let me illustrate once more. To know a thing, what we can really call knowing, a man must first love the thing, which means that he can sympathize vividly with it. Egypt thus knew the lotus and translated the flower to the dignified stone forms of her architecture. Such was the lotus conventionalized. Greece knew and idealized the acanthus in stone translations. Thus was the acanthus conventionalized. If Egypt or Greece had plucked the lotus as it grew and given us a mere imitation of it in stone, the stone forms would have died with the original. In translating, however, its very life-principle into terms of stone well adapted to grace a column capital, the Egyptian artist made it pass through a rarefying spiritual process, whereby its natural character was really intensified and revealed in terms of stone adapted to an architectural use. The lotus gained thus imperishable significance; for the life-principle in the flower is transmuted in terms of building stone to idealize a need. This is conventionalization. It is reality because it is poetry. As the Egyptian took the lotus, the Greek the acanthus, and the Japanese every natural thing on earth, and as we may adapt to our highest use in our own way a natural flower or thing—so civilization must take the natural man to fit him for his place in this great piece of architecture we call the social state. Today, as centuries ago, it is the prophetic artist eye that must reveal this natural state thus idealized, conventionalized harmoniously with the life-principle of all men. How otherwise shall culture be discerned? All the wisdom of science, the cunning of politics, and the prayers of religion can but stand and wait for the revelation—awaiting at the hands of the artist "conventionalization," that free expression of life-principle which shall make our social living beautiful because organically true. Behind all institutions or dogmatic schemes, whatever their worth may be, or their venerable antiquity, behind them all is something produced and preserved for its aesthetic worth: the song of the poet, some artist vision, the pattern seen in the mount.

Now speaking a language all the clearer because not native to us, beggared as we are by material riches, the humble artist of old Japan has become greatly significant as interpreter of the one thing that can make the concerns, the forms, of his everyday life—whether laws, customs, manners, costumes, utensils, or ceremonials—harmonious with the life-principle of his race—and so living native forms, humanly significant, humanly joy giving—an art, a religion, as in ever varied moods, in evanescent loveliness he has made Fujiyama—that image of man in the vast—the God of Nippon.

NOTES

1. From Thomas Carlyle, "The Hero as Poet. Dante: Shakespeare," Lecture III of *On Heroes and Hero Worship and the Heroic in History* (1841), which reads: "a beautiful eye looking out on you, from the great inner Sea of Beauty."

2. Another name for Mount Fuji, at 12,388 feet, the highest peak in Japan.

3. See Document 6, n. 2.

4. See Document 6, n. 2.

5. A vertical scroll painting meant to be wall-hung.

6. Torii Kiyonaga (1752–1815), scroll painter, and Utagawa Toyokuni (1777–1835), printmaker of actors and theatrical scenes. Several of the artists mentioned here used more than one name.

7. Ichikawa Danjuro was a stage name taken by Kabuki actors of the Ichikawa family beginning with Danjuro (1660–1704), some of whom were depicted by Katsukawa Shunsho (1726–92), a prominent painter and printmaker of theatrical scenes and personalities.

8. Historically, and still, the red-light, public-bath district of Tokyo.

9. A courtesan, mistress, or companion in ancient Greece as, for example, Aspasia, mistress of Pericles. "The Little Clay Cart" (c. second century BCE), one of the earliest known Sanskrit plays, features Vasantisena, a nagarvadhu, or courtesan.

10. Wright cites Pierre Puvis de Chavannes (1824–98) and Maurice Boutet de Monvel (1855–1913) as exemplars of the "'Plein-air' school of France" who painted outdoors in order to study the effect of changing light on color.

11. Suzuki Harunobuo (1724–70) popularized multicolor woodblock print-making; Ando Hiroshige (1797–1858) was a painter and printmaker known for his landscapes.

12. In 1890, Thomas Hovenden (1840–95), Irish born American painter, produced *Breaking Home Ties*, which subsequently achieved enormous commercial success as a print. Norman Rockwell (1899–1978) produced a painting by the same title in 1954.

13. From his New York City factory John Rogers (1829–1904) manufactured perhaps 100,000 copies of his eighty-five patented plaster castings of small groups (families, soldiers, scenes from literature and the stage), all eight to forty-six inches high, earning him over $1,000,000 during his lifetime.

14. Wright likely refers to *Venus de Milo* (Aphrodite of Milos), thought to have been sculpted by Alexandros of Antioch (c. 130–90 BCE), and to *The Victory* (aka *The Winged Victory* and *The Winged Victory of Samothrace*), depicting the Greek goddess Nike (Victory), tentatively dated anywhere from 288 to 170 BCE, by an unknown sculptor.

EIGHT

In the Cause of Architecture: Second Paper (1914)

In this angry, bitter essay Wright contends that the "premature success" of his Prairie period work had the unanticipated consequence of preventing the principles of organic architecture from taking root. His striking new forms had been marketed to clients desperate for "something different" by "architectural babes and sucklings" including his own employees, eager to make names for themselves. In the process his philosophy, the substance of his work, what mattered most, had been ignored. Without explicitly saying so, Wright hints that his ideas had been stolen by former friends and colleagues whose highest priority was commercial "success."

This is the first appearance in the architectural press of what might be called the "persecuted genius" persona he had introduced in the Chicago newspapers in late 1911 in response to the widespread condemnation of his private life (outlined in the introduction to this volume). Here, in 1914, the personal becomes professional.

He had begun working for "the cause," he insists, "twenty-five years ago . . . alone—absolutely alone." From the start (contrary to evidence, it must be said) his efforts were abused, scorned, ridiculed, and prostituted by, among others, the very "comrades" and "loyal assistants" he had embraced in his 1908 essay (Document 4). Unfortunately, "architects, as a class, in this region at least," turned out to have an "almost total lack of any standard of artistic integrity." He added, for good measure, having been excoriated for immorality in a November 1910 Western Architect editorial, that critics and editors are a "narrow," "ignorant," "provincial," and "cowardly" lot, writing "for profit or bias [in] an advertising game."

Later on, the fully developed persona would include the contention that although he had fought for "the cause" from day one against impossible odds, he had nevertheless succeeded in creating a truly American architecture all by himself (sometimes he added that Louis Sullivan helped). This is hinted at here when he implies that only organic architecture—he being its sole practitioner now—has any "lasting value."

Despite its contentiousness, there are good reasons to consider this essay essential, aside from what has already been said. Understanding an architect's work in part requires understanding the architect, and increasingly after 1914, Wright's "persecuted genius" persona shaped not only his personal style and public image but also his professional posture. It helps explain his (usually disdainful) remarks about other architects and their work, his (non)relationships with professional organizations, his (paternalistic) treatment of apprentices, and his (sometimes casual) attitude about client budgets. It also helps explain his (increasingly impenetrable) prose, his (flamboyant) wardrobe, his (cavalier) attitude toward creditors, and the (baronial) living arrangements at his Taliesin estates in Spring Green, Wisconsin, and Scottsdale, Arizona. Fully developed by the early 1930s at the latest, Wright's self-image was of a "devil-may-care" genius, pontificating on any and all subjects including those he knew nothing about, doing exactly what he wanted when he wanted to, and the hell with you!

But more important is this essay's not-so-hidden assumption— ironically enough—that artistic achievement is socially conditioned, that architectural art is not a rarefied phenomenon existing in and of itself as "art for art's sake" advocates would have it, but is a social act shaping and being shaped by social life. Despite his concern toward *this essay's conclusion about "false Democracy," Wright clung to the belief that artistic individuality and integrity would in the end prevail because individuality and integrity were deeply ingrained American characteristics. Despite what he writes here, until the day he died he remained optimistic about the future of his nation and its architectural possibilities.*

From the Architectural Record, *34 (May 1914).*

"Style, therefore, will be the man. It is his. Let his forms alone."

"Nature has made creatures only; Art has made men." [1] Nevertheless, or perhaps for that very reason, every struggle for truth in the arts and for the freedom that should go with the truth has always had its own peculiar load of disciples, neophytes and quacks. The young work in architecture here in the Middle West, owing to a measure of premature success, has for some time past been daily rediscovered, heralded and drowned in noise by this new characteristic feature of its struggle. The so-called "movement" threatens to explode soon in foolish exploitation of unripe performances or topple over in pretentious attempts to "speak the language." The broker, too, has made his appearance to deal in its slender stock in trade, not a wholly new form of artistic activity certainly, but one serving to indicate how profitable this intensive rush for a place in the "new school" has become.

Just at this time it may be well to remember that "every form of artistic activity is not Art."

Obviously this stage of development was to be expected and has its humorous side. It has also unexpected and dangerous effects, astonishingly in line with certain prophetic letters written by honest "conservatives" upon the publication of the former paper of 1908.

Although an utterance from me of a critical nature is painful, because it must be a personal matter, perhaps a seeming retraction on my part, still all that ever really happens is "personal matter" and the time has come when forbearance ceases to be either virtue or convenience. A promising garden seems to be rapidly overgrown with weeds, notwithstanding the fact that "all may raise the flowers now, for all have got the seed."[2] But the seed has not been planted—transplanting is preferred, but it cannot raise the needed flowers.

To stultify or corrupt our architectural possibilities is to corrupt our aesthetic life at the fountain head. Her Architecture is the most precious of the susceptibilities of a young, constructive country in this constructive stage of development; and maintaining its integrity in this respect, therefore, distinctly a cause.

When, twenty-one years ago, I took my stand, alone in my field,[3] the cause was unprofitable, seemingly impossible, almost unknown, or, if known, was, as a rule, unhonored and ridiculed— Montgomery Schuyler was the one notable exception to the rule.[4] So swiftly do things "come on" in this vigorous and invigorating age that although the cause itself has had little or no recognition, the work has more than its share of attention and has attracted to itself abuses seldom described—never openly attacked—but which a perspective of the past six years will enable me to describe, as I feel they must render the finer values in this work abortive for the time being, if they do not wholly defeat its aim. Many a similar work in the past has gone prematurely to ruin owing to similar abuses—to rise again, it is true, but retarded generations in time.

I still believe that the ideal of an organic* architecture forms the origin and source, the strength and, fundamentally, the significance of everything ever worthy the name of architecture.

---

*By organic architecture I mean an architecture that *develops* from within outward in harmony with the conditions of its being as distinguished from one that is *applied* from without.

And I know that the sense of an organic architecture, once grasped, carries with it in its very nature the discipline of an ideal at whatever cost to self interest or the established order.

It is itself a standard and an ideal.

And I maintain that only earnest artist integrity, both of instinct and of intelligence, can make any forward movement of this nature in architecture of lasting value.

The ideal of an organic architecture for America is no mere license for doing the thing that you please to do as you please to do it in order to hold up the strange thing when done with the "see-what-I-have-made" of childish pride. Nor is it achieved by speaking the fancied language of "form and function"—cant terms learned by rote—or prating foolishly of "Progress before Precedent" [5]—that unthinking, unthinkable thing. In fact, it is precisely the total absence of any conception of this ideal standard that is made conspicuous by this folly and the practices that go with it. To reiterate the statement made in 1908:

This ideal of an organic architecture for America was touched by Richardson and Root, and perhaps other men, but was developing consciously twenty-eight years ago in the practice of Adler & Sullivan, when I went to work in their office. [6] This ideal combination of Adler & Sullivan was then working to produce what no other combination of architects nor any individual architect at that time dared even preach—a sentient, rational building that would owe its "style" to the integrity with which it was individually fashioned to serve its particular purpose—a "thinking" as well as "feeling" process, requiring the independent work of true artist imagination—an ideal that is dynamite, cap and fuse, in selfish, insensible hands—personal ambition, the lighted match.

At the expiration of a six year apprenticeship, during which time Louis Sullivan was my master and inspiration, twenty-one years ago, I entered a field he had not, in any new spirit, touched—

the field of domestic architecture—and began to break ground and make the forms I needed, alone—absolutely alone.

These forms were the result of a conscientious study of materials and of the machine which is the real tool, whether we like it or not, that we must use to give shape to our ideals—a tool which at that time had received no such artistic consideration from artist or architect. And that my work now has individuality, the strength to stand by itself, honors Mr. Sullivan the more. The principles, however, underlying the fundamental ideal of an organic architecture, common to his work and to mine, are common to all work that ever rang true in the architecture of the world, and free as air to any pair of honest young lungs that will breathe deeply enough. But I have occasion to refer here only to that element in this so-called "new movement" which I have characterized by my own work and which should and, in a more advanced stage of culture, would be responsible to me for use or abuse of the forms and privileges of that work. Specifically, I speak only to that element within this element, now beyond private reach or control, ruthlessly characterizing and publicly exploiting the cause it does not comprehend or else that it cannot serve.

Some one for the sake of that cause must have some conscience in the matter and tell the truth. Since disciples, neophytes and brokers will not, critics do not, and the public cannot—I will. I will be suspected of the unbecoming motives usually ascribed to any man who comes to the front in behalf of an ideal, or his own; nevertheless, somehow, this incipient movement, which it has been my life work to help outfit and launch, must be protected or directed in its course. An enlightened public opinion would take care of this, but there is no such opinion. In time there will be; meantime good work is being wasted, opportunities destroyed or worse, architectural mortgages on future generations forged wholesale: and in architecture they must be paid with usurious interest.

The sins of the Architect are permanent sins.

To promote good work it is necessary to characterize bad work as bad.

Half-baked, imitative designs—fictitious semblances—pretentiously put forward in the name of a movement or a cause, particularly while novelty is the chief popular standard, endanger the cause, weaken the efficiency of genuine work, for the time being at least; lower the standard of artistic integrity permanently; demor alize all values artistically; until utter prostitution results. This prostitution has resulted in the new work partly, I have now to confess, as a by-product of an intimate, personal touch with the work, hitherto untried in the office of an American architect; and partly, too, perhaps, as one result of an ideal of individuality in architecture, administered in doses too strong, too soon, for architectural babes and sucklings; but chiefly, I believe, owing to almost total lack of any standard of artist integrity among architects, as a class, in this region at least. Of ethics we hear something occasionally, but only in regard to the relation of architects to each other when a client is in question—never in relation to sources of inspiration, the finer material the architect uses in shaping the thing he gives to his client. Ethics that promote integrity in this respect are as yet unformed and the young man in architecture is adrift in the most vitally important of his experiences, he cannot know where he stands in the absence of any well-defined principles on the part of his confreres or his elders.

If I had a right to project myself in the direction of an organic architecture twenty-one years ago, it entailed the right to my work and, so far as I am able, a right to defend my aim. Also—yet not so clearly—I am bound to do what I can to save the public from untoward effects that follow in the wake of my own break with traditions. I deliberately chose to break with traditions in order to be more true to Tradition than current conventions and ideals in architecture would permit. The more vital course is usually the rougher one and lies through conventions oftentimes settled into laws that must be broken, with consequent liberation of other forces that cannot stand freedom. So a break of this nature is a thing dangerous, nevertheless indispensable, to society. Society recognizes the danger and makes the break usually fatal to the man who makes it. It should not be made without reckoning the danger and sacrifice, without ability to stand severe punishment, nor without sincere faith that the end will justify the means; nor do I believe it can be effectively made without all these. But who can reckon with the folly bred by temporal success in a country that has as yet no artistic standards, no other god so potent as that same Success? For every thousand men nature enables to stand adversity, she, perhaps, makes one man capable of surviving success. An unenlightened public is at its mercy always—the "success" of the one thousand as well as of the one in a thousand; were it not for the resistance of honest enmity, society, nature herself even, would soon cycle madly to disaster. So reaction is essential to progress, and enemies as valuable an asset in any forward movement as friends, provided only they be honest; if intelligent as well as honest, they are invaluable. Some time ago this work reached the stage where it sorely needed honest enemies if it was to survive. It has had some honest enemies whose honest fears were expressed in the prophetic letters I have mentioned.

But the enemies of this work, with an exception or two, have not served it well. They have been either unintelligent or careless of the gist of the whole matter. It fact, its avowed enemies have generally been of the same superficial, time serving spirit as many of its present load of disciples and neophytes. Nowhere even now, save in Europe, with some few notable exceptions in this country, has the organic character of the work been fairly recognized and valued—the character that is perhaps the only feature of lasting vital consequence.

As for its peculiarities—if my own share in this work has a distinguished trait, it has individuality undefiled. It has gone forward unswerving from the beginning, unchanging, yet developing, in this quality of individuality, and stands, as it has stood for nineteen years at least, an individual entity, clearly defined. Such as it is, its "individuality" is as irrevocably mine as the work of any painter, sculptor or poet who ever lived was irrevocably his. The form of a work that has this quality of individuality is never the product of a composite. An artist knows this; but the general public, near-artist and perhaps "critic," too, may have to be reminded or informed. To grant a work this quality is to absolve it without further argument from anything like composite origin, and *to fix its limitations.*

There are enough types and forms in my work to characterize the work of an architect, but certainly not enough to characterize an architecture. Nothing to my mind could be worse imposition than to have some individual, even temporarily, deliberately fix the outward forms of his concept of beauty upon the future of a free people or even of a growing city. A tentative, advantageous forecast of probable future utilitarian development goes far enough in this direction. Any individual willing to undertake more would thereby only prove his unfitness for the task, assuming the task possible or desirable. A socialist might shut out the sunlight from a free and developing people with his own shadow, in this way. An artist is too true an individualist to suffer such an imposition, much less perpetrate it; his problems are quite other. The manner of any work (and all work of any quality has its manner) may be for the time being a strength, but finally it is a weakness; and as the returns come in, it seems as though not only the manner of this work or its "clothes," but also its strength in this very quality of individuality, which is a matter of its soul as well as of its forms, would soon prove its undoing, to be worn to shreds and tatters by foolish, conscienceless imitation. As for the vital principle of the work—the quality of an organic architecture—that has been lost to sight, even by pupils. But I still believe as firmly as ever that without artist integrity and this consequent individuality manifesting itself in multifarious forms, there can be no great architecture, no great artists, no great civilization, no worthy life. Is, then, the very strength of such a work as this is its weakness? Is it so because of a false democratic system naturally inimical to art? or is it so because the commercialization of art leaves no noble standards? Is it because architects have less personal honor than sculptors, painters or poets? Or is it because fine buildings are less important now than fine pictures and good books?

In any case, judging from what is exploited as such, most of what is beginning to be called the "New School of the Middle West" is not only far from the ideal of an organic architecture, but getting farther away from it every day.

A study of similar situations in the past will show that any departure from beaten paths must stand and grow in organic character or soon fall, leaving permanent waste and desolation in final ruin; *it dare not trade long on mere forms,* no matter how inevitable they seem. Trading in the letter has cursed art for centuries past, but in architecture it has usually been rather an impersonal letter of those decently cold in their graves for some time.

One may submit to the flattery of imitation or to caricature personally; every one who marches or strays from beaten paths must submit to one or to both, but never will one submit tamely to caricature of that which one loves. Personally, I, too, am heartily sick of being commercialized and traded in and upon; but most of all I dread to see the types I have worked with so long and patiently drifting toward speculative builders, cheapened or befooled by senseless changes, robbed of quality and distinction, dead forms or grinning originalities for the sake of originality, an endless string of hacked carcasses, to encumber democratic front yards for five decades or more. This, however, is only the personal side of the matter and to be endured in silence were there any profit in it to come to the future architecture of the "melting pot."

The more serious side and the occasion for this second paper is the fact that emboldened or befooled by its measure of "Success," the new work has been showing weaknesses instead of the character it might have shown some years hence were it more enlightened and discreet, more sincere and modest, prepared to wait, to wait to prepare.

The average American man or woman who wants to build a house wants something different—"something different" is what they say they want, and most of them want it in a hurry. That this is the fertile soil upon which an undisciplined "language speaking" neophyte may grow his crop to the top of his ambition is deplorable in one sense, but none the less hopeful in another and more vital sense. The average man of business in America has truer intuition, and so a more nearly just estimate of artistic values, when he has a chance to judge between good and bad, than a man of similar class in any other country. But he is prone to take that "something different" anyhow; if not good, then bad. He is rapidly outgrowing the provincialism that needs a foreign-made label upon "Art," and so, at the present moment, not only is he in danger of being swindled, but likely to find something peculiarly his own, in time, and valuable to him, if he can last. I hope and believe he can last. At any rate, there is no way of preventing him from getting either swindled or something merely "different"; nor do I believe it would be desirable if he could be, until the inorganic thing he usually gets in the form of this "something different" is put forward and publicly advertised as of that character of the young work for which I must feel myself responsible.

I do not admit that my disciples or pupils, be they artists, neophytes or brokers, are responsible for worse buildings than nine-tenths of the work done by average architects who are "good school"—in fact, I think the worst of them do better—although they sometimes justify themselves in equivocal positions by reference to this fact. Were no more to come of my work than is evident at present, the architecture of the country would have received an impetus that will finally resolve itself into good. But to me the exasperating fact is that it might aid vitally the great things we all desire, if it were treated on its merits, used and not abused. Selling even good versions of an original at second hand is in the circumstances not good enough. It is cheap and bad—demoralizing in every sense. But, unhappily, I have to confess that the situation seems worse where originality, as such, has thus far been attempted, because it seems to have been attempted chiefly *for its own sake,* and the results bear about the same resemblance to an organic architecture as might be shown were one to take a classic column and, breaking it, let the upper half lie carelessly at the foot of the lower, then setting the capital picturesquely askew against the half thus prostrate, one were to settle the whole arrangement as some structural feature of street or garden.

For worker or broker to exhibit such "designs" as efforts of creative architects, before the ink is yet dry on either work or worker, is easily done under present standards with "success," but the exploit finally reflects a poor sort of credit upon the exploited architect and the cause. As for the cause, any growth that comes to it in a "spread" of this kind is unwholesome. I insist that this sort of thing is not "new school," nor this the way to develop one. This is piracy, lunacy, plunder, imitation, adulation, or what you will; it is not a developing architecture when worked in this fashion, nor will it ever become one until purged of this spirit; least of all is it an organic architecture. Its practices belie any such character.

"Disciples" aside, some fifteen young people, all entirely inexperienced and unformed—but few had even college educations—attracted by the character of my work, sought me as their employer.[7] I am no teacher; I am a worker—but I gave to all, impartially, the freedom of my work room, my work and myself, to imbue them with the spirit of the performances for their own sakes, and with the letter for my sake, so that they might become useful to me; because the nature of my endeavor was such that I had to train my own help and pay current wages while I trained them.

The nature of the profession these young people were to make when they assumed to practice architecture entails much more careful preparation than that of the "good school" architect; theirs is a far more difficult thing to do technically and artistically, if they would do something of their own. To my chagrin, too many are content to take it "ready made," and with no further preparation hasten to compete for clients of their own. Now fifteen good, bad and indifferent are practicing architecture in the Middle West, South and Far West, and with considerable "success." In common with the work of numerous disciples (judging from such work as has been put forward publicly), there is a restless jockeying with members, one left off here, another added there, with varying intent—in some a vain endeavor to reindividualize the old types; in others an attempt to conceal their origin, but always—ad nauseam—the inevitable reiteration of the features that gave the original work its style and individuality. To find fault with this were unfair. It is not unexpected nor unpromising except in those unbearable cases where badly modified *inorganic* results seem to satisfy their authors' conception of originality; and banalities of form and proportion are accordingly advertised in haste as work of creative architects of a *"new school."* That some uniformity in performance should have obtained for some years is natural; it could not be otherwise, unless unaware I had harbored marked geniuses. But when the genius arrives nobody will take his work for mine—least of all will he mistake my work for his.

"The letter killeth." In this young work at this time, still it is the letter that killeth, and emulation of the "letter" that gives the illusion or delusion of "movement." There is no doubt, however, but that the sentiment is awakened which will mean progressive movement in time. And there are many working quietly who, I am sure, will give a good account of themselves.

Meanwhile, the spirit in which this use of the letter has its rise is important to any noble future still left to the cause. If the practices that disgrace and demoralize the soul of the young man in architecture could be made plain to him; if he could be shown that inevitably equivocation dwarfs and eventually destroys what creative faculty he may possess—that designing lies, in design to deceive himself or others, shuts him out absolutely from realizing upon his own gifts—no matter how flattering his opportunities may be—if he could realize that the artist heart is one uncompromising core of truth in seeking, in giving or in taking—a precious service could be rendered him. The young architect who is artist enough to know where he stands and man enough to use honestly his parent forms as such, conservatively, until he feels his own strength within him, is only exercising an artistic birthright in the interest of a good cause—he has the character at least from which great things may come. But the boy who steals his forms—"steals" them because he sells them as his own for the moment of superficial distinction he gains by trading on the results—is no artist, has not the sense of the first principles of the ideal that he poses and the forms that he abuses. He denies his birthright, an act characteristic and unimportant; but for a mess of pottage, he endangers the chances of a genuine forward movement, insults both cause and precedent with an astounding insolence quite peculiar to these matters in the United States, ruthlessly sucks what blood may be left in the tortured and abused forms he caricatures and exploits—like the parasite he is.

Another condition as far removed from creative work is the state of mind of those who, having in the course of their day's labor put some stitches into the "clothes" of the work, assume, therefore, that style and pattern are rightfully theirs and wear them defiantly unregenerate. The gist of the whole matter artistically has entirely eluded them. This may be the so-called "democratic" point of view: at any rate it is the immemorial error of the rabble. No great artist nor work of art ever proceeded from that conception, nor ever will.

Then there is the soiled and soiling fringe of all creative effort, a type common to all work everywhere that meets with any degree of success, although it may be more virulent here because of low standards; those who benefit by the use of another's work and to justify themselves depreciate both the work and worker they took it from—the type that will declare, "In the first place, I never had your shovel; in the second place, I never broke your shovel; and in the third place, it was broken when I got it, anyway"—the type that with more crafty intelligence develops into the "coffin worm." One of Whistler's "coffin worms" has just wriggled in and out.[8]

But underneath all, I am constrained to believe, lies the feverish ambition to get fame or fortune "quick," characteristic of the rush of commercial standards that rule in place of artist standards, and consequent unwillingness to wait to prepare thoroughly.

"Art to one is high as a heavenly goddess: to another only the thrifty cow that gives him his butter," said Schiller;[9] and who will deny that our profession is prostitute to the cow, meager in ideals, cheap in performance, commercial in spirit; demoralized by ignoble ambition? A foolish optimism regarding this only serves to perpetuate it. Foolish optimism and the vanity of fear of ridicule or "failure" are both friends of ignorance.

In no country in the world do disciples, neophytes or brokers pass artist counterfeit so easily as in these United States. Art is commercialized here rather more than anything else, although the arts should be as free from this taint as religion. But has religion escaped?

So the standard of criticism is not only low—it is often dishonest or faked somewhere between the two, largely manufactured to order for profit or bias. Criticism is worked as an advertising game, traders' instincts subject to the prevailing commercial taint. Therein lies a radically evil imposition that harms the public; that also further distorts, confuses and injures values and promotes bad work; that tends to render the integrity of artist and commerce alike a stale and unprofitable joke, and to make honest enemies even harder to find than honest friends. The spirit of fair play, the endeavor to preserve the integrity of values, intelligently, on a high plane in order to help in raising the level of the standard of achievement in the country, and to refrain from throwing the senseless weight of the mediocre and bad upon it— all this is unhappily too rare among editors. The average editor has a "constituency," not a standard. This constituency is largely the average architect who has bought the "artistic" in his architecture as one of its dubious and minor aspects, or the sophisticated neophyte, the broker and the quack, to whom printers' ink is ego-balm and fortune.

So until the standard is raised, any plea for artist integrity is like a cry for water in the Painted Desert. As for competent criticism, the honest word of illuminating insight, where is it? Nothing is more precious or essential to progress. Where is the editor or critic not narrow or provincial? Or loose and ignorant? Or cleverly or superficially or cowardly commercial? Let him raise this standard! Friend or foe, there is still a demand for him even here; but if he did, he would fail—gloriously fail—of "success."

Is architecture, then, no longer to be practiced as an art? Has its practice permanently descended to a form of mere "artistic activity"?

The art of architecture has fallen from a high estate—lower steadily since the Men of Florence patched together fragments of the art of Greece and Rome and in vain endeavor to re-establish its eminence manufactured the Renaissance. It has fallen—from the heavenly Goddess of Antiquity and the Middle Ages to the thrifty cow of the present day. To touch upon these matters in this country is doubly unkind, for it is to touch upon the question of "bread and butter" chiefly. Aside from the conscienceless ambition of the near artist—more sordid than any greed of gold—and beneath this thin pretense of the ideal that veneers the curious compound of broker and neophyte there lurks, I know, for any young architect an ever present dread of the kind of "failure" that is the obverse of the kind of "success" that commercialized standards demand of him if he is to survive. Whosoever would worship his heavenly goddess has small choice—he must keep his eye on the thrifty cow or give up his dream of "success"; and the power of discrimination possessed by the cow promises ill for the future integrity of an organic architecture. The net result of present standards is likely to be a poor wretch, a coward who aspires pretentiously or theoretically, advertises cleverly and milks surreptitiously. There is no real connection between aspiration and practice except a tissue of lies and deceit; there never can be. The young architect before he ventures to practice architecture with an ideal, today, should first be sure of his goddess and then, somehow, be connected with a base of supplies from which he cannot be cut off, or else fall in with the rank and file of the "good school" of the hour. Any one who has tried it knows this; that is, if he is honest and is going to use his own material as soon as he is able. So the ever present economic question underlies this question of artist integrity, at this stage of our development, like quicksand beneath the footing of a needed foundation, and the structure itself seems doomed to shreds and cracks and shores and patches, the deadening compromises and pitiful makeshifts of the struggle to *"succeed!"* Even the cry for this integrity will bind the legion together, as one man, against the crier and the cry.

This is Art, then, in a sentimental Democracy, which seems to be only another form of self-same hypocrisy? Show me a man who prates of such "Democracy" as a basis for artist endeavor, and I will show you an inordinately foolish egotist or a quack. The "Democracy" of the man in the American street is no more than the Gospel of Mediocrity. When it is understood that a great

Democracy is the highest form of Aristocracy conceivable, not of birth or place or wealth, but of those qualities that give distinction to the man as a man, and that as a social state it must be characterized by the honesty and responsibility of the absolute individualist as the unit of its structure, then only can we have an Art worthy the name. The rule of mankind by mankind is one thing; but false "Democracy"—the hypocritical sentimentality politically practiced and preached here, usually the sheep's clothing of the proverbial wolf, or the egotistic dream of self-constituted patron saints—is quite another thing. "The letter killeth"; yes, but more deadly still is the undertow of false democracy that poses the man as a creative artist and starves him to death unless he fakes his goddess or persuades himself, with "language," that the cow is really she. Is the lack of an artist-conscience, then, simply the helpless surrender of the would-be artist to this wherewithal Democracy with which a nation soothes itself into subjection? Is the integrity for which I plead here no part of this time and place? And is no young aspirant or hardened sinner to blame for lacking it? It may be so. If it is, we can at least be honest about that, too. But what aspiring artist could knowingly face such a condition? He would choose to dig in the ditch and trace his dreams by lamplight, on scrap paper, for the good of his own soul—a sweet and honorable, if commercially futile, occupation.

It has been my hope to have inspired among my pupils a personality or two to contribute to this work, some day, forms of their own devising, with an artistic integrity that will help to establish upon a firmer basis the efforts that have gone before them and enable them in more propitious times to carry on their practice with a personal gentleness, wisdom and reverence denied to the pioneers who broke rough ground for them, with a wistful eye to better conditions for their future.

And I believe that, cleared of the superficial pose and push that is the inevitable abuse of its opportunity and its nature, and against which I ungraciously urge myself here, there will be found good work in a cause that deserves honest friends and honest enemies among the better architects of the country. Let us have done with "language" and unfair use of borrowed forms; understand that such practices or products are not of the character of this young work. This work is a sincere endeavor to establish the ideal of an organic architecture in a new country; a type of endeavor that alone can give lasting value to any architecture and that is in line with the spirit of every great and noble precedent in the world of forms that has come to us as the heritage of the great life that has been lived, and in the spirit of which all great life to be will still be lived.

And this thing that eludes the disciple, remains in hiding from the neophyte, and in the name of which the broker seduces his client—what is it? This mystery requiring the catch phrases of a new language to abate the agonies of the convert and in the name of which ubiquitous atrocities have been and will continue to be committed, with the deadly enthusiasm of the ego-mania that is its plague? First, a study of the nature of materials you elect to use and the tools you must use with them, searching to find the characteristic qualities in both that are suited to your purpose. Second, with an ideal of organic nature as a guide, so to unite these qualities to serve that purpose, that the fashion of what you do has integrity or is *natively fit,* regardless of preconceived notions of style. *Style* is a by-product of the process and comes of the man or the mind in the process. The style of the thing, therefore, will be the man—it is his. *Let his forms alone.*

To adopt a "style" as a motive is to put the cart before the horse and get nowhere beyond the "Styles"—never to reach *Style.*

It is obvious that this is neither ideal nor work for fakirs or tyros; for unless this process is finally so imbued, informed, with a feeling for the beautiful that grace and proportion are inevitable, the result cannot get beyond good engineering.

A light matter this, altogether? And yet an organic architecture must take this course and belie nothing, shirk nothing. Discipline! The architect who undertakes his work seriously on these lines is emancipated and imprisoned at the same time. His work may be severe; it cannot be foolish. It may lack grace; it cannot lack fitness altogether. It may seem ugly; it will not be false. No wonder, however, that the practice of architecture in this sense is the height of ambition and the depth of poverty!

Nothing is more difficult to achieve than the integral simplicity of organic nature, amid the tangled confusions of the innumerable relics of form that encumber life for us. To achieve it in any degree means a serious devotion to the "underneath" in an attempt to grasp the *nature* of building a beautiful building beautifully, as organically true in itself, to itself and to its purpose, as any tree or flower.

That is the need, and the need is demoralized, not served, by the same superficial emulation of the letter in the new work that has heretofore characterized the performances of those who start out to practice architecture by selecting and electing to work in a ready-made "style."

NOTES

1. From Friedrich Schiller (1759–1805), *On the Aesthetic Education of Man in a Series of Letters* (1794).

2. Adapted from Lord Alfred Tennyson's 1864 poem "The Flower" which reads: "Most can raise the flowers now/For all have got the seed."

3. After Wright left Adler & Sullivan, he opened an independent practice in 1893.

4. Montgomery Schuyler (1843–1914), a prominent critic, was a founder of *Architectural Record* in 1891.

5. "Progress Before Precedent" was adopted in 1900 as the motto of the Architectural League of America, founded the year before. Wright published a critical but not hostile comment about it in *The Brickbuilder,* 9 (May 1900).

6. "Twenty-eight years ago" would have been 1886, but Wright, infrequently careful with dates, most likely entered Adler & Sullivan's employ early in 1888.

7. Wright names twelve employees in "In the Cause of Architecture" (1908), Document 4.

8. "Coffin worms" (that eat the dead after burial), a term employed by Charles Baudelaire, William Butler Yeats, and John Keats, is a colloquialism old enough also to have been used by William Shakespeare, although apparently not by James McNeill Whistler, as a search of his correspondence archives reveals. If Wright misremembered his literary source, he nevertheless uses "coffin worms" to condemn those who "soil" the creative work of others—namely himself—by appropriating it as their own. I owe this information to Marjorie Munsterburg via Harriet Senie of the Art History Department, the City College of New York.

9. From *Xenien*, a collection of distichs (in modern parlance couplets) jointly composed by Schiller and Johann Wolfgang Goethe (1749–1832) in 1795–96. This one about "scholarship" reads: "To some she is the high and mighty goddess; to others she is a useful cow providing them with butter."

NINE

The American System of House Building (1916)

Prominent architects' reputations are usually based upon highly visible, large-scale, "foreground" buildings for corporations, institutions, governments, and the like. But for the most part Wright's reputation stems from detached, single-family dwellings, accounting for perhaps three-quarters of all his commissions. Most were for comfortably middle-class clients, to be sure, or for others even wealthier, but in 1916 he began to address the problem of affordable, moderate-income housing, a preoccupation for the rest of his life.

His "American System Ready-Cut Houses" were small-to-medium-size single-family residences and four-unit duplex apartment buildings up to three stories tall of wood and/or stucco in several design types, the least expensive advertised in the Chicago Tribune in 1917 for $2,730. Because room plans within types were standardized, they could be variously arranged according to preference or site condition; because their wooden elements—framing, flooring, molding, trim, and so on—were premeasured and precut at the Arthur L. Richards Company factory in Milwaukee, they could be installed at reduced cost. As such, "Ready-Cuts" constituted a pioneering attempt to mass-produce partially prefabricated housing.

It is unknown how many were erected. Wright's office did not supervise construction because orders were placed directly with the Richards Company, now long defunct with records lost. One authority *reports that Wright produced over nine hundred drawings and sketches that another authority maintains constitute the single largest collection in the Wright archive. It is estimated, however, that ten to fifteen Ready-Cuts are scattered around the Midwest, roughly half in Milwaukee, others in and around Chicago, one in Gary, Indiana. Given renewed interest, it is likely more will be discovered.*

Shortages of building material after the United States entered World War One in 1917, coupled with disputes between Wright and Richards over money, plus the primitive state of mass-production technology and distribution, especially for the housing market, ended the experiment in 1917. But the few extant Ready-Cuts bear witness to Wright's desire to offer "organic architecture" to as wide an audience as possible.

This excerpt from Wright's "recent" speech to an unidentified gathering of Chicago businessmen (most likely realtors) was published in the Western Architect, *24 (September 1916).*

I hesitated a long time before I decided that I would undertake a thing of this nature. It is something I have always believed could be done here in America better than anywhere else in the world. In all of my work from the beginning, I have had faith in the machine as the characteristic tool of my times, therefore an artist's tool. I have believed that this tool put into an artist's hand could be a real benefit to our civilization. I believe that the architecture in America that fails to take into account the machine and modern organization tendencies is going to be of no great benefit to the people. Of course, I know that it is going to take a more subtle art within more severe limitation to build houses beautifully while utilizing the machine. But I believe this effort is the logical conclusion of my studies and my architectural practice.

I believe the world will find in the American System of House construction, the only instance in the world today of a work which has absolute individuality due to a central idea which is the organic integrity of the work.

If the whole organization of the plan by which the American models are to be merchandised is worked out in a broad, healthy way, great things will come of it. Naturally, I do not want it exploited like a flash in the pan, nor do I want anything done that will make the plan seem an expedient of the moment.

The idea back of the American System has been in my head for years. I have guarded it carefully. I wanted time to think in quiet of how the idea might be brought to the public without injury to the integrity of my own art. Any student of design will know that the designs of these houses are not architectural attempts at reform. They are developed according to a principle. They grow from the inside out, just as trees or flowers grow. They have that integrity. The difference between my work and the work of other men is all a difference in grasp and treatment of old principles.

I do not want any mistake made about this new "System." These buildings are not in any sense the ready cut buildings we have all heard of where a little package of material is sold to be stuck together in any fashion. The American System-Built House is not a ready cut house, but a house built by an organization, systematized in such a way that the result is guaranteed the fellow that buys the house. I want to deliver beautiful houses to people at a certain price, key in packet. If I have made progress in the art of architecture, I want to be able to offer this to the people intact. I think the idea will appeal also to the man in the street. Every man would love to have a beautiful house if he could pay for the tremendous amount of waste usually involved in building such a house. The American Plan you see, simply cuts out the tremendous waste that has in the past made house-building on a beautiful scale possible only to the very rich, and any integrity in the result possible only to the especially enlightened individual. Unlimited money has failed there most loudly.

Somehow in America, architecture has never been appreciated. We are perhaps the greatest nation of house builders in the world, and the most slip-shod nation of home builders. Architecture has for the most part, been let go by the board, because we have had to have buildings, and have them quick.

The result is that the old log cabin, built in the woods by the frontiersmen, is really much more beautiful than the modern house with all its affectation, fussiness and ugly waste.

Now, I believe that the coming of the machine has so altered the conditions of home building that something like this American System was inevitable, but I have not borne in mind purely the economical side of it. I would like to explain to you men some of the impulses back of my work in this direction.

When I, as a young American architect, went abroad, I found many things that astonished me. I expected to find over there, a great variety—great interest. I went from one city to another, and for the most part found beauty in the very old buildings only. The Germans who really built German buildings, and the Italians who built really Italian buildings, built beautifully. I naturally came to the conclusion that much of the hideousness in the architecture of modern day was due to the academic "Renaissance," that Europe has so nearly standardized. To my mind, the renaissance, although academic, never was organic. And, for centuries, architecture, like other arts, touched by the renaissance, had been divorced from life, divorced from any organic relation of cause and effect.

Now, when we go back to the old architecture, we find something quite different. The Gothic, for example, was a true style. It was a real architecture. It was an organic architecture. In all of my work I have always tried to make my work organic.

Now, in America, you understand that we have been all of these years borrowing bad forms. The result is that our buildings have no life, no meaning in them, and if we are ever going to have a living architecture again—an architecture in which there is really joy and which gives joy—we have got to go back to first principles. We have got to go beyond the renaissance to reality, to truth.

And now there comes a thought which is really back of this whole effort and which to you business men may sound like a highly sophisticated affair. You see, you in America have been led to believe that an artist is necessarily a queer fellow—one divorced from the life about him. The contrary is true. The perfect artist should be a better business man than any of you here sitting before me and he would be if he had time and the need.

In America, the natural tendency of our times is away from the old handcraft. The railroad locomotive, the great electrical dynamo—these are some of our truly beautiful products—beautiful because of their perfect adaptation of means to ends. Now, I do not believe any architecture in the time of commercialism, of industrialism, and of huge organization, can be real architecture unless it uses beautifully all of these great tools of modern life. And that is just what the American System of building houses proposes to do.

Of course, I realized the danger in all this. I would not dare go into it if I did not believe I could in the midst of industrialism and commercialism, keep on top with my art. In the designing of all these houses, I have kept close to first principles, but I look with horror at what might easily happen in spite of all the care with which I have handled this matter. I do not want to lose sight of the central idea of using the machine and all modern industrialism to produce beauty. I asked you men to be patient with me if I sometimes insisted upon things that you do not understand the meaning of. Simply selling houses at less cost means nothing at all to me. To sell beautiful houses at less cost means everything. A beautiful house means a truer, better house in every way.

TEN

In the Cause of Architecture:
The New Imperial Hotel, Tokio
(1923)

Wright's second visit to Japan, from January to May 1913, was at the behest of Imperial Hotel management, which, shortly after he returned home, tentatively offered the commission to replace its inadequate structure. Design work during the next three and a half years was repeatedly interrupted by personal preoccupations, other professional obligations, and management indecision, but as soon as he was officially commissioned late in 1916, he returned to Tokyo to arrange construction. All in all, Wright spent approximately forty-five months in Japan over the course of five extended trips from January 1913 to July 1922, working there and here on one of the largest, longest-in-gestation, costliest, most widely discussed and controversial buildings of his career.

He was not present the day the last portion of the New Imperial opened. September 1, 1923, was also the day an earthquake, not the one of which he writes, took at least 92,000 lives, injuring many more. The hotel's location at the periphery of the shock, plus the ingenious foundation system of which he does write, enabled it to survive with minimal damage. United States firebombing during the latter stages of World War Two took a much greater toll.

By the 1960s the Imperial had outlived its usefulness. Its original raison d'être as the emperor's social center for international visitors had given way to upscale commercial enterprise long before the empire collapsed in 1945. Nearby subway excavations had further weakened foundations already so compromised by shifting alluvial subsoil that portions of the building had sunk three and a half feet. With modern high-rise hotels catering to a new generation of tourists, and at three stories but fewer than 250 rooms set in extensive gardens consuming an enormous parcel of prime real estate, it had become a financial white elephant.

Still gorgeous, a favorite of nostalgic travelers, but undeniably shabby and ill maintained, the Imperial closed in November 1967 and was immediately demolished, except for a small portion reconstructed at an architecture museum near Nagoya and the Old Imperial Bar rebuilt in its replacement. The decidedly undistinguished seventeen-story glass and steel "new" New Imperial opened in 1970.

Even before Wright's Imperial opened, it was criticized for being too American, not Japanese enough, too modern for Japan, and too old-fashioned compared to the new European architecture he would soon condemn (in Documents 12a to d). But that was precisely the point, for Wright's objective was neither to look forward or backward nor to East or West, but to erect something organically Japanese by blending local materials, garden vegetation, labor practices, construction technologies, social conventions, and "the spirit of Oriental art"—emphasis on "spirit"—into "one fabric," as he puts it, a seamless, timeless "harmonious whole."

That it took nine years to design and build but lasted a mere forty-four does not necessarily negate another of Wright's contentions: that the Imperial was his "missionary with a sense of beauty." Perhaps it was presumptuous of him to "conventionalize" another society's ideas for its own instruction, but if this were cultural imperialism, it paled in comparison to the emerging notion that the European-based "International Style" was suitable for any culture anywhere. For as Wright so often wrote, working in a style was a far lesser thing than having style itself.

Originally published as "In the Cause of Architecture: The New Imperial Hotel, Tokio, Frank Lloyd Wright, Architect," Western Architect, *32 (April 1923).*

I. The Purpose of the Building

The Imperial Hotel is not a hotel at all in the accepted sense of that term. It is a delightful place of sojourn for travellers and a place of varied entertainment for the social functions of the life of Tokio, the Japanese Capital.

The Imperial is the first important protest against the Gargantuan waste adopted by Japan from old German precedents when there were no worse ones. It is a conservation of space, energy and time by concentration and the invention of practical ways and means to that end. Just such conservation as this existed in Old Japan, and is at work in this building to help establish in the new life now inevitable to them that same wonderful unity.

Every utilitarian need is insisted upon as an ordered thing in a harmonious whole; that is what the old Japanese life insisted upon with telling and beautiful effect.

The Imperial has no quarrel with life as lived upon any civilized basis now, but at the present time it does belong in point of character and purpose to the more advanced stage of culture, because it insists upon utilitarian needs as ordered features of a sentient whole, and finds its "effects" in making them so.

The Imperial Hotel has therefore, in most essential respects, been fixed ahead of the abuse and waste of the hour—to be, in the meantime, attacked as a challenge to that old waste and abuse. This would be true of any building, doing in its own way the thing that has always been done in a more familiar way.

The "Hotel," however, is less than one-half the substance of the whole, or its function, or its cost. It is—as it has always been— a concession to the foreign invasion, rather than an investment.

There is also a centre of entertainment which is more important and profitable, and an investment rather than a concession. This centre is a clearing house for Japan's social obligations to "the foreigner," and the Japanese social life of the Capital. This central group contains a masonry promenade, or central paved court 300 feet long by 20 feet wide, 16 various private supper rooms and various parlors being appropriately grouped about it; a masonry theatre seating one thousand people, opening directly from it. The theatre has a revolving stage. There is, below the theatre, also opening directly from the promenade, a terraced cabaret seating at tables 300 people, with dancing space and stage. Above the theatre, reached directly from the promenade, is a spacious foyer opening to the main roof garden—above this is a banquet hall with capacity to seat a thousand at table. A splay and cantilever gallery is continued all around this room, springing upward to a pendentive roof. Like the theatre this room too, is done in imperishable materials—a great building in itself. These various rooms for important public functions have adequate toilet accommodations, service rooms and galleries or avenues of inter-communication, and are all associated directly with enclosed gardens, terraces and balconies. The Imperial Hotel, therefore, is not designed as a profitable undertaking in the ordinary commercial sense, but it is so as a distinguished center of social entertainment for the life of the capital, in a sense that is unique.

II. The Nature of the Imperial and Its Problem

In a pool of conflicting ideas and competitive races like Tokio, there is always much that is obscure, lurking behind walls that are unknown languages. But the thing that stands out to me most sharply in this experience is the incapacity for any sacrifice of habitual "use and wont" on the part of the average human being. Not only that, but the bitterness with which any suggestion of the sort is resented as a personal affront. Instead of being intrigued and interested by an attempt to inculcate a finer and better "use and wont," one more in keeping with true civilization, civilization seems to have been abandoned by the average guest in an oriental hotel at Yen twenty per day.

A hotel primarily is a place for human creatures certainly. And a hotel is a dangerous place in which to put a premium upon human intelligence, human aesthetic needs, or human appreciation of a beautiful environment.

In the confusion consequent upon English, German, French, Chinese or Russian ideas of "the right thing" there does seem to be a consensus of opinion regarding "the right thing" in a hotel. It is a guest room that is a vast compound, the vaster the better, in which to spread around a freight car load of luggage; a big tub in another nearby room; plenty of big windows on at least two sides of the compound, three preferred; an enormous upholstered platform, seven feet square three feet above the floor to sleep on; another big room with an outside window in which to throw things or hang them; no sense of a ceiling at all; an aggregation of oversized, over-stuffed furniture that can be dragged about regardless or pushed aside entirely; food and water always handy; boy San just outside the door day and night; a cuspidor.

As for light and heat, plenty of both, with doors and windows wide open.

But the Imperial has aimed higher than to stall and feed and groom and bed that captious animal with quite all the license which would be popular. The Imperial therefore is not a hotel. The creature comforts are all there but also an aspiration to something better although not so big and less barbarous; something more on the order of what might be found in a gentleman's home in a modern country house.

In the Imperial therefore, the Art of Architecture comes to grips with reality for the sake of a better order, a popular mission, but one that will not immediately be popular. A management imbued with this idea is as essential to its success as are the features of the building itself, and more so. The old management by whom the building was initiated changed during the course of construction. Aisaku Hayashi was the managing director. Another manager, H. S. K. Yamaguchi, personally popular and successful in the conduct of a resort hotel, was appointed, and while undertaking an enterprise shaped in detail to suit the ideas of another manager, he has attacked the problem with spirit and a desire to succeed in every feature of his responsibility. What Mr. Yamaguchi, in his difficult position will achieve, remains to be seen.

The enterprise, although initiated many years ago by the Imperial Household as a social necessity in connection with Japanese official life in contact with the foreigner, has proved profitable. As the social life of the Capital has grown in foreign style, it became desirable to expand and date the enterprise somewhat ahead in order to keep it, as it always has been, the social center of the life of the Japanese Capital. So, while it has been, and will be profitable under good management, it is, as was stated above, not a commercial venture, not an investment in an ordinary sense.

That is why it was laid out as a group of buildings in a system of gardens and terraces and not as an "office building hotel" along American lines. That is why the attributes of culture have been sought in its design and appointments; that is why a love for beauty must characterize the guest who really belongs to the Imperial.

The world moves with incredible rapidity. Concentration of space by means of concentrated conveniences has already gone far. The ship began it, the Pullman car took it up, the ocean liner went further and now the high-class hotel on costly ground is at work upon it all over the world.

In the New Imperial the quality of beauty and integrity of the whole is established by making each unit (albeit a smaller unit) an integral part of a great and harmonious whole. That broader relationship affords a richer experience, a fuller life for each individual than could possibly be where more license in more space would turn that individual loose at the expense of the whole. In all this there is the economic limit—that is, the degree to which the human animal will submit to the larger and the finer interest. Who can say just where that limit lies, or should lie, except that, in an effort to establish a superior thing, that limit should be fixed ahead of the abuse and waste of the hour?

III. The Aesthetic Motif

The Imperial Hotel is designed as a system of gardens and sunken gardens and terraced gardens—of balconies that are gardens and loggias that are also gardens and roofs that are gardens—until the whole arrangement becomes an interpenetration of gardens. Japan is Garden-land.

This is not realized in the photographs as they were made before the building was entirely finished, and before this part of the work was fairly begun. Until the intended foliage develops in relation to enclosures and preparations made for it in the structural scheme, the Imperial is something like a sycamore without its leaves. Its structure asserts itself so boldly as to pain the sensitive beholder committed by use and wont to the modifying member. Having devoted my life to getting rid of that expedient in Architecture, or in Society or in Life—it is with difficulty that I realize the shock to sensitive Renaissance nerves, the utter neglect of this member causes, and the sense of outrage the frustrated sensibilities of the school-bred architect receives from such bold assertions and contrasts as confront him and bear him down in this building.

The Imperial is perhaps the most "shameless offense against the modifying member" that has ever been committed. There is a strength of purpose behind the thrust of slab and spread of the cantilever in this structure that is without a parallel. So much so that modified and modifying architects gravely decide that it were better had it never been built at all. What a small world is the world of the "modifying member!" In any serious analysis, how lacking in any fundamental character. It is the world of yesterday in a futile endeavor to foreclose upon today, in order that tomorrow may be as yesterday.

Therefore, this modifying member, graceless and stultifying hypocrite that it is, is here rejected, and the structure appeals directly to nature for modification. In course of time the building will receive it richly and wear it nobly, as an appropriate raiment, the one enhancing the other.

I am not of those who conceive a building as a carved and sculptured block of building material. That is two dimension thinking. A room or group of rooms expressed in an arrangement and grouping of wall enclosures, together with the surmounting slabs or planes: fenestration not embrasures merely, but knitting all together in one fabric as a harmonious whole; that, is a building.

This sense of building is the three-dimension conception of Architecture. In this conception, integral effects in both materials and methods are the only effects.

The question I would ask concerning any architect or his building would be, is the architect's mind or is his work in two or in three dimensions? Is his work extraneous—applied from without, or an integral development from within?

This is not the standard of the schools. This is a far more subtle and difficult standard. This criterion must be found *inside* and not picked up outside.

It is the Imagination that is challenged, and not the Memory.

Whatever, in an aesthetic sense, the faults of the Imperial may be, I can truly say that it is all of one piece in honest materials, honestly made; that it is a virile study in coherent scale and that scale broadly adapted and adjusted to the human figure; a strong and purposeful foil for natural foliage and verdure—enhanced by it and enhancing it; it belies nothing intentionally, copies nothing, but reveres the spirit of Oriental Art, without losing its own individuality; a missionary with a sense of beauty, believing in the importance of preserving the individuality of the soul to whom it would minister. It has consistent style as a whole, although owing nothing to styles.

Faults or no faults, sincere work of this type ought to be valuable at this stage of Japan's culture, and to the thoughtful it will be so.

It would be equally valuable to us if we would look at it, for what it has to give, because our own architectural situation is not so different from Japan's as we like to think it is. We are under the same necessity to develop an indigenous architecture. The Japanese once had such an architecture and now must create it again for a changed life condition. We have never had it and have only mixed traditions of many races almost as unsuited to our present use as are the old Japanese traditions to their use. We too must create an architecture for our own changed life conditions.

A western editor of an Architectural Journal laments that the export of "American Architecture" to Japan is likely to be damaged by this "experiment." Japanese architects, "American trained," are insulted by it,—he thinks, and he says they have a right to feel cheated. If the western editor is right I am not sorry.

The Imperial is a protest in every sense against the commercialism that would standardize a world to make a market even for "American Architecture." If only the United States might look that architecture squarely in the face with the eyes of the Beaux-Arts or the European architects who despise it for the servile thing it really is, and if they would deprive the commercial sheep who commend and sell it,—of their "franchise,"—but what vain hope! Architecture "ready-made" like our manners or our institutions is a necessity to us, as to Japan, for but slightly different reasons. There is no remedy except one to come afterward that will tear down what the fashion-monger builded upon the labor of the hard pressed and hard working pioneer, or none that will not eventually have to throw away the product of the fashionable accidents or social indiscretions that have "Art" in charge—shall I say in trust—for the moment.

And what a sacrilege it is, to see Japan taking this performance or betrayal from us second hand, upon faith!

In several of the photographs of the Imperial hotel, the environment of Japanese modern civilization in Tokio may be glimpsed. Japanese culture has met with Occidental Architecture as a beautiful work of Art might meet with a terrible "accident." It is trampled and obliterated by the waste of senseless German precedents or literally ironed flat by sordid facts brought over from America in ships.

American commercial buildings ten stories tall, or more, steel frames, inserted walls, are ravaging Tokio's architectural possibilities just as the "Derby hat" and "Boston gaiters," or the "hard-straw" have already insulted the Kimono and Geta.

The present plight of Japan in this matter of "civilization" is pathetic. To participate in this masked form of commercial subjugation, would be to participate in a crime Japan is deliberately invited by Western "interests" to commit.

Therefore, the New Imperial Hotel is not an American building in Tokio any more than was inevitable in the circumstances. It is not a Japanese building, however, nor intended to be an Oriental building. It is an architect's sincere tribute to an unique nation, a building that respects Oriental tradition, at the same time that it keeps its own individuality as a sympathetic friend on Japanese soil.

I have been astonished to find such bitterness and such confusion of opinion concerning this attempt to assist Japan to her
own architectural feet, to help find an equivalent for her ancient
supremacy in Art.

The Imperial does not profess to be that new form, but it does
break away in that direction, a revolt and a suggestion. This simple statement of motive taken in connection with the photographs
may serve to enlighten some, but will probably only deepen the
chiaroscuro into which the whole seems to be thrown for the time
being, by and for others: so helpless are authorities and "profes-
sions" when deprived of their accepted "standards."

The animosity of Morality has often shocked and revolted me,
but the citizen's "sneer" directed in a democracy toward an idea or
an individual suspected of the idea that he has an idea, is always at
every turn a disagreeable surprise. Democracy has benefits, but
liberality toward ideals not one's own is not one of them. At least
among those "professing" anything.

Tastes or methods may well differ, but when principles are at
cross purpose, or when Principle encounters Sham, or Sham to
preserve itself, obscures Principle, there can be no peace.

Man is mocked by events in his struggle to express his little vision of great Truths. Out of every great endeavor perhaps some little good here or significance there will eventually be gathered into
the "common-good," just as thoughts great hearts once broke for,
we now breathe cheaply as the common air. What virtue lies in any
effort will survive—although the whole result be turned down as
outrageous by senseless "authority," or be aborted of its aims by
officious interference.

This is faith—and essential to all good work for human
progress.

Naturally I believe the Imperial right and square on the center line of human progress, and I know very well why I believe it.

•

IV. The Building of the Building

The difficulties overcome to acquire the proper materials, many of them made for the first time in Japan, and to instruct and control the industrial and commercial elements in the doing of a new thing in unfamiliar materials and by many methods necessarily new in a strange country where I could not speak the language and only a few assistants could speak mine, may be imagined.

Masonry building is still in its infancy in Japan.

The scheme of construction as fabricated upon a 4'-0" unit, was simple, so far as possible suited to hand-labor conditions as they still exist in that country. There was a stone and brick outer and inner shell, the outer shell the finished surface of the building, both outer and inner shells laid up to certain practicable heights and then concrete poured between them after laying in the necessary steel work for reinforcement. The outside brick shell was laid of bricks, especially made, that formed a 2 inch wall with 4 inch spurs, within the wall 4'-0" on centers. The inside face of the walls was laid up with 4" x 12" tile blocks with dovetailed grooves which, made by ourselves, were used for the first time in Japan. Intensive hand methods were necessary to avoid wrecking the fragile shells in pouring the concrete.

The third material, which was the plastic material used to articulate and decorate the structure, was a lava which I found was used as the ordinary "stone" of the region. We located a superior quarry and quarried it ourselves. This light lava, weighing 96 pounds per cubic foot, is easily worked when fresh from the quarry. It is an admirable material that has stood the test of centuries—similar to Travertine in character but with a more picturesque quality. Objection was made to using so common a material for a fine building, but the objection was overcome and a great part of the forms that articulate the structure and into which it is actually cast, are of this material, or itself cast into the structure like the bricks and the reinforcement tied in to it from behind. The edges of the projecting reinforced concrete slabs were all faced with this lava. The cornices or eaves are all projecting floor or roof slabs, perforated, faced with lava, and interlaced with copper. The lava was easily cut or carved, and the Japanese were especially skillful in this work, so this cut lava became, naturally, the characteristic ornamentation of the structure. Wherever it was felt necessary to relieve it, copper turned turquoise blue by surface treatment—an anticipation of the work of time—was cast in with it, and gold mosaic was inlaid in the pattern of the carving.

The "fusing" together of these materials perfectly was under the constant supervision of Paul Mueller,[1] whose devotion to the work for nearly four years is the best guarantee of thorough stability any work could have. To build this building we took a central organization accustomed to building docks and warehouses for the navy department and augmented it by such labor as could be picked up in Tokio or the provinces. This provincial labor made it necessary to quarter about 300 workmen and their families on the building site in addition to those who resided in Tokio.

For four years the site was a swarming hive of human activity and the work made more than usually difficult by this congestion, but a congestion natural enough, nearly everywhere in Tokio.

In planting this building upon soft ground in an earthquake country, the mud cushion 60 feet in depth was good insurance if the strength of a sufficient depth of it could be made available at the surface. I intended to do this by boring 9-inch holes 2'-0" on centers, 9'-0" [deep] and filling them with concrete, or the holes to go to a proper depth to be ascertained by tests. These holes were to be bored over the area required to give sufficient strength to carry the loads with a certain squeeze that could be allowed with safety to the structure: pins of sufficient number, in a pin cushion.

The tests were made, but in executing the foundation along these lines the ground was found to be full of boulders and old piles, and so Mr. Mueller punched the holes with a tapered wooden pile instead of boring them as intended. The friction was less and the ground shaken, but the result was sufficiently good.

As a proof of the method of construction and the faithfulness with which it was executed there came the earthquake of April, 1922, the most severe Tokio had experienced in more than fifty years—three years after the foundation had been put in. Levels taken along the base line of the building afterwards showed no deviation whatever due to seismic disturbance. Except where movement was allowed for, at the expansion joints, not a check or a crack or fallen piece of stone could be found as a result of this terrific distortion which caused every workman in the building to throw aside his tools and rush outside to the street. I myself, caught in the upper story of the wing where the architect's office was located, walked out onto the roofs with Endo San,[2] who had remained with me, and looked down at the excited crowd—gesticulating and badly frightened—in the street below. I was dripping with perspiration myself, knees none too steady. But I knew now by actual test the building was safe, several terrific crashes that had occurred during the quake being the falling of chimneys of the old Imperial at the rear, chimneys that had been left standing seventy feet high after the burning of the hotel a short time before.

It is useless to attempt to describe the troubles that beset the great enterprise from beginning to end. They were the troubles that beset any unusual thorough work that is an invention and innovation, anywhere, but complicated by the difficulty of communicating freely and directly with the forces actually at work. This was offset by the unfailing politeness and willingness of the workmen, the faithfulness too, of all those concerned in the work, except those entrusted with contracts who were no better and no worse than their equivalent in our own country.

•

V. A Labor of Mind and Body

Whatever the faults of their building may be, in building it the Japanese have shown a capacity for devotion to an ideal rare in any country. As a people they are sensitive to criticism. Hitherto they were protected by a completely established custom and code in which they had refuge or could take refuge at any time. Now they are easily bewildered or confused by the conflicting ideas or the contradictory testimony of the "new civilization."

They are prone to regard every matter as "personal," and the Oriental sense of "fate" and love of luxury is at work always in them. Their endurance at long-drawn-out, hard labor, mental or physical, is less than that of western races. Their efficiency, in our sense of the term, is therefore less.

In their language is no word to translate our word "Integrity;" none for "Love;" none for "Art" except "bijitsu," another form of the wrestling "jiujitzu"—clever tricks. "Beauty" is a word they seldom use and never as we use it. With them the word refers to something like a painted lady, cheap and on the surface.

But probably this is because a Japanese never speaks of that most sacred to him. To show deep feeling or to bare his inmost thoughts, is to wear his heart upon his sleeve, a vulgarity impossible to him. They have many words in their language which show a deep sense of all the things signified to us by the words quoted above, but in a more subtle sense than conveyed by our own words.

The Japanese people is a pleasure-loving, emotional people deeply inhibited by centuries of discipline so severe as to be unthinkable to us. They have been fused or welded into a homogeneous mass in which the friendliness and forbearance practiced toward one another is very beautiful.

The Japanese workman has a higher sense of his own worth and his own way than our workmen, and his position in Japan is more independent in most essential respects than that of the members of our unions. He seems to have, naturally, with no "unions," a community of interest and a solidarity of purpose which "unions" were necessary to effect in western countries.

The Japanese craftsman, when personally interested, is the finest craftsman in the world; but he likes to be an independent worker in his own behalf. To him piece work is a far more satisfactory basis than day's work, and also for his employer. The old system of labor brokerage is still in force, a certain broker controlling and selling the labor of many men who are still his henchmen. This broker delivers them to the work, but there his responsibility ceases. They are then free to work as they please to produce the desired results.

As the countenance of the building began to emerge, the workmen became intensely interested and with an intelligence of appreciation unrivalled anywhere in my experience. I shall never forget their touching farewells nor the sense of kindly co-operation in what all believed to be great work for the future of Japan.

Among the Japanese workmen there is a true gentleness and fineness to be found here only among truly cultured people. The Imperial—shall I say "Hotel?"—means to me the labor of this sympathetic group of freemen in concrete form, a thing wrought as I imagine the great buildings of the middle ages were wrought, to stand for centuries as a supreme achievement of human imagination and human cooperation: massed effort directed toward a certain achievement in which all shared.

The very bricks and lava, steel and concrete, stay but to record the passing of the fingers and brains that laid and left them in place. A tremendous, vital, voluntary force swept through great piles of inert matter and gave form and life for all time to a great building—belonging first to that voluntary force. Whoever may "own" the result is merely a custodian, who, on trial, takes on trust the labor of mind and body recorded in the thing now called the New Imperial.

NOTES

1. Paul F. P. Mueller (1864–1934) of Chicago, a building contractor with whom Wright often worked.

2. Endo San was one of Wright's assistants on the project.

ELEVEN

Louis Sullivan

(1924)

Louis Sullivan died on April 14, 1924, the day after Wright visited him on his deathbed. Thus ended an on-off-on-again relationship begun in 1888 when Adler & Sullivan hired Wright as a draughtsman. By 1890 he had risen to chief draughtsman, with his own office connecting to Sullivan's in a two-story suite high atop the Auditorium Building, Adler & Sullivan's triumph that had only recently opened.

Wright recalled in his autobiography and elsewhere the many late-night conversations in that tower suite from which he absorbed Sullivan's design philosophy. Sitting at his master's feet and working by his side on an array of major and minor projects could not have been better training. By the time he left the firm in 1893 after a dispute about the conditions of his contract, he was well prepared to go it alone.

As Sullivan's career foundered after the turn of the twentieth century, he and Wright gradually reestablished their former "loving relationship" but with a kind of role reversal. In 1923 and 1924 Architectural Record *essays on the New Imperial Hotel, for example, Sullivan declared his former protégé to be "a seer and a prophet, a craftsman, a masterbuilder," whose hotel was "the high water mark thus far attained by any modern architect." Sullivan passed the torch just months before he died.*

In the first tribute to his "beloved master" penned shortly afterward, Wright reviews the hostile cultural climate in which Sullivan struggled and was ultimately neglected, nevertheless leaving a philosophical legacy from which "great things will yet be born." The second focuses more on the work, speculating that had his legacy consisted only of the Auditorium, Transportation, and Wainwright buildings, and the Getty Tomb, it would still have been enough "to show the great reach of the creative activity that was Louis Sullivan's genius."

Without doubt these essays contain the kindest words Wright ever wrote about another architect. They also highlight what he believed to be Sullivan's import for American culture and, by indirection, for Wright himself.

"Louis Henry Sullivan: Beloved Master" was published in the Western Architect, *33 (June 1924) and "Louis Sullivan—His Work" in the* Architectural Record, *56 (July 1924), the latter reprinted with permission from Architectural Record © 1924, The McGraw-Hill Companies. Visit www.architecturalrecord.com for more information.*

11a Louis Henry Sullivan: Beloved Master (1924)

The beloved Master who knew how to be a great friend is dead. My young mind turned to him in hope and affection at eighteen,[1] and now, at middle age, I am to miss him and look back upon a long and loving association to which no new days, no new experiences may be added.

He needs no eulogy from me, this man of men, this highminded workman—who would not sell out! He would take no less than his price—and his price was too high for his time! His price for Louis Sullivan, the Architect, was as high as principle is high: for Louis Sullivan, the sentient human being, his price was not high enough. He was prodigal with his bodily heritage. Recklessly he flung it into the crucible that was his soul, or carelessly he wasted it in physical reactions to dispel loneliness, the loneliness that is the result of disillusionment—the loneliness that every great, uncompromising mind knows well and dreads and inherits, together with those who have gone the lonely road before him where only one at a time may tread. His lesser self was his, to do with as he pleased. He spent it with that extravagance that goes with the opulent nature, rich in resources, and we had him for a shorter time in consequence. The loss was ours—perhaps it was not his.

To know him well was to love him well. I never liked the name Frank until I would hear him say it, and the quiet breath he gave it made it beautiful in my ears and I would remember it was the name of freemen—meant free. The deep quiet of his temper had great charm for me. The rich humour that was lurking in the deeps within him and that sat in his eyes whatever his mouth might be saying, however earnest the moment might be, was rich and rare in human quality. He had remarkable and beautiful eyes—true windows for the soul of him. Meredith's portrait of Beethoven—"The hand of the Wind was in his hair—he seemed to hear with his eyes," is a portrait I have never forgotten.[2] If someone could give the warmer, different line, that would give the Master's quality! I feel it and I have tried—but I cannot write it.

I left him just after the Transportation Building brought him fame—to "make my own," and did not find him again until he was in trouble—some nine years ago, and needed me. Since that time the relation between us, established so early and lasting at that early period seven years, seemed, although the interruption was seventeen years long,[3] to be resumed with little or no lapse of time. We understood each other as we had done always.

Somehow I am in no mood to talk about his work. I know well its vital significance, its great value, the beautiful quality of its strain. I know too, now, what was the matter with it, but where it fell short, it fell short of his own ideal. He could not build so well as he knew nor so true to his thought as he could think, sometimes, but sometimes he did better than either.

Genius he had as surely as there is Genius in the great work called Man. The quality of that Genius his country needed as the parched leaf or the drying fields need dew or rain. A fine depth was in him and he was broad enough, without reducing the scale of it, or showing up the quiet strength of it. And yet his country did not know him!

He loved appreciation. He was pleased as a child is pleased with praise. No measure of it was too much for him, because he well knew that no such measure could reach his powers, much less go beyond them. And any achievement visible as praiseworthy he knew was as nothing compared to what already was achieved in the consciousness that was his.

He was a fine workman. He could draw with consummate skillfulness. He could draw as beautifully as he could think and he was one of the few architects of the age who could really think. I used to fear his graphic facility—this virtuosity of his, as an enemy to him in the higher reaches of his genius. It was not so. The very extravagance of his gift was a quality of its beauty in an age when all in similar effort is niggardly or cowardly or stale.

I feel the emptiness where he was wont to work. The sterility of my time closes in upon his place. Machine-made life in a Machine-age that steadily automatizes, standardizes, amortizes the living beauty of the Life he knew and loved and served so well seems desolation, damnation! Without him the battle seems suddenly to have gone wrong, the victory in doubt!

•

Here, in our country, where individual distinction of the highest order must be distorted or swamped in the cloying surge of "good taste!"

Here where free initiative is treated as dangerous or regarded as absurd!

Here, where the Gift is suspected, feared or hated unless entertainment can be got out of it!

Here, where the plain man has, in a bogus Democracy, license to sneer at all above him or sit on all below him!

Here, where thought is ankle-deep, activity non-creative, but both, in motion and quantity, over all heads!

Here, in a country so nobly dedicated, root and branch, to Truth and Freedom as no more than Justice, yet where the government itself officially encourages the mental grip of "the middle," the sacred average that all but paralyzes head and heart and hand!

Here where a stupendous, mechanized industry is fast becoming reflected in mechanized mentality, sterilizing Life, Love, Hope—standardization, without light from within is stagnation!

Here where there are religions but no Religion!

Here where there are arts but no Art!

Here where religion and art are utterly divorced from life and automatic substitutes everywhere are in the shop windows, in the streets, in the seats of the mighty, in the retreats of the humble, in the sanctuaries of the Soul!

Here where Institutes turn out droves of illustrators and egotists—mannikins, instead of interpreters and givers!

Here where tainted minor-arts make shift in profusion and disorder upon the ruins of the great Arts!

Here, in this blind aggregation of wealth and power, a great Master was, in despair, forced to relinquish his chosen work in *Architecture,* the great Art of Civilization needed now as of time immemorial, the Art of all arts most needed by his country—and was compelled to win recognition in a medium that is the all-devouring monster of the age—the literal art that has sapped the life and strength of all the other great Arts and to no good purpose: no, to the everlasting harm of culture and good life, to the eventual impoverishment of the human establishment! Inasmuch as there are five senses, five avenues open to man's communion with Life—four-fifths of human sensibility is lost when one Art usurps the place of the other four. Human beings are fast becoming human documents, Humanity, a litany!

Here, in free America, this prophetic mind with trained and gifted capacity for the regeneration of this now ugly, awkward work of this world, in *living* forms of Beauty, was little used and passed by, that the process, inexorable as Fate, might not be interrupted—nor little hoards of little men be unduly squandered above the animal plane of economic satisfaction!

That a country in such need, his country, any country, at such a time—a crisis—should have failed to use one of her great men—in many respects, her greatest man—to do the work he loved and in which he was not only competent but prophetic—is terrible proof of how much more disastrous is half-knowledge, than either Ignorance or Folly could ever be. This I call Tragedy!

And now this book. "The Autobiography of an Idea"[4] his book, has come to convince an unwilling world, tainted with that hatred for superiority that characterizes a false Democracy, of what it missed in leaving a man of such quality to turn from the rare work he could do, to give, in a book, proof of that quality in a medium his kindred had learned to understand—proof of his quality—too late.

It is a characteristic triumph of Genius such as his that he should lay this book upon the library table of the nation he loved, as he died! His fertility was great enough to scatter seed no matter what the disability, no matter what the obstruction. If the eye of his country was uneducated, inept, objective, illiterate or merely *literal*; if its sense of Beauty of Form as Idea or beauty of Idea as Form was unawakened, he took literature, the literal medium by which the literal may most easily be reached and, perhaps, literally made to understand—grasped it and made himself known—the Master still.

But he was most needed where the workmen wait for the Plan—where the directing Imagination must get the work of the world done in such master-fashion that mankind may see and forever more believe that Spirit and Matter are one—when both are real. Realize that Form and Idea are one and inseparable—as he showed them to be in that master-key to the Skyscraper as Architecture—the Wainwright Building.[5] To this high task he came as an anointed prophet—to turn disillusioned to the cloister as so many have turned before him and will so turn still—although his cloister was the printed page—the book, that, opened now, all may read.

Any appreciation of the Master must be an arraignment of the time, the place, the people that needed and hungered for what he had to give, but all but wasted him when he was fit and ready to give. Yes, in the neglect of this great man's genius and his power to get many more noble buildings built for his country than he was allowed to build—we see the hideous cruelty of America's blind infatuation with the Expedient—this deadly, grinding spoilation of the Beautiful.

Louis Sullivan was a sacrifice to the God of Temporal Things by a hard working, pioneering people, too vain of the culture of lies in their heads, over empty, hungry hearts, a heedless people living a hectic life no full hands may ever make worth while—and who either could not or would not know him. The regret and shame those feel who knew his quality—who knew what his hand held ready to give to truly enrich his kind, the impotent rage that all but chokes utterance that this treasure of a greatly rich and powerful nation was neglected, was comparatively unknown—when the opportunism of the inferior, the fashionable, the imitative were in favor, is hard to bear.

What is left to us is the least of him—but it will serve.

Out of the fragments of his dreams that were his buildings—out of the sense of Architecture as entering a new phase as a *plastic Art*—great things will yet be born. Every thing he did has some fine quality, was some solution of a difficult problem—some sorely needed light on practical affairs. Practical? Truly here was a practical man in a radical sense—rooted in Principle, and as richly gifted as he was impressionable—as deep-sighted as he was far-seeing.

The work the master did may die with him—no great matter. What he represented has lived in spite of all drift—all friction, all waste, all slip—since time began for man. In this sense was Louis Sullivan true to tradition—in this sense will the divine spark, given to him from the deep centre of the universe and to which he held true, be handed on the fresher, more vital, more potent, enriched a little, perhaps much by the individuality that was his. There is no occasion for deep despair—although chagrin, frustrated hopes, broken lives and broken promises strew the way with gruesome wreckage. The light that was in him lives—and will go on—forever.

Later when I have him more in perspective I intend to write about and illustrate his work. It is too soon, now.[6] I hope to make clear in unmistakable concrete terms, what is now necessarily abstract. A privilege I feel as mine and one I know from him that he would be pleased that I should take, as I have assured him I sometime would do.

NOTES

1. Wright was born June 8, 1867, not 1869, as he claimed, and most likely entered the firm of Adler & Sullivan early in 1888 when he was twenty.

2. From Book 3 of English writer George Meredith's 1864 novel *Emily in England*, retitled *Sandra Belloni* in 1887. The passage reads: "I have seen his picture in shop windows: the wind seemed in his hair, and he seemed to hear with his eyes."

3. Wright worked for Adler & Sullivan approximately five years, not seven as he often said, leaving the firm probably early in 1893 as a result of bitter disputes with his employers, opening a serious breech, especially with Sullivan. (See Twombly, *Frank Lloyd Wright: His Life and His Architecture* [New York: John Wiley & Sons, 1979], 22–23.) Wright states correctly here that "I left him [Sullivan] just after the Transportation Building [for the 1893 World's Columbian Exposition] brought him fame" but then incorrectly adds that I "did not find him again until . . . some nine years ago," or 1915, and that "the interruption was seventeen years long," which would date its beginning in 1898, not 1893. But a reconciliation of sorts with Sullivan may have actually begun long before Wright says he "found him again" in 1915, that is, in 1900 (the year Dankmar Adler died) at the Architectural League of America's annual convention in Chicago, when immediately after Sullivan's extemporaneous remarks Wright prefaced his own prepared speech (Document 1) by saying "after listening to the master it hardly seem[s] proper to listen to the disciple." (See Twombly, *Louis Sullivan: His Life and Work* [New York: Viking Press, 1986], 365.)

4. Sullivan's book was initially published in sixteen issues of the *Journal of the American Institute of Architects* from June 1922 to September 1923, then in book form in 1924 by the Press of the American Institute of Architects, Washington, D.C.

5. St. Louis, 1890.

6. Wright did so in 1949 with *Genius and the Mobocracy* (New York: Duell, Sloan & Pearce). On April 13, 1924, the day before he died, Sullivan gave Wright a portfolio of 132 drawings (117 of his own, fifteen by others), thirty-nine of which Wright reproduced in *Genius* to accompany his memoir.

11b Louis Sullivan—His Work (1924)

Louis Sullivan's great value as an Artist-Architect—alive or dead—lies in his firm grasp of principle. He knew the truths of Architecture as I believe no one before him knew them. And profoundly he realized them.

This illumination of his was the more remarkable a vision when all around him cultural mists hung low to obscure or blight every dawning hope of a finer beauty in the matter of this world.

As "the name of God has fenced about all crime with holiness"[1] so in the name of Architecture the "Classic" perpetually invents skillful lies to hide ignorance or impotence and belie creation.

But the Master's was true creative activity—not deceived nor deceiving. He was a radical and so one knew, always, where to find him. His sense and thought and spirit were deep-rooted in that high quality of old and new which make them one and thereby he was apprised of the falsity of outward shows that duped his fellows, and that dupe them still.

The names, attributes and passions of earth's creatures change, but—that creation changes never; his sane and passionate vision leaves testimony here on earth in fragments of his dreams—his work.

His work! Who may gauge the worth of the work of such a man? Who shall say what his influence was, or is, or will be? Not I.

That his work was done at all was marvelous. That it could *be*, under the circumstances we call Democracy and that so mock his own fine sense of that much abused idea, was prophetic and for his country the greatest and most potent suggestion.

Here in this aspiring land of the impertinent, impermanent and of commercial importunity, he never struck his colors. The buildings he has left us are the least of him—in the heart of him.

He was of infinite value to the country that wasted him because it could not know him.

Work must be studied in relation to the time in which it presented its contrasts, insisted upon its virtues and got itself into human view. Remember if you can the contemporaries of Louis Sullivan's first great work, the Chicago Auditorium.[2] Those contemporaries were a lot of unregenerate sinners in the grammar of the insensate period of General Grant Gothic.

Imagine this noble calm of the Auditorium exterior, the beautiful free room within, so beautifully conceived as a unit, with its *plastic* ornamentation, the quiet of its deep cream and soft gold scheme of color, the imaginative *plastic* richness of this interior, and compare both with the cut, butt and slash of that period—the meaningless stiffness that sterilized the Chicago buildings for all their ambitious attitudes and grand gestures. They belonged to a world to which the sense of the word *"plastic"* had not been born. That the word itself could get itself understood in relation to architecture is doubtful—and then see what Louis Sullivan's creative activity from that time on meant to Architecture as an art.

Back of that first great performance of his was a deepening knowledge, a tightening grasp on essentials. Much in the great effort got away from him; it wore him out; it was all at tremendous pressure, against fearful odds—but the Chicago Auditorium is good enough yet to be the most successful room for opera in the world. I think I have seen them all. His genius burst into full bloom with the impetus of the success and fame that great enterprise brought to him and to Adler. Dankmar Adler, his partner, was a fine critic, a master of the plan and of men. His influence over Louis Sullivan at that time was great and good.

The Getty tomb was a work that soon followed the Auditorium as did the Wainwright Building in St. Louis to greater purpose. The Getty tomb in Graceland Cemetery was a piece of sculpture, a statue, an elegiac poem addressed to the sensibilities as such.[3] It was Architecture in a detached and romantic phase, a beautiful burial casket, "in memoriam" but—a memorial to the architect whose work it was. His "type," the form that was peculiarly his was never better expressed.

When he brought in the board with the motive of the Wainwright Building outlined in profile and in scheme upon it and threw it down on my table, I was perfectly aware of what had happened. This was Louis Sullivan's greatest moment—his greatest effort. The "skyscraper," as a new thing beneath the sun, an entity with virtue, individuality and beauty all its own, was born.

Until Louis Sullivan showed the way the masses of the tall buildings were never a complete whole in themselves. They were ugly, harsh aggregates with no sense of unity, fighting tallness instead of accepting it. What unity those masses now have, that pile up toward New York and Chicago skies, is due to the Master-mind that first perceived one as a harmonious unit—its height triumphant.

The Wainwright Building cleared the way and to this day remains the master key to the skyscraper as a matter of architecture in the work of the world. The Wainwright and its group were Architecture living again as such in a new age—the Steel Age—*living in the work of the world!* The Practical therein achieving expression as Beauty. A true service rendered humanity in that here was proof of the oneness of Spirit and Matter, *when both are real*—a synthesis the world awaits as the service of the artist and a benediction it will receive when false ideas as to the nature and limitation of art and the functions of the artist disappear.

The Transportation Building at the Columbian Exposition cost him most trouble of anything he ever did.[4] He got the great doorway "straight away," but the rest hung fire. I had never seen him anxious before, but anxious he then was. How eventually successful this beautiful contribution to that fine collection of picture-buildings was, itself shows. But the Transportation Building was no solution of the work of the world as was the Wain-wright Building. It was a "picture-building"—but one with rhyme and reason and, above all, individuality; a real picture, not a mere pose of the picturesque. It was not architecture in its highest sense, except as a great theme suggested, an idea of violent changes in scale exemplified, noble contrasts effected—meanwhile its excuse for existence being the enclosure of exhibition space devoted to transportation. It was no masterful solution of a practical problem. It was a holiday circumstance and superb entertainment, which is what it was intended to be. It was original, the fresh individual note of vitality at the Fair—inspiring, a thing created but—something in itself, for itself alone. Except that if here—where a mischief was done to architectural America from which it has never recovered, by the introduction of "the classic," so called, in the Fair buildings, as the "Ideal,"—had that note of individual vitality as expressed in the Transportation Building been heeded for what it was worth, that mischief might largely have been averted. Only the Chicago Auditorium, the Transportation Building, the Getty Tomb, the Wainright Building are necessary to show the great reach of the creative activity that was Louis Sullivan's genius. The other buildings he did are blossoms, more or less individual, upon these stems. Some were grafted from one to the other of them, some were grown from them, but all are relatively inferior in point of that quality which we finally associate with the primitive strength of the thing that got itself done regardless and "stark" to the Idea: sheer, significant, vital.

As to materials, the grasp of the Master's imagination gripped them all pretty much alike. As to relying upon them for beauties of their own, he had no need—no patience. They were stuff to bear the stamp of his imagination and bear it they did, cast iron, wrought iron, marble, plaster, concrete, wood. In this respect he did not live up to his principle. He was too rich in fancy to allow anything to come for its own sake between him and the goal of his desire. It would have been to him like naturalistic noises in the orchestra.

Where his work fell short, it fell short of his ideal. He could not build so well as he knew nor so true to his thought as he was able to think—often. But some times he did better than either.

I see his individual quality in that feature of his work that was his sensuous ornament—as I see the wondrous smile upon his face—a charm, a personal appealing charm. So very like and so very much his own. It will be cherished long because no one has had the quality to produce out of himself such a gracious, beautiful response, so lovely a smile evoked by love of beauty. The capacity for love, ardent, true, poetic, was great in him as this alone would prove. His work in this was interior, esoteric, peculiar to himself. It is none the less precious for that. Do you prefer the Greek? Why not? Do you admire the Chinese? Why not, as a matter of course? Do you prefer the Romanesque? It is your privilege. Perhaps you respond to old Baroque? Your reactions to Gothic you find more satisfying? Doubtless. But do you realize that here is no body of culture evolving through centuries of time a "style," but an *individual* in the poetry-crushing environment of a cruel materialism, who, in this, invoked the Goddess that hitherto whole civilizations strove for centuries to win, and won her with this charming smile—the fruit of his own spirit.

Ah, that supreme, erotic, high adventure of the mind that was his ornament! Often I would see him, his back bent over his drawing board, intent upon what? I knew his symbolism—I caught his feelings as he worked. A Casanova on his rounds? Beside this sensuous master of adventure with tenuous, vibrant, plastic form, Casanova was a duffer; Gil Blas a torn chapeau; Bocaccio's [sic] imagination no higher than a stable-boy's. Compared to this high quest the Don's was as Sancho Panza's ass. The soul of Rabelais alone could have understood and would have called him brother.[5] How often have I held his cloak and sword while he adventured in the realm within, to win his mistress; and while he wooed the mistress. I would woo the maid! Those days! And now, I say, this caress that was his own should be his own, forever sacred to him and treasured high for its own sake—this rhythmic pulse of the wings of America's creative genius. Who has the temerity to undertake to imitate it will fail. Take his principle who will, none may do better—and try the wings that nature gave to you. Do not try to soar with his. Has the time come when every man may have that precious quality called style for his very own? Then where, I ask you, are the others? Eros is a fickle god and hard to please. Musing with blinded eyes he has heard from earth the music of an immortal strain; henceforth will take no less.

Genius the Master had—or rather it had him. It possessed him, he revelled in it, squandered it and the lesser part of him was squandered by it. He lived! And compared to what came to him in life from his effort, the effort itself being a quality of it, the greatly successful careers were, I imagine, relatively lifeless.

Yes, genius he had in most unequivocal sense—true genius—there is no other kind—the effect of which is not seen in his own time, nor can it ever be seen. Human affairs are of themselves plastic in spite of names and man's ill advised endeavors to make them static to his will. As a pebble cast into the ocean sets up reactions lost in distance and time, so one man's genius goes on infinitely forever because it is always an expression of *principle*. And therefore, in no way does it ever run counter to another's genius. The Master's genius is perhaps itself a reaction, the initial force of which we can not—need not—see.

Of one thing we may be sure—the intuitions of such a nature, the work to which he put his hand, no less than the suggestion he himself was to kindred or aspiring natures, is worth more to the future in any conservative or progressive sense than all the work of all the schools, just as example is more valuable than precept.

Is it not true that *individuality* is the supreme entertainment of life? Surely it is the quality most precious in it and most worthy of conservation; veritably the visible hand of the Creator! Here in Louis Sullivan was an example as clear and convincing as any, anywhere, at any time, under conditions as unpromising to fulfilment as ever existed.

Is it not probable that the social solidarity that produced the great "styles" exists no longer in the same sense and that never more will such a manifestation appear, especially in a nation composed of nationalities like ours? But, as free opportunity offers, when America awakens spiritually or is awakened by Spirit, individuality will come to flower in almost as many styles as there are individuals capable of style. And there will arise more and more men who are capable of it. Until we have a wealth of vital expression. We will then only need order in the aggregate—an "order" which will be established eventually by the nature of the individual intelligence capable of style—*itself* perceiving the necessity for it and making it therefore a veritable condition of every such individual expression. The nature capable of style is more capable than any other of the appropriate conduct of that power when and wherever need be.

Is not that a more desirable and logical conclusion to draw from the principle upon which this country was founded than that the dead level of a mongrelized version of the "Classic," a renaissance of Renaissance, should be allowed to characterize the mongrel as mongrel—and nothing more?

H. H. Richardson, great emotionalist in architecture that he was, elected to work in the "style" Romanesque. The Master dug deeper and made style for himself out of the same stuff the Romanesque was made from, and the Gothic too. With all these examples before us of "styles," surely man may penetrate to the heart of *Style* and unveiling its secret be master of his own. And as a master of this type was Louis Sullivan—esoteric though his synthetic style may be. The leadership of Stanford White was exoteric, his mind that of a connoisseur. His gift was selective and we owe to him and his kind the architectural army of "good taste" that smothers the practical in applied expedients—an army whose beauty-worship is content with the beauty of the painted lady, the henna, paste and rouge; or the more earnest kind, the avid antiquarian or the far too credulous historian.[6] What does it matter if Tradition's followers fail to see that Louis Sullivan's loyalty to Tradition was wholly complete and utterly profound? His loyalty was greater than theirs, as the Spirit transcends the Letter. What lives in New York architecture is little enough, and in spite of its grammar and far beyond the style-mongering it receives in the Atelier. It is the force of circumstance piling itself inexorably by mere mass into the sky—the darkening canyons that are paths leading into darkness, or to Death! It seems incredible now, but such unity as those tall masses may have is due to the master-mind, that first conceived and contributed one as a unit. The Wainwright Building cleared the way for them—and to this day remains the master key to the skyscraper as Architecture the world over. Why is it so difficult for standardization to receive to a greater degree the illumination from within that would mean Life instead of Death? Why is the vision of such a master-mind lost in the competitive confusion of so-called ideas and jostling ambitions? Why is the matter, except for him, still all from the outside—culture nowhere sane nor safe except as the imitation or the innocuous is safe—which it never is, or was. Look backward toward Rome!

Yes, the great Master's contribution as to form may die with him. No great matter. This Way-shower needs no piles of perishable granite, no sightly shapes to secure his immortality or make good his fame. It is his fortune that in the hearts of his fellows his gift was real. The boon to us of his journey on this earth, in the span of life allotted to him, is beyond all question, all calculation. His work was the work of a man for men—for sincere humanity.

The look of the thing he did may or may not appeal to the imagination trained to regard certain rhythms, spacings, forms and figures as architecture. Many faults may be laid to him, but they are the rough hewn edges of the real thing. And what he did, even more than the way he did it, will always repay painstaking study if it is free study. It can only vex and puzzle the pedantic mind and end in its hostility—the hostility that never more than entertained and amused him although eventually it did destroy his usefulness. That hostility of the provincial mind is found on the farm, in the small town, on Main Street, on Fifth Avenue, in the Seats of the Mighty, in the Church, in New York and in Hollywood. Wherever that type of mind is found it will accept no radical, because anything radical is the death of the provincial. Instinctively the provincial mentality feels this, and fears it and therefore hates. And Louis Sullivan was a radical in the same sense that the Ideal-Man was the consummate radical of human history.

Not long ago—weary—he said to me in a despondent moment that it would be far more difficult now to do the radical work he did—more difficult to get accepted than when he worked. The dead level of mediocrity had risen to the point where herd-psychology had accepted as normal the "good form" of the schools, and stopped thinking. The inevitable drift had set in. But no, it is not so! The torch flung to the Master hand from the depths of antiquity, from the heart of the world, and held faithfully and firmly alight and aloft for thirty years at least by him, shall not go out. It has never yet, since time began for man, gone out. Willing hands have already caught the divine sparks and little running fires are lighted on the hills and glimmer in the dark; some flickering and feeble; some with more smoke than fire; some guttering in candle grease; but some—clear, candescent flame— that shall rise high and higher until the darkness the tired, wayworn Master saw—that spectre looming as the horror of his country's shade—will fade in true illumination. Hope too long deferred will make the strongest hearts foreboding. For the consummate radical the Kingdom on Earth was "at hand" nineteen hundred years ago. It is a little nearer now. This laborer in the same vineyard with a similar hope to the same purpose has gone, his hope still high. The sire of an immortal strain has gone unterrified into the gulf which we call Death. A great chief among men's spirits, he has been made one with Nature—and now he is a presence to be felt and known in darkness and in light, spreading a vital and benign influence wherever quick dreams spring from youthful minds or careworn, toil-stained comrades to his thought may need—"that Light whose smile kindles the universe. That Beauty in which all things work and move."

"He lives, he wakes, 'tis Death is dead—not he."[7] Not he, who, in a world that chains and fetters humankind, was Life's green tree. A benediction, he, that will outlive the Curse—live down the Lie.

NOTES

1. From Percy Bysshe Shelley, *Queen Mab*, Book VII (1821), a lengthy philosophical poem.

2. The Auditorium Building (1886–90), Chicago.

3. The Wainwright Building, St. Louis, and the Carrie Elizabeth Getty Tomb, Chicago, both 1890.

4. The Transportation Building (1891) for the 1893 World's Columbian Exposition, Chicago.

5. Giacomo Casanova (1725–98), Venetian writer, musician, entrepreneur, and adventurer best known during his lifetime and to history as a world-class womanizer. Gil Blas is the title character of *The Adventures of Gil Blas of Santillane* (published in twelve books from 1715 to 1747) by Alain-René Lesage (1668–1747), French novelist and playwright. Giovanni Boccaccio (1315–75), Italian writer and poet best known for *Decameron* (c. 1349–52, revised 1370–71). Sancho Panza renamed himself as the title character of *Don Quixote*—

published in two parts in 1605 and 1615 by the Spaniard Don Miguel de Cer-
vantes Saavedra (1547–1616)—when he set out on his donkey in search of
adventure. Francis Rabelais (c. 1494–1553), a physician and teacher of medi-
cine, was a major French Renaissance writer. Here Wright associates Sullivan's
ornament—"that supreme, erotic, high adventure of the mind"—with the
"heretical" activities of Casanova, Blas, Boccaccio, Panza, and Rabelais.

6. Wright unfavorably compares Stanford White to Henry Hobson Richardson,
    for whom White worked from 1870 to 1878.

7. From Shelley's poem "Adonais," 1821.

Taliesin, Spring Green, Wisconsin, *c.* 1913.

Larkin Company
Administration
Building, Buffalo,
New York, *c.* 1903–06,
demolished 1950. From
Inland Architect (July 1907).

Larkin Company Administration Building, interior, Buffalo, New York, *c.* 1903-06, demolished 1950. From *Inland Architect* (July 1907).

F. B. Henderson residence, Elmhurst, Illinois, 1901. An example of "low-pitched hip roofs, heaped together in pyramidal fashion," the first type from "In the Cause of Architecture" (1908). Photo by Robert Twombly.

Harlan Bradley (top) and Warren Hickox residences, Kankakee, Illinois, both 1900. Examples of "low roofs with simple pediments countering on long ridges," the second type from "In the Cause of Architecture" (1908). From *The Architectural Record* (July 1905).

Elizabeth Gale residence, Oak Park, Illinois, 1909. An example of "simple slab" roofs, the third type from "In the Cause of Architecture" (1908). Photo by Robert Twombly.

Edward E. Boynton residence, Rochester, New York, 1908. A prairie house interior; view from dining through living room to roofed terrace. Photo by Sue Miller, courtesy Mr. and Mrs. Louis M. Clark, Jr.

"Ausgeführte Bauten und Entwürfe von Frank Lloyd Wright"

Two portfolios 17½" x 25½" in size; of lithographed plates showing plans, elevations, and perspectives of seventy buildings by this architect. Published by Ernst Wasmuth, of Berlin. Special arrangements have been made for selling this work direct to the purchaser. Write for descriptive circular to

FRANK LLOYD WRIGHT, 605 Orchestra Hall, Chicago

Advertisement for *Ausgeführte Bauten und Entwürfe von Frank Lloyd Wright* (1910) depicting the Avery Coonley residence living room, Riverside, Illinois, 1907. From *The Architectural Record* (January 1913).

Two of the four-unit "American System Ready-Cut Houses" known as the Arthur Richards Apartments, Milwaukee, Wisconsin, 1916. Photo by Robert Twombly.

The Imperial Hotel, Tokyo, Japan, 1913–23, demolished 1967. Photo by David Roessler.

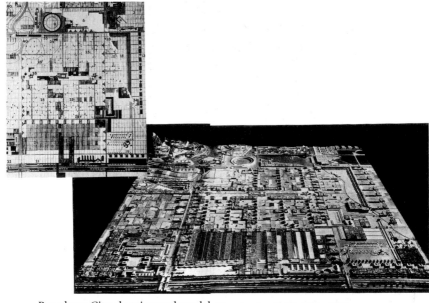

Broadacre City, drawing and model. From *American Architect* (May 1935).

First Usonian house for Herbert Jacobs, garden view, Madison, Wisconsin, 1936–37. Courtesy of The Art Institute of Chicago.

First Usonian house for Herbert Jacobs, street view, Madison, Wisconsin, 1936–37. Courtesy of The Art Institute of Chicago.

Nathan G. Moore residence, Oak Park, Illinois, 1895, 1923. This residence is mentioned in Wright's 1949 acceptance speech for the American Institute of Architects' Gold Medal. Photo by Robert Twombly.

Robert H. Sunday residence, a "second phase" Usonian house, Marshalltown, Iowa, 1958–59. Photo by Robert Twombly.

Hiram Baldwin residence, Kenilworth, Illinois, 1905. This residence is mentioned in Wright's 1949 acceptance speech for the American Institute of Architects' Gold Medal. Photo by Robert Twombly.

Taliesin West, Scottsdale, Arizona, 1937 and after. From *Arizona Highways* (February 1956).

TWELVE

The International Style
(1928–32)

"Towards a New Architecture," Wright's "review" of the 1927 English edition of Le Corbusier's 1923 book of that name, is his first literary confrontation with what in short order would be called "the International Style." He applauds Le Corbusier for his design simplifications, his necessary "dressing down" of neoclassicism, and his recognition of machine-age beauty. But he condemns the work for being two dimensional "surface and mass" without depth, thereby ignoring all that he and Louis Sullivan had accomplished years before in their "minority report." He hints that his own "three dimensional" work begins with conceptualizing interior space—depth—which generates appropriate exteriors or, put another way, that plans precede elevations. Le Corbusier has it backward, Wright thinks, designing "picture-building" façades first, fitting interiors to match.

In "The Logic of Contemporary Architecture" he wonders why architecture should be "castrated by a factory-aesthetic" resembling "machines for living in," as Le Corbusier put it. When buildings are "stripped clean of all considerations but Function and Utility," he laments, they lose "Romance—the essential Joy of Living." "For All May Raise the Flowers Now" argues that "internationalist" architects are little more than "up-to-date eclectics" reproducing interchangeable forms from agreed-upon formulae that to his disgust are already penetrating Japan and Argentina as well as the United States.

"Of Thee I Sing" is Wright's rebuttal of the 1932 "Modern Archi-tecture—International Exhibition" at New York's Museum of Mod-ern Art, which later toured the country. This major attempt to popularize the new European architecture and its American deriva-tives was organized by museum director Alfred Barr, exhibition di-rector Philip Johnson, and guest director and historian Henry-Russell Hitchcock, a "self-appointed committee" Wright says are simply propagandists for a movement he fears will undermine (his own) homegrown efforts to develop a democratic architecture. Wright consented to participate anyway, sharing a room with J. J. P. Oud, Le Corbusier, and Mies van der Rohe, hoping to counteract their "miscarriage of a machine-age that would sterilize itself," but worse, sterilize organic design.

These (and several other essays) launch the critique of "mod-ernism" Wright would endlessly repeat for the remainder of his life, in prose now so jargonistic, mangled, and self-referential as to be al-most impenetrable at times. He damns the International Style as a foreign, therefore irrelevant collection of easily cloned clichés, a nega-tion of the difficult work and hard thought organic architecture re-quires. In 1914 (in Document 8) he had chastised his midwestern colleagues for appropriating his forms without absorbing their sub-stance. Now he lambastes a younger, more global generation for bas-tardizing his substance with inappropriate forms. These essays place Wright squarely in opposition to the modern movement, an ersatz style yet a very real threat, as he sees it, to the emergence of an au-thentic national architecture.

Wright's critique of the International Style presupposes that Eu-ropean modernism was nothing more than a misunderstanding of his own work exported back to the United States as something new, and that neither its European creators nor their American followers acknowledged his pioneering ideas, albeit bastardized, as the basis of their own. Hence his patronizing characterization of Philip Johnson in Document 12c.

"Towards a New Architecture," appeared in World Unity Magazine, *2 (September 1928); "The Logic of Contemporary Architecture as an Expression of This Age" in* Architectural Forum, *52 (May 1930); "For All May Raise the Flowers Now for All Have Got the Seed" in* T-Square, *2 (February 1932); and "Of Thee I Sing" in* Shelter, *2 (April 1932).*

12a "Towards a New Architecture" (1928)

In a style as stark as one of the gas-pipe railings at the edge of one of his "new" cantilever-porches, Le Corbusier, no sentimentalist, comes to us to tell us that this machine age has "surface and mass" effects neglected in our architecture. He points to the clean lines and surfaces of the aeroplane, the ocean greyhounds, and to certain machinery,—having no other motif than to express in the simplest terms the nature of its necessity,—as the "new" beauty. He is right.

"Styles," says he, "are no more than the feather in madam's hat." His way of putting our own minority report.

France, our fashion-monger, has thus arrived at the psychological moment to set a fashion for us in architecture,—to pull the plumes from the hat we call our "Classic," and maybe get the hat itself.

The fact that all Le Corbusier says or means was at home here in architecture in America in the work of Louis Sullivan and myself—more than twenty-five years ago, and is fully on record in both building and writing here and abroad, has no meaning for him in this connection.

There, in those countries, the matter for which Le Corbusier claims two dimensions has been at work all these years, while here in America it was at work in full three dimensions. True—a minority report it was, and still is. But as John Bright was fond of pointing to History to prove—the Minority has always been right.[1]

What then will happen should a fashion now be made of the minority report in American Architecture? The truth will move on and be found elsewhere in another minority report to be "discovered" again at some future time as usual,—but "progress" is ahead no less.

Our "American Classic" needs this dressing-down, from the "abroad" it has itself aped and imitated. Therefore, France will be more effective and convincing in this matter than anything anyone at home could say or do, especially as it comes just when Manhattan's commercial Machine has triumphed over Architects and compelled their cornice (our feathered hat) to go.

This testimony from the passing stranger applauds *that* triumph and not at all deplores the blow the Machine dealt the Classic. The Machine is showing its strength. The feathered hat is already on askew. This fresh breeze blowing from abroad for some years past and now renewed from the cradle of Liberty itself,— well,—hat and all is going to go. Our psychology in affairs of the Arts is notorious.

And yet this pronouncement by Monsieur—what is it? Really it is essentially a plea for another kind of picture-building. It is only more appropriate now to leave off all the "trimming" and keep all severely plain.

In this matter of Art, the Frenchman has seldom got inside. He has usually discovered the surface "effects" best suited to the time, the place and the hour. It is no small virtue in him and has heaped honors upon his Nation.

But that "flair" is no longer good enough. In this architectural matter, France may for once find herself behind. America's minority report—already handed in—goes deeper and the French movement may soon lose its two dimensions, "surface and mass," within the three that characterize the American work. The third dimension we already have to be added to the two of France is *depth*.

It is this quality of *depth* that alone can give life or purpose to the other two dimensions and result in that integrity in Architecture that makes the building no less organic than the tree itself.

"Surface and mass," which the talented Frenchman (true to the custom of his people since time began) declares the chief *elements* of Architecture with which the Architect has to deal—are in reality not *elements*—but products. Length, width and thickness make after all but two dimensions,—the superficial ones. Until that third element as the quality of depth that makes all *integral* has entered, nothing has happened in Architecture beyond a refreshing *semblance* of simplicity.

A spiritual interpretation must be given length, width and thickness; length as "continuity," width as "breadth," thickness as "depth"—and all be made homogeneous.

We are learning to see from the outside the "effects" produced by such homogeneity and to desire them. We are beginning to hunger for them really. But we will not learn to produce them by studying them outside. We will get at them from "within" or we will *create* nothing. We will only be giving an imitation of the more appropriate aspect of the thing we see—making more picture-buildings—adding another *ist* to affect only another *ism*—among so many gone down before.

But I wish everyone engaged in making or breaking these United States would read the Le Corbusier book. Universities especially should read it. And as for world unity—it seems that in so far as this ideal of America is a spirit,—America already, except for the minority report, is found much more abroad than at home in this great matter of Architecture. We are, by nature of our opportunity, time and place, the logical people to give highest expression to the "New." We *are* the great thing in this sense. We fail to see it in ourselves because we have been imitating an old-world that now sees in us, neglected, a higher estate than it has ever known in its own sense of itself.

So, welcome Holland, Germany, Austria and France! What you take from us we receive from you gratefully. Had you not taken it, we as a Nation might never have been aware of it, never, even, have seen it!

NOTES

1. John Bright (1811–89), from 1843 to 1870 a Quaker member of the English House of Commons and holder of other government posts, was an outspoken advocate of minority causes—including universal suffrage and publicly funded education—ultimately enacted into law.

"Those countries" are Germany, Austria, the Netherlands, and Sweden.

12b The Logic of Contemporary Architecture as an Expression of This Age (1930)

I do not like this title because it seems to me either too obvious or too ambiguous. But it is the Editor's and so I shall keep it. Is it logical to assume that this age may find Expression in contemporary architecture, that is to say, in an Architecture of its own? I wonder, because contemporary architecture in this age has neither logic nor expression. The Age has, so far, given itself away! But, is it logical that a contemporary architecture should express its own age?

Is the rising sun logical, Mr. Editor? It is natural, and that is better.

It is just as natural as that the sun should rise that contemporary architecture should also rise to express its own "age"—in this instance—our own time. To express our own time would be to characterize our age for all time. An Architecture might be borrowed for this purpose, but only to stigmatize the age! An Architecture might be conceived and taught as something fine in itself, much admired as such, to no greater end than to sentimentalize and therefore stultify the age.

To no greater end, I say, because only contemporary Architecture could possibly express this age or has ever expressed any other age,—such as the Architecture or the Age happened to be. What other Architecture could express the age except the architecture of the age itself?

Of course we may imagine an era wherein there was nothing architectural to express or there were no architects to express whatever there was, and recourse had to plan-factories, academies, and schools to supply the lack out of the world's stock to save the situation,—so to say. And that would be about all the "contemporary" architecture that particular era or age would get,—or deserve to get,—as "expression"—even if that lack were ever so quickly and richly supplied and every fine thing that ever happened in ancient Architecture was externally applied as "Contemporary Architecture." That shame would really be the "logic of Contemporary Architecture" as an "expression of that age"—the expression of the fact that the age had no architecture of its own and had tried on at least 57 Varieties to find one ready-made to fit.

It is no exaggeration to say that the *expression* of this Machine Age has, so far, been waste and *repression*. How about the wasted timber resources—the lost trees of a new-continent to merely rot or burn as "mill-work"? How about the butchery by machinery of every traditional-form ever borrowed and worn to win the contempt of the civilized world, especially of the Beaux-Arts—that was supposedly its advocate? How about neglect and insult by way of Traditions to great, new materials, and the separation in consequence of Engineering and Architecture: and the great change in human-thought the ideal of Democracy represents, left without any interpretation in Architecture whatsoever?

Traditions had for us the vitality of inertia—the "vitality" of the ball and chain, instead of the inspiration of traditional-forms loved only as an expression of the age to which they were "contemporary." That love would honor Tradition as distinguished from the abuse of traditions. And that love might have instructed us and saved our age for a great Architecture of our own. What made Traditional-Architecture modern and living in its own age—that was the only business we had with Tradition in Architecture. And that was great business.

But twentieth-century America must pay a ghastly price for nineteenth century grave-robbing in architecture, a price that staggers reason, and pay it all back for lack of a simple sense of Tradition that would allow America to live its own life, and by so doing, greatly honor Tradition. Imitation may be the sincerest form of flattery, but whom have we flattered, and how—and, for what?

Creation knows Imitation only as a form of self-abuse. It takes creative imagination to see stone as stone, see steel as steel, see glass as glass, and to view traditions as Tradition. Perhaps that was too much to expect, but where, I ask, is there one honest, living word Tradition as a vital-force has been allowed to say for itself anywhere in this area prostitute to traditions, 2,000 miles North to South and 4,000 miles East to West, that is to say, the length and breadth of this great new ground of ours—let the climate rage or smile upon it how it may? If the Editor of THE FORUM will compile a list, I will take it up item by item and either convince myself or convict him.

This is the Machine Age as distinguished from all other ages; this is the age too, of steel and steam. Ours is the age of the individual, supreme as such, in a life that he can call his own. These great new needs in Art were the Architect's great opportunity. His great office consisted in the fact that Human thought is, here and now, stripping off old ideas like old garments, and such cutting, fitting and trying on as we have done—to find ready-made to wear—all ends naturally in a mis-fit.

All are a mis-fit. But the age is still young and healthy. It seems at last to have shaken off the expedient-interest and be willing now to find the great urge to awaken the creative-faculty that has been lying sterile, neglecting the wretched need of great imaginative interpretation in good work for four hundred and thirty-eight years.

If great Life is sure of great Art, and it is—how can America fail of great Life—once this confusion of ideas, arising perhaps from the Babel of tongues and the embarrassment of the riches of a great, but antiquated inheritance passes—and the great immediate facts of the Life that is her destiny stand out clearly before her people?

For America's future none but the working of Principle is safe Tradition. The only precedent she can find worthy is Principle. If, now, modern-architecture may be both Modern and Architecture, we realize great Architecture as greatest proof of human greatness as it ever was before and in all ages.

Architecture is the scientific art of making structure express Ideas.

Architecture is the triumph of Human Imagination over materials, methods, and men, to put man into possession of his own Earth.

Architecture is man's great sense of himself embodied in a world of his own making. It may rise as high in quality only as its source, because Great Art is Great Life!

Now what is the American Ideal of Great Life?

Liberty is the foreground, middle-distance, and future of that Life. Toleration and Liberty are the foundations of this Great Republic?

Notwithstanding all powerful threats—of a Machine Age—to this Ideal, why not the hope in American hearts that Liberty in Art

will be the native offspring of Political Liberty? And for a new people—a new Architecture!

The old culture itself, for nearly five-hundred years, miserably
failed with the form-language of the human-heart and mind in
Architecture. The Renaissance was that failure and the pseudo-Re-
naissance in America was a tragic betrayal of such ideals as we are
learning now to love to call "American."

The sense of Romance suffered most by the betrayal. But this
sense is already shifting its circumference, therefore its horizon, as it
has done before and will continue to do, for Romance is Immortal.

Industry in the Machine Age can only become a machine
without it. Modern Architecture itself will become a poor, flat-
faced thing of steel-bones, box outlines, gas-pipe and hand-rail
fittings—as sun-receptive as a concrete side-walk or a glass tank,
without Romance,—the essential Joy of Living as distinguished
from Pleasure,—alive in it.

Architecture without that Joy could inspire nothing but mediocre emulation and would degenerate to a box fit merely to contain
the objects of Art and Decoration it should itself create and maintain.

Constructing architectural features and parts to give the decorative effect of simplicity is not good enough. It comes to just the
same thing in the end as—America's disgrace,—now.

Why should Architecture or objects of Art in the Machine
Age, because they are made by Machines, resemble Machinery?
Because they were so made might be the best of reasons why they
should not. Nor is there good reason why Forms stripped clean of
all considerations but Function and Utility should be admirable
beyond that standpoint. They may be abominable from the human standpoint. Let us have no fear, therefore, of Liberalism in
our Art of Architecture, nor in our Industries.

Romance, all great poets are agreed, is only Liberalism in Art.
It never did apply to "make believe" or to constructing Architectural features and parts for ornamental effect, or to falsifying, or

to degenerate to sentimentality—except as it was betrayed by the Renaissance.

The taste for mediocrity grows by what it feeds upon, therefore the public of this Republic is more than ever likely to find the love of commonplace-elegance that curses it, and that was gratified by the sentimentality of the ornamental, now replaced by a pleasure in the ornamentality of affected-simplicity, or a reaction toward the sterility of ornaphobia.

Yes, this Machine Age, especially now at the moment of awakening from damnation by senseless sentimentality, may be in danger of being sterilized,—castrated by a factory-aesthetic.

The Machine is the brainless craftsman of a new-freedom in social order. Untried and unqualified this "New" is a dangerous means to great-realization in Architecture.

But,—Scientists and Philosophers!—convention us no narrow *conventions,* New or Old, to rise up in middle-minds and get into selfish, meddling hands as *preventions* in this Modern World that,—thanks to an Organic-Architecture,—we are going to build upon fertile new ground. As Sons-of-Liberty we are going to build that New Freedom in Art upon ground fertilized by the Old,—ground in which the carcasses of ancient Architecture lie rotting beneath our feet if Traditions are to die where and how and when they should die that Tradition may nobly live.

Until the dead-past has buried its dead—Life is poisoned and itself dies of its own dead.

12c For All May Raise the Flowers Now for All Have Got the Seed (1932)

It is a weakness of our American system that any energetic, unscrupulous individual with something of the instinct of the salesman, may get a fortune in a few years.

With no culture, but much will and desire, power comes with money. He gets himself "fixed" with "makings" as no one of his quality could do in any other country.

His ability to sell lands him in an incongruous self-made shell. His ability to use his power is all out of drawing with his ability to administer it as his money systematically comes alive and goes on, itself working, to multiply itself.

He knows nothing of the real meaning of what he now gathers. He does not know what art is, but he knows what he likes. It is ready-made. The country is free.

So here is the cultural weed.

He goes to seed. And more weeds by way of "ready-made."

Exaggerated power is aggravated by such ready-made culture as he can (or will) provide.

The salesman is . . . "Success."

Now, salesman cuts salesman. In architecture—and it is the culture most important to him—it is his counterpart that sells it to him by way of similar success.

It is only ready-made culture that he will buy.

And, to him, that is European. Europeans themselves come and find this out and soon become expert salesmen in the American scene by the American method.

This salesmanship we call propaganda.

The propagandist at the present moment is the "internationalist."

Is architecture "modern" because alter-egos need some formula to follow any individual initiative and overtaking it, as they imagine, may thus manage soon to ride the initiative to death? How much is being written and how little built and how little sense in cause or contra shows clearly *why* the straight-line and flat-plane (both abstractions), and the single curved-surface added to make of the whole another abstraction, have come to be expedient "modern" architecture.

Why is the formula expedient? Is it in order that the original impotence—eclecticism—may be now "improved" as modernistic—or modernism—and function as the inevitable ism, ist, or ite, to make a "*movement*"? A movement of this sort depends upon the obvious and easy for the nearsighted near-great, the smaller and small men to play up for selfish purposes in small ways to again kill such initiative as lives, or might live, in our architecture.

A "movement" is usually exploitation, not initiative. Taking all this together, it becomes personal to me because the cause of an organic-architecture runs well beyond the yard-stick and plain-plaster by which busybodies, in their extremity, obscure a simple issue as "modern."

A bee in their bonnets!

They are doing some harm, I believe, and unless there is enough vitality in the great cause of architecture itself to rebuke and shake them off, they intend doing not only more but all the harm there is in them. It may not be so much in the long run, but it discourages all true creative initiative meantime.

But trust the reactionary alter-ego—anyone's alterego—to make the great small, the little big and both of not much consequence so far as his own ability goes.

I said doing harm.

Let's be specific.

Poor Japan, who eagerly copies the latest in Western haberdashery or art—impartially—not knowing what either is all about, and . . . gets kicked out!

I loved Japan and reverently took off my hat to its nativity when asked there to build a building. The Japanese are Oriental, not Occidental, hard as they may try to be Occidental. They are trying pitifully hard, but there is a chasm between the races where art is concerned wholly in favor of the Oriental.

Yet, see all the internationalists busy over there encouraging that ambitious, industrious nation to belie and stultify itself by an aggravated architectural version of the Derby hat, kimono and Boston gaiters. Tokio is becoming a profane sight in consequence. To anyone who loves these sensitive, ambitious people who call Tokio capital, here is deplorable butchery.

The East still thinks the West knows what it is about and promptly gets after whatever is after the West, too quick to grab and fall in line. Japan's national weakness.

Some day the East will learn that the West itself is a formula-chaser or an imitator, instead of a culture builder. Any formula derived from its experimental civilization can only be a brand, or a fraud, upon the East.

The Japanese will some day wake to curse the abuse they were encouraged to practice upon themselves.

The Japanese house—a perfect expression of organic architecture—is being made over into a Western garage, instead of being organically developed into a suitable place for the same life rising from its knees to its feet.

On the verge—another instance.

Rio de Janeiro—the capital of a romantic people in love with loveliness.

There I found some seven hundred art students of the Bellas Artes on "strike"—as they built our word into their Portuguese language. These students wanted to go forward instead of backward, and the Beaux-Arts arm-chairs couldn't allow that, so they couldn't get the students back to work. These high-spirited young people were regarding "the formula" as it had found its way there over-seas by way of a Russian working for a German on the tropical mountain-side, at Copacabana. A good "internationalist" example. As good as any.[1]

These young people were regarding it proudly but uneasily. Something was out of "drawing."

In tropical sunshine, the flat-faced hard-head was glaring shamelessly at a high-spirited romantic people regardless of climate or environment, and they were trying to see it, whole, as the right thing. Not quite so gullible as the poor Japanese where the West is concerned, they were suspicious.

The students had gathered there and invited me to tell them if that was "modern architecture."

I said the equivocal term might mean that it was, probably did. But it wasn't architecture at all where they were concerned, because it ignored their natures, their climate, and the character of their environment.

A cheer went up, and smiles broke out. They were relieved. As I told them why, in more detail, the sky cleared for a moment.

But propaganda is at work on them, too. They have no models otherwise. They have no one directly to stimulate their imaginations along lines natural to them, unless Lucio Costa or Araujo.[2]

What are they to do?

Here is our own nation.

Eclecticism, a form of self-abuse too long practiced, has rendered us impotent. Such architecture as we have, we got that way. We are prostitute to any formula because we are prostitute to the machine.

Now comes this "internationalist" formula deduced from such initiative as we have had in our own architecture. Such as it is, it is all too easy for eclectics to seize it. And soon—regardless of native characteristics and fitness to climate or environment, we may see the formula in Miami, Minneapolis, Alaska, Arizona, the Philippines, and Texas.

And this is what the little minds of the propagandists for "the international" call success.

All formulae have pedigrees. Yes . . . this one, as many pedigrees as there are peddlers.

This one has bad ones from the time it became a formula.

The creative artists, whose initiative is capitalized and exploited in this formula, would none of them own it. They would, and they do, abominate it.

And they would, and do, despise the peddlers whose "pedigree" it is to trade in it or on it regardless of depth or quality or fitness to purpose just because they can only "elect" some style or pass up an exploit in salesmanship.

If these busybodies would get down to work, put up more, and shut off propaganda for a while I, for one, might have some belief in their sincerity and the character of their effort, half-baked though it must be.

H. Th. Wijdeveld[3] recently told me of "a propagandist" who got to Amsterdam and, asked to speak, wore out the "audience" with 62 out of 76 lantern slides of a by no means unusual or remarkable "internationalist" house built by himself. He will probably not lecture again in Amsterdam. But he is by no means unusual. In this busybody propaganda wherever it is found, the cackling outdoes the egg.

No genuine art ever sought expression by way of such calculated selfishness.

Now it is another weakness of our American system that the national mind seems never to believe that a man may be actuated by principles to speak his own mind, loving principle more than himself and willing to eat the dirt thrown into his mouth every time he opens it rather than let the principle in him go by default. No. The instinct of the salesman immediately places him as not "having got his." To a salesman, all men are salesmen. So where financial interests have any concern in architecture (and where are they not concerned?)—it is all the man's socio-economic life is worth to voice dissent where money is tied up or tied in. There is but one voice where there is "investment." Hence the default, or the combined ballyhoo of salesmanship to drown the voice.

One of those unfortunate men who live to be the envy and the reproach of the alter-ego, I often have occasion to reflect upon the disadvantage I offer—by being alive and more productive than ever—to callous or flighty disciples or perhaps callow apprentices now full-fledged and eager to fly. As somebody said at the "League" last year—was it "Little Napoleon" number three?—"We always come to the realization that Wright is alive with a kind of shock." 4

And I am writing this with an enemy in each eye. Two extremes.

The predatory eclectic in the right eye.

The predatory "internationalist" in the left eye.

The one elects forms "ready-made" from an architecture dead.

The other elects a formula derived from an architecture living, or just beginning to live, and kills the architecture.

I am not at the moment cross-eyed because both the old and improved eclectic come from the same stock and amount to the same thing. I can see straight through both eyes, because the "internationalist" is only the modern improvement on the old eclectic. He is the up-to-date eclectic.

Now, eclecticism, unimproved, was obnoxious to me. And eclecticism improved seems no less obnoxious because, while the unimproved peddled the dead, to peddle the improvement the living must lose its life.

Special activity, now, to juggle and fake history by warped and twisted pedigrees by specialists important in Europe, according to themselves, when in America and important in America, according to themselves, when in Europe . . . until "modern" architecture is a bone for any stray dog to gnaw. But the bone holds its shape. Contention or no contention.

Architecture is architecture.

Standards as they go about with the predatory "international-ist" are weaknesses all too near the weakness of our own American socio-economic system to be lightly encouraged for personal profit.

What creative mind wants emulation? What he-architect wants disciples?

Not one.

He wants work.

The man wants to see the principles he loves, live.

He wants life to go on growing, not by emulation but by depth of individual experience. Not by *peddling* but by *working*.

The man may be kind, easily flattered and fond of the mirror in personal matters.

But the very life in him is the honor of his art if he is an architect.

And any man's art is dishonored by imitation.

Any nation's life is dishonored by seizing formulae instead of perceiving principles. And, especially, it will pay a hard price for any formula in the freedom that we, as Usonians in America, must learn to see as democracy.

I love my country, and I would that my country love me. But not by way of flattery or imitation, coming or going, will I give or accept love.

To such I, now, prefer hate.

If only our country would "*raise the flowers, now that all have got the seed,*" from seed: principle, the seed, transplanting not preferred . . . what a country!

NOTES

1. Wright was invited to Rio de Janeiro in 1931 to judge the Christopher Columbus Memorial Lighthouse competition. He likely refers here to Gregori Warchavchik (1896–1972), Odessa-born migrant to Brazil in 1923, influenced

by the ideas of Walter Gropius and Mies van der Rohe. In 1931, Warchavchik designed a restaurant on the beach at Copacabana.

2. Wright certainly means Brazilian architect Lúcio Costa (1902–98) and perhaps refers to Manuel de Araújo Porto-alegre (neé Manuel José de Araújo (1806–79), who in addition to being an architect was a painter, playwright, poet, and diplomat among several other things.

3. Architect Hendrik Theodorus Wijdeveld (1885–1987) was a member and principal publicist of the "Amsterdam School," a Dutch version of expressive modernism, though *Wendingen* (1918–1931), the journal he founded and edited.

4. Wright refers to Philip Johnson, at the time architectural curator at the Museum of Modern Art in New York City, who had spoken at the Architectural League of New York's annual exhibition in February 1931.

12d Of Thee I Sing (1932)[1]

I find myself standing now against the "Geist der Kleinlichkeit," [2] to strike for an architecture for the individual instead of tamely recognizing senility in the guise of a new invention . . . the so-called international style.

No unusual vision is required to see in this alleged invention an attempt to strip hide and horns from the living breathing organism that is modern architecture of the past twenty-five years and, by beating the tom-tom, try to make the hide come alive, or, in despair, tack the "skin" on America's barn-door for a pattern.

Such, I believe, is the nature of this ulterior "invention."

Architecture was made for man, not man made for architecture. And since when then, has the man sunk so low, even by way of the machine, that a self-elected group of formalizers could predetermine his literature, his music, or his architecture for him?

I know the European neuter's argument: "the Western soul is dead; Western intelligence, though keen, is therefore sterile and can realize an impression but not expression of life except as life may be recognized as some intellectual formula."

But I think such confession of genital impotence, while valid enough where this cliché is concerned, a senility that healthy youth North, South, East or West is bound to ridicule and repudiate.

Youth is not going to take its architecture or its life that way.

Form, and such style as it may own, comes out of structure industrial, social, architectural.

Principles of construction employing suitable materials for the definite purposes of industry or society, in living hands, will result in style. The changing methods and materials of a changing life should keep the road open for developing variety of expression, spontaneous so long as human imagination lives.

The imagination that makes a building into architecture as mathematics is made into music is not the quality of mind that makes a professor of mathematics or makes a building engineer or makes a short-cut aesthete. *Nor is it ever a matter of a "style."*

Mass-machine-production needs a conscience but needs no aesthetic formula as a short cut to any style. It is itself a deadly formula. Machinery needs the creative force that can seize it, as it is, for what it is worth, to get the work of the world done by it and gradually make that work no less an expression of the spontaneous human spirit than ever before. We must make the expression of life as much richer as it is bound to be more general in realization. Or, by way of machine worship, go machine mad.

Do you think that, as a style, any aesthetic formula forced upon this work of ours in our country can do more than stultify this reasonable hope for a life of the soul?

A creative architecture for America can only mean an architecture for the individual.

The community interest in these United States is not communism or communistic as the internationalists' formula for a "style" presents itself. Its language aside, communistic the proposition is. Communistic in communism's most objectionable phase: the sterility of the individual its end if not its aim and . . . in the name of "discipline"!

Life needs and gets interior discipline according to its ideal. The higher the ideal, the greater the discipline.

But this communistic formula proposes to get rid of this constructive interior discipline's anxieties (and joys) by the surrender that ends all in all and for all, by way of a preconceived style for life—conceived by the few to be imposed upon all alike.

Such communistic "ism" belongs to inverted capitalism. Some good, undoubtedly, the inversion if only to demonstrate the cruelty of both capitalism and such communism. Out of any sincere struggle, something comes for the growth of humanity. But, for a free democracy to accept a communistic tenet of this breed disguised as aesthetic formula for architecture is a confession of failure I do not believe we, as a people, are ready to make.

Centralization (a form of every man for himself and the devil for the hindmost) is what is the matter with us. We are suffering from an abuse of individuality in this virulent form, instead of enjoying the ideal of integration natural to democracy.

We are sickened by capitalistic centralization but not so sick, I believe, that we need confess impotence by embracing a communistic exterior discipline in architecture to kill finally what spontaneous life we have left in the circumstances.

As for discipline?

Do you know the living discipline of an ideal of life as organic architecture or architecture as organic life? Those who do know the interior discipline of this ideal look upon surrender to any style formula whatever as dead exterior discipline. Imprisonment in impotence.

"Besonnenheit?"

"Entsagung?" [3]

Well . . . if an effect is produced at all in organic architecture, it must proceed from the interior of the work. It must be of the very organism created.

Try that for discipline in our democracy!

It is an inflexible will, bridling a rich and powerful ego, that is necessary to the creation of any building as architecture or the living of any life in a free democracy. Call it individual. And it is ever so.

And any great thing is too much of whatever it is: it is a quality of greatness.

"Excess of contrast, in genius, brings about a mighty equilibrium." [4]

But "Geist der Kleinlichkeit" will take the excess and capitalize it as a "style." Never will it take the principle or its essence. But it will take the excess and prescribe a *pattern*. In this case an excess of the original protest.

Styles are anterior, posterior or ulterior.

Why should pretentious formalizers worry about the discipline of a "style" for Americans before either they or America yet know style?

The methods, materials and life of our country are common discipline to any right idea of work. Allowed to exercise at our best such wholesouled individuality as we may find among us, the common use of the common tools and materials of a common life will so discipline individual effort that centuries forward men will look back and recognize the work of the democratic life of the Twentieth Century as a great, not a dead, style. The honest buildings from which this proposed internationalist style is derived were made that way. We can build many more buildings in that same brave, independent, liberal spirit.

So we need no "Geist der Kleinlichkeit" touting a style at us. No, Herr Spengler, we are not yet impotent.

We will, given our own principle, with no self-conscious effort make a great one.

By force of circumstances freely acting upon what is great and alive in us,–and that is our democratic principle of freedom–we will make our own.

It is true that we understand imperfectly our own ideal of democracy, and so we have shamefully abused it.

We have allowed our ideal to foster offensive privatism that is exaggerated selfishness in the name of individualism. Selfish beyond any monarchy. But do you imagine communism eradicates selfishness? It may suppress it or submerge it.

Nor can socialism eradicate selfishness. It gives it another turn. Democracy cannot eradicate it. No, but democracy alone can turn it into a noble, creative selfhood.

And that is best of all for all.

So out of my own life-experience as an architect, I earnestly say: what our country needs in order to realize a great architecture for a great life is only to realize and release a high ideal of democracy, the ideal upon which the new life here was founded on new ground, and humbly try to learn how to live up to its principles.

I am sure, too, that the work of an organic architecture, for the individual, had gone so far in the work of the world before this self-seeking propaganda came up, as to enable anyone with ordinary vision to see it coming naturally as our future architecture, propagandists aside. So why, now, as a self-appointed committee on a *style*, do promoting propagandists imagine they can steal the hide and horns of this living, breathing, healthy, young organism and vaingloriously parade the hide and shake the horns to make Americans think it is the living creature?

Granted they are sincere: having confessed impotence, do they urge others to confess too?

Granted they are ambitious: they wish to be inventors as an eunuch might wish to be a father.

Granted they are impecunious: do they wish to get work to do under false pretenses?

Granted they are aesthetes: they are superficial and ignorant of the depths of nature.

Granted they are as intelligent and hard and scientific as they think they are: they are miscarriage of a machine-age that would sterilize itself, if it could, to avoid continuing to propagate the race.

Youth asks for life, and this "Geist der Kleinlichkeit" would hand out a recipe in the form of a pattern of itself?

The letter is more than the spirit only to artists of the second rank.

It is the thing said that is more important, now, than the manner of saying it.

Our pioneer days are not over.

NOTES

1. Wright takes his title from George and Ira Gershwin, George S. Kaufman, and Morrie Ryskind's 1931 Broadway musical.

2. The spirit of smallness.

3. *Besonnenheit*: Roughly, a highly developed level of self-consciousness through which we know that we know, including characteristics of the external world. *Entsagung*: Roughly, doing honestly what we know must be done by obeying the laws of one's own nature.

4. From Romain Rolland (1866–1944), *Beethoven the Creator* (1929). The passage reads: "Whoever would understand him must be able to embrace the excess of his contrasts, that bring about his mighty equilibrium." In the preceding paragraph Rolland discusses "that spirit of smallness" (*Geist der Kleinlichkeit*) which Beethoven abominated.

THIRTEEN

Broadacre City: A New Community Plan (1935)

Wright had been thinking a lot and writing a little about decentral-
ization well before he directly addressed the issue in The Disappear-
ing City *and a* New York Times Magazine *piece, both in 1932. By*
the spring of 1935 his apprentices had constructed a twelve-by-
twelve-foot Broadacre City model that depicted an exemplary four-
square-mile county, suggesting what a decentralized America might
be like. This text was intended to accompany the model's exhibition
at New York's Rockefeller Center that April.

 Based on the recognition that high-speed transportation and
communication had breached temporal and spatial barriers, en-
abling people to spread out but not be isolated, Wright adopted the
county as Broadacre's basic administrative unit, eliminating states
and municipalities. Services would be directed by the County Archi-
tect, its highest official, to ensure that all structures were aesthetically
pleasing and that everything affecting collective life was humanely
and efficiently administered.

 Ten-lane auto routes with median strip monorail and submerged
flanking truck lanes with warehousing were located at boundaries to
serve counties on either side. Parallel zones of roadside businesses,
markets, light manufacturing, power plants, gas stations, and other
potentially unsightly county-wide necessities were screened by vine-
yards, orchards, and blue-collar housing from the large central area

of small detached houses arranged in loosely defined neighborhoods, each with its own schools, libraries, parks, places of worship, garages, and shops. On both macro and micro levels, counties were thus discreetly segregated into more and less aesthetically pleasing, more and less sensorially polluting, clusters.

Land was allocated on the basis of one acre per household member to be held as long as productively used. Wright expected most families to maintain vegetable gardens, perhaps keep a chicken or two, and to help erect their own standardized housing that could be expanded or contracted as circumstances dictated (see Document 14a). For those unable to make the transition to a land-based life style or who preferred to live alone, Wright provided apartment buildings inconspicuously tucked here and there.

He offered this scheme because he was convinced that cities were overdeveloped and dehumanizing, to enhance individualism and self-sufficiency, as a way of ending the Depression (without explaining how), and as an alternative to high-rise cities Le Corbusier and other prominent (mostly European) architects had been proposing for years. Making no suggestion for how to implement the plan knowing it would never happen, he nonetheless acted as if it would, periodically tinkering with his model and drawings, lecturing and writing about it for the rest of his life.

One historian called Broadacre City "the chief work of Wright's mature life," while another noted its "profound effect on establishing the need for" post-World War Two new towns and regional planning.[1] Both observations have merit, and a third is that one cannot fully grasp Wright's last great design achievement, the Usonian House (Documents 14a to c), without understanding its centrality in a "Broadacred" America.

From The Architectural Record, 74 (April 1935), reprinted with permission from Architectural Record © 1935, the McGraw-Hill Companies. Visit www.architecturalrecord.com for more information.

Given the simple exercise of several inherently just rights of man, the freedom to decentralize, to redistribute and to correlate the properties of the life of man on earth to his birthright—the ground itself—and Broadacre City becomes reality.

As I see Architecture, the best architect is he who will devise forms nearest organic as features of human growth by way of changes natural to that growth. Civilization is itself inevitably a form but not, if democracy is sanity, is it necessarily the fixation called "academic." All regimentation is a form of death which may sometimes serve life but more often imposes upon it. In Broadacres all is symmetrical but it is seldom obviously and never academically so.

Whatever forms issue are capable of normal growth without destruction of such pattern as they may have. Nor is there much obvious repetition in the new city. Where regiment and row serve the general harmony of arrangement both are present, but generally both are absent except where planting and cultivation are naturally a process or walls afford a desired seclusion. Rhythm is the substitute for such repetitions everywhere. Wherever repetition (standardization) enters, it has been modified by inner rhythms either by art or by nature as it must, to be of any lasting human value.

The three major inventions already at work building Broadacres, whether the powers that over-built the old cities otherwise like it or not are:

1. The motor car: general mobilization of the human being.
2. Radio, telephone and telegraph: electrical intercommunication becoming complete.
3. Standardized machine-shop production: machine invention plus scientific discovery.

The price of the major three to America has been the exploitation we see everywhere around us in waste and in ugly scaffolding that may now be thrown away. The price has not been so great if by way of popular government we are able to exercise the use of three inherent rights of any man:

1. His social right to a direct medium of exchange in place of gold as a commodity: some form of social credit.
2. His social right to his place on the ground as he has had it in the sun and air: land to be held only by use and improvements.
3. His social right to the ideas by which and for which he lives: public ownership of invention and scientific discoveries that concern the life of the people.

The only assumption made by Broadacres as ideal is that these three rights will be the citizen's so soon as the folly of endeavoring to cheat him of their democratic values becomes apparent to those who hold (feudal survivors or survivals), as it is becoming apparent to the thinking people who are held blindly abject or subject against their will.

The landlord is no happier than the tenant. The speculator can no longer win much at a game about played out. The present success-ideal placing, as it does, premiums upon the wolf, the fox and the rat in human affairs and above all, upon the parasite, is growing more evident every day as a falsity just as injurious to the "successful" as to the victims of such success.

Well—sociologically, Broadacres is release from all that fatal "success" which is after all, only excess. So I have called it a new freedom for living in America. It has thrown the scaffolding aside. It sets up a new ideal of success.

In Broadacres, by elimination of cities and towns the present curse of petty and minor officialdom, government, has been reduced to one minor government for each county. The waste motion, the back and forth haul, that today makes so much idle business is gone. Distribution becomes automatic and direct; taking place mostly in the region of origin. Methods of distribution of everything are simple and direct. From the maker to the consumer by the most direct route.

Coal (one third the tonnage of the haul of our railways) is eliminated by burning it at the mines and transferring that power, making it easier to take over the great railroad rights of way; to take off the cumbersome rolling stock and put the right of way into general service as the great arterial on which truck traffic is concentrated on lower side lanes, many lanes of speed traffic above and monorail speed trains at the center, continuously running. Because traffic may take off or take on at any given point, these arterials are traffic not dated but fluescent [*sic*]. And the great arterial as well as all the highways become great architecture, automatically affording within their structure all necessary storage facilities of raw materials, the elimination of all unsightly piles of raw material.

In the hands of the state, but by way of the county, is all redistribution of land—a minimum of one acre going to the childless family and more to the larger family as effected by the state. The agent of the state in all matters of land allotment or improvement, or in matters affecting the harmony of the whole, is the architect. All building is subject to his sense of the whole as organic architecture. Here architecture is landscape and landscape takes on the character of architecture by way of the simple process of cultivation.

All public utilities are concentrated in the hands of the state and county government as are matters of administration, patrol, fire, post, banking license and record, making politics a vital matter to every one in the new city instead of the old case where hopeless indifference makes "politics" a grafter's profession.

In the buildings for Broadacres no distinction exists between much and little, more and less. Quality is in all, for all, alike. The thought entering into the first or last estate is of the best. What differs is only individuality and extent. There is nothing poor or mean in Broadacres.

Nor does Broadacres issue any dictum or see any finality in the matter either of pattern or style.

Organic character is style. Such style has myriad forms inherently good. Growth is possible to Broadacres as a fundamental form: not as mere accident of change but as integral pattern unfolding from within.

Here now may be seen the elemental units of our social structure: The correlated farm, the factory—its smoke and gases eliminated by burning coal at places of origin, the decentralized school, the various conditions of residence, the home offices, safe traffic, simplified government. All common interests take place in a simple coordination wherein all are employed: *little* farms, *little* homes for industry, *little* factories, *little* schools, a *little* university going to the people mostly by way of their interest in the ground, *little* laboratories on their own ground for professional men. And the farm itself, notwithstanding its animals, becomes the most attractive unit of the city. The husbandry of animals at last is in decent association with them and with all else as well. True farm relief.

To build Broadacres as conceived would automatically end unemployment and all its evils forever. There would never be labor enough nor could under-consumption ever ensue. Whatever a man did would be done—obviously and directly—mostly by himself in his own interest under the most valuable inspiration and direction: under training, certainly, if necessary. Economic independence would be near, a subsistence certain; life varied and interesting.

Every kind of builder would be likely to have a jealous eye to the harmony of the whole within broad limits fixed by the county architect, an architect chosen by the county itself. Each county would thus naturally develop an individuality of its own. Architecture—in the broad sense—would thrive.

In an organic architecture the ground itself predetermines all features; the climate modifies them; available means limit them; function shapes them.

Form and function are one in Broadacres. But Broadacres is no finality. The model shows four square miles of a typical countryside developed on the acre as unit according to conditions in the temperate zone and accommodating some 1,400 families. It would swing north or swing south in type as conditions, climate and topography of the region changed.

In the model the emphasis has been placed upon diversity in unity, recognizing the necessity of cultivation as a need for formality in most of the planting. By a simple government subsidy certain specific acres or groups of acre units are, in every generation, planted to useful trees, meantime beautiful, giving privacy and various rural divisions. There are no rows of trees alongside the roads to shut out the view. Rows where they occur are perpendicular to the road or the trees are planted in groups. Useful trees like white pine, walnut, birch, beech, fir, would come to maturity as well as fruit and nut trees and they would come as a profitable crop meantime giving character, privacy and comfort to the whole city. The general park is a flowered meadow beside the stream and is bordered with ranks of trees, tiers gradually rising in height above the flowers at the ground level. A music-garden is sequestered from noise at one end. Much is made of general sports and festivals by way of the stadium, zoo, aquarium, arboretum and the arts.

The traffic problem has been given special attention, as the more mobilization is made a comfort and a facility the sooner will Broadacres arrive. Every Broadacre citizen has his own car. Multiple-lane highways make travel safe and enjoyable. There are no grade crossings nor left turns on grade. The road system and construction is such that no signals nor any lamp-posts need be seen. No ditches are alongside the roads. No curbs either. An inlaid purfling over which the car cannot come without damage to itself takes its place to protect the pedestrian.

In the affair of air transport Broadacres rejects the present airplane and substitutes the self-contained mechanical unit that is sure to come: an aerotor capable of rising straight up and by reversible rotors able to travel in any given direction under radio control at a maximum speed of, say, 200 miles an hour, and able to descend safely into the hexacomb from which it arose or anywhere else. By a doorstep if desired.

The only fixed transport trains kept on the arterial are the long-distance monorail cars traveling at a speed (already established in Germany) of 220 miles per hour. All other traffic is by motor car on the twelve lane levels or the triple truck lanes on the lower levels which have on both sides the advantage of delivery direct to warehousing or from warehouses to consumer. Local trucks may get to warehouse-storage on lower levels under the main arterial itself. A local truck road parallels the swifter lanes.

Houses in the new city are varied: make much of fireproof synthetic materials, factory-fabricated units adapted to free assembly and varied arrangement, but do not neglect the older nature-materials wherever they are desired and available. Householders' utilities are nearly all planned in prefabricated utility stacks or units, simplifying construction and reducing building costs to a certainty. There is the professional's house with its laboratory, the minimum house with its workshop, the medium house ditto, the larger house and the house of machine-age-luxury. We might speak of them as a one-car house, a two-car house, a three-car house and a five-car house. Glass is extensively used as are roofless rooms. The roof is used often as a trellis or a garden. But where glass is extensively used it is usually for domestic purposes in the shadow of protecting overhangs.

Copper for roofs is indicated generally on the model as a permanent cover capable of being worked in many appropriate ways and giving a general harmonious color effect to the whole.

Electricity, oil and gas are the only popular fuels. Each land allotment has a pit near the public lighting fixture where access to the three and to water and sewer may be had without tearing up the pavements.

The school problem is solved by segregating a group of low buildings in the interior spaces of the city where the children can go without crossing traffic. The school building group includes galleries for loan collections from the museum, a concert and lecture hall, small gardens for the children in small groups and well-lighted cubicles for individual outdoor study: there is a small zoo, large pools and green playgrounds.

This group is at the very center of the model and contains at its center the higher school adapted to the segregation of the students into small groups.

This tract of four miles square, by way of such liberal general allotment determined by acreage and type of ground, including apartment buildings and hotel facilities, provides for about 1,400 families at, say, an average of five or more persons to the family.

To reiterate: the basis of the whole is general decentralization as an applied principle and architectural reintegration of all units into one fabric; free use of the ground held only by use and improvements; public utilities and government itself owned by the people of Broadacre City; privacy on one's own ground for all and a fair means of subsistence for all by way of their own work on their own ground or in their own laboratory or in common offices serving the life of the whole.

There are too many details involved in the model of Broadacres to permit complete explanation. Study of the model itself is necessary study. Most details are explained by way of collateral models of the various types of construction shown: highway construction, left turns, crossovers, underpasses and various houses and public buildings.

Any one studying the model should bear in mind the thesis upon which the design has been built by the Taliesin Fellowship,[2] built carefully not as a finality in any sense but as an interpretation of the changes inevitable to our growth as a people and a nation.

Individuality established on such terms must thrive. Unwholesome life would get no encouragement and the ghastly heritage left by overcrowding in overdone ultra-capitalistic centers would be likely to disappear in three or four generations. The old success ideals having no chance at all, new ones more natural to the best in man would be given a fresh opportunity to develop naturally.

NOTES

1. John Sergeant, *Frank Lloyd Wright's Usonian Houses: The Case for Organic Architecture* (New York: Watson-Guptill, 1976), 125; Donald Leslie Johnson, *Frank Lloyd Wright versus America: The 1930s* (Cambridge, MA: MIT Press, 1990), 151.

2. The Taliesin Fellowship, founded by Wright in 1932 at Taliesin, his Spring Green, Wisconsin estate, was an architectural training program organized around the apprentice system. See Myron A. and Shirley L. Marty, *Frank Lloyd Wright's Taliesin Fellowship* (Kirkland, MO: Truman State University Press, 1999) and Roger Friedland and Harold Zellman, *The Fellowship: The Untold Story of Frank Lloyd Wright and the Taliesin Fellowship* (New York: Regan, 2006).

FOURTEEN

The Usonian House

(1932–38)

Wright used the acronym "Usonian" to refer to the "United States of North America," to a handful of residential communities laid out in the 1930s, 1940s, and 1950s, to forty or so houses of five basic types designed from 1936 to 1941, and finally to all his work after World War Two. It is the prewar residences to which the following texts refer.

The defining features of a typical (but not every) prewar Usonian House are: radiant floor heating, a single story with flat roof and widely cantilevered eaves, floor-to-ceiling windows and doors opening to a garden with patio, a kitchen-bathroom unit slightly elevated above roof line, a bedroom zone, a kitchen-dining-living zone semi-divided by function, partially prefabricated walls that could be assembled on site (or potentially in a factory) and raised into place, street-facing clerestory windows and, next to the entry, a roofed but open-ended carport, a term Wright coined. The intention was to offer comparatively inexpensive housing to moderate income people.

The Usonian idea had been brewing for some time, reflecting social and architectural change during the quarter century since Wright's Prairie period. The Usonian house can in fact be considered an updated Prairie house, more open in plan and to the outdoors, easily maintained without servants, addressing the increased casualness of a new generation's lifestyles. It built upon the incipient standardization and prefabrication he had hoped to utilize more fully ever since his 1916 "American Ready-Cuts" (Document 9). Although Wright never admitted it, Usonians reinterpreted the sleek, stripped-down, efficient appearance and organization of "internationalist" work he had railed against (Documents 12a–d). And from the beginning of its gestation it was part and parcel of his developing thoughts on decentralization.

He made this clear whenever he called it a "missionary" for Broadacre City, an example of the kinds of residences people might expect there. He made it clear when he told clients to select building sites ten times farther away from urban agglomerations than they had thought necessary, when he included workshops and vegetable gardens in plans and prospectives, and when he urged clients to help erect their own houses, as a few actually did. Along with his two Taliesin estates, Wright's new dwellings served in his mind as "little experiment stations in out of the way places."

Without using the word Usonian or mentioning Broadacre City although alluding to it, he floated his latest ideas in "The House of the Future" speech (Document 14a). He put them into preliminary form in a handful of built and unbuilt projects from 1934 to 1936 and into final form in the 1936–37 Herbert Jacobs residence, generally acknowledged to be the first true Usonian, discussed in "The House of Moderate Cost" (Document 14b). The new concept attracted immediate attention. Time, Life, Architectural Forum, and other prominent publications gave it extensive coverage, and commissions flowed in until American entry into World War Two ended residential construction.

After the war when construction resumed, when Wright's practice burgeoned and the socioeconomic standing of his clients was higher, Usonian features like partial prefabrication appeared less often and materials more substantial than wood more often, bringing the period of "true" Usonians to an end. But since he continued to *use the word, perhaps it is more accurate to say that the relative modesty of Usonia "phase one" gave way to a more upscale "phase two," for most of the defining features remained and Wright continued to experiment with other ways to contain cost.*

"To the Blackbourns" (Document 14c), a personalized application of general principles outlined in "The House of Moderate Cost," is Wright's proposal for a specific $5,000-to-$6,000-income "typical family selected by Life" *magazine. It was not built, but the twenty-plus "true" or "phase one" Usonians still standing and an equal number never erected may be considered Wright's last design breakthrough (he turned seventy-four in 1941), his subsequent residential work being variations on a theme. But this is only to say that if his philosophy of house design did not change after "phase one," his implementations thereof, as with nonresidential work, remained a potpourri of visual treats.*

"The House of the Future" is an excerpt from an address delivered to the National Association of Real Estate Boards meeting in Cincinnati, published in National Real Estate Journal, *33 (July 1932), "reprinted with permission from National Real Estate Journal, July 1932, © National Association of Realtors®. All rights reserved." Readers may also consult "Machine Made Simplicity in Homes," a differently worded "digest" of the speech, in the Chicago-based* Real Estate: The Weekly for Owners, Realtors, and Builders *(9 July 1932).*

"The House of Moderate Cost" is an excerpt from a much longer essay in Architectural Forum, *68 (January 1938), an issue designed by and entirely devoted to Wright. "To the Blackbourns" is from* Architectural Forum, *69 (November 1938).*

14a The House of the Future (1932)

I shall call the thing the "assembled house." I do not think there is a big concern in the United States that has not been flirting with it more or less, that has not done some research work along the line of a standardized, machine-made house.

At first, of course, the house itself is going to take on some of the characteristics that Henry's Model T took on when it was in Henry's hands, when it was in the inventor's hands. An inventor is not an architect. The house will be ugly in the beginning, but it will get into the hands of the creative architect or the artist who can evolve a scheme or a plan by which it can be made an harmonious whole. There is no reason why the assembled house, fabricated in the factory, should not be made as beautiful and as efficient as the modern automobile.

You will see a few appearing, and will turn away from them and say: "My God, anything but that." But that is the way everything that is new and effective has found its way into civilization.

When we have established a few models that are usable, beautiful and livable, there is no question but that the people will like them.

There will be as great a difference between this new house and the old house as between the old caravel in which Columbus discovered America and a beautiful stream-lined rotor ship. You will see that a new element esthetically has entered into modern life by way of the very things that are now doing more to destroy that life than to make it.

There will be a new simplicity, a machine-made simplicity. Now, a good machine is good to look at. There is no reason why a house should look like a machine, but there is no reason why it should not be just as good to look at as a machine, and for just the same reason.

That is an entirely new basis for architecture and for thought and for life.

Now, in working out this "assembled house" we have already the bathroom as a single unit to draw upon. We will call it unit No. 1. You can now get a bathroom with a bath tub and the bowl and the water closet in one fixture, and all that is to be done is to make the connection to the sewer we have provided, and screw it up. There it is.

Now your kitchen has been worked out in many ways. I think there are at least five now available where you can get a complete and a more practical, a more beautiful kitchen, than almost any architect could himself design. Unit No. 2. And in connection with that unit you have the heating of the house—the heat which you use for your kitchen for cooking—an immense economy. All that needs is a single connection, screwing it up and putting it together.

The appurtenant systems in any house are more than one-third of the cost of the house. As the cost of the building comes down the proportion rises. Once we have those things completely established as certain parts are established in your car, and they have nothing whatever to do with the general effect of the house as a whole, we have established one very essential economy, and we have then something at last toward the building of this modern house.

Now, in addition to that it is just as easy to standardize a bed-room unit which is ideal and which does not have the old stuffy closet. We do not have closets any more in the older sense. We architects, in spite of our impracticability, have seen the consequences of providing the housewife with a hole in which to chuck things. Our closet is not essential any more and we do not have it. We have the wardrobe instead, which is a ventilated affair, which can be easily kept in order.

The bed-room unit can be in various sizes; it can be assembled in various ways with the other units.

Then we can have a living room unit of two or three sizes. In fact, all the features which are characteristic of modern life and modern living, we can buy on some standardized scheme of arrangement.

These can be laid out on a unit system so that they all come together in an organic style, and the design of these things in the first place can be of such a character that in the final assembly no wrong or bad thing can happen.

In putting these units together according to your means, you may be able to have a three-unit house. You will probably have to have a bathroom, a kitchen unit, and a bedroom—three units at the minimum. Then you can go on and you can amplify that house until you have it surrounding an interior court. And this thing can all come knocked down to you in metal, metal slabs pressed on each side with some heat resisting or cold resisting insulation. In fact, you can have the slabs 10 feet or you can have them 12 feet long and 8 to 9 feet high in the knock-down shape and put together on the job with a B.T.U. resistance equal to that of an 8-inch brick wall.

Now, in connection with this assembled house a man need not go so heavily into debt to own his house as he has to do now. He will not have to encourage the mortgage banker to quite such an extent. As his means grow and his family grows, his house can grow. And I can demonstrate to you with perspectives and models which are being prepared, that none of these houses in any way you can put them together will be other than good to look at.

They are characteristic of the age. You can drive a car up to the door of one of these little houses, or big houses, however they may be extended, drive into the garage, and it will all look as though it belonged together—as the costume of the modern woman as she is dressed today also belongs to that house and to that car. The men's costume does not simply because the women won't let us change. We ought to have something simpler than we are putting on in order to be modern. We are dreadfully old-fashioned when we hook up about 43 buttons and go through all our pockets, and finally take stock of the gadgets which go to make us complete.

Simplification is the slogan of the machine age, a new significance for the car, for the house, for madam's dress, for monsieur, eventually, but we have got to fight for that freedom; it is not coming unless we do fight for it.

Well, now, I have laid before you a simple outline and the gist of this thing that we call modern. I have given you an outline here of the main characteristics and the thought behind modern architecture. It is not well to laugh at it, and it is not well to put it aside. You can't. I have seen it during the 30 years which it has been my pleasure and privilege to try to build houses for people. I have seen it growing and growing, going abroad, becoming the characteristic thing in Holland, in Germany, in Switzerland, Czecho-Slovakia, Poland and France. Our own country has been the only country satisfied with its own little plaster caverns, its own gadgets, its own little pretty things which it is willing to set up in some style or other and try to live in.

Now, it seems to me that the most valuable thing for a body of Realtors to get into their systems is the idea, first, that we have got to make spaciousness more characteristic of modern life. It is the natural thing for democracy to get space. The modern city works against it. All of you Realtors have worked against it all your lives. The finer you could get the thing, and the smaller the pieces you could pass around, why the more successful you were. That time has gone by, I believe.

There is a lot of ground in this country. In fact if all the people of the world were to be put together on the Island of Bermuda, they would not cover it standing up—I do not know about sitting down. And there is just about 53 acres, at any rate about 50 acres in this country, for every man, woman and child in it if it were to be divided up on that basis.

Now, it is senseless getting the thing in a heap, pig-piling, to pigpile some more. Believe me, it is old-fashioned. It is not in the keeping of our modern opportunities. It is not in the keeping of our modern thought. It is dead.

Probably you do not even know now when you see the little gas station out there on the prairie that that is the advance agent of decentralization. Distribution is changing. Whole agencies are changing. Your telephone poles could be down tomorrow if it was not for the investment in them. The whole expression and guide of modern living has gained fluidity, spontaneity. What before took 10 years is now spontaneous.

Have we got to go on building buildings, partitioning ground, setting up institutions along these dead old lines, and crucifying human life to make a little money? We are all where we are now, flat on our backs, gasping for a little sustenance—I guess we call it cash—just because we can't keep pace with the modern thought that is building the modern world. We have had before us a spectacle of what we call depression. I suppose we call it a "depression" to be nice, just the way the car people when they take your car call it "repossession."

But I do not believe that this is a depression. I believe that we are at the end of an epoch, and I believe that unless real estate men put their ears to their own ground and get this message: Decentralization—Reintegration—Organic Architecture—The Use of Our Other Resources—we are faced with a very serious situation. Those things seem insignificant, but God knows what they can do. Glass, steel, the automobile, mobilization of the whole community. Why, it has changed the entire face of civilization and the universe.

And until we can grasp that, until we can interpret it, until we can capitalize it for the people, we have not got a civilization.

•

14b The House of Moderate Cost (1938)

The house of moderate cost is not only America's major architectural problem but the problem most difficult for her major architects. As for me, I would rather solve it with satisfaction to myself and Usonia, than build anything I can think of at the moment except the modern theater now needed by the legitimate drama unless "the stage" is to be done to death by "the movies."

In our country the chief obstacle to any real solution of the moderate-cost house problem is the fact that our people do not really know how to live, imagining their idiosyncrasies to be their "tastes," their prejudices to be their predilections and their ignorance to be virtue where any beauty of living is concerned.

To be more specific, a small house on the side street might have charm if it didn't ape the big house on the avenue, just as the Usonian village itself might have great charm if it didn't ape the big town. Likewise, Marybud on the old farm might be charming in clothes befitting her state and her work, but is only silly in the Sears-Roebuck finery that imitates the clothes of her city sisters who imitate Hollywood stars with their lipstick, rouge, high heels, silk stockings, bell skirt and cock-eyed hat. Exactly that sort of "monkeyfied" business is the obstacle to architectural achievement in our U.S.A. This provincial "culture-lag" does not allow the person, thing or thought to be simply and naturally itself: the true basis of genuine culture.

I am certain that any approach to the new house needed by indigenous culture—why worry about the house wanted by provincial ignorance—is fundamentally different. That house must be a pattern for more simple and, at the same time, more gracious living: new, but suitable to living conditions as they might so well be in the country we live in today.

This needed house of moderate cost must sometime face reality. Why not now? The houses built by the million, which journals propagate, do no such thing. To me such houses are "escapist" houses, putting on some style or other, really having none. Style *is* important. *A* style is not. There is all the difference when we work *with* style and not for *a* style. But so little honest thought has been allowed to penetrate to living conditions among us that to write about them and even to build for them seems foolish enough although seen to be necessary.

A pressing, needy, hungry, confused issue is the American "small house" problem. But where is a better thing to come from while government housing itself is only perpetuating the old stupidities?[1] I do not believe the needed house can come from current education, from big business, or by way of smart advertising experts. I do not think it will be a matter of expert salesmanship at all unless common sense has dropped to that level in America. It is, first, common sense that might take us along the road to the better thing.

What would be really sensible in this matter? Let's see how far the Herbert Jacobs house[2] at Madison, Wisconsin, is a sensible house. This house for a young journalist, his wife, and small daughter, is now under roof: cost $5,500, including architect's fee of $450. Contract let to Bert Groves.

To give the little Jacobs family the benefit of industrial advantages of the era in which they live, something else must be done for them than to plant another little imitation of a mansion. Simplifications must take place. Mr. and Mrs. Jacobs must themselves see life in somewhat simplified terms. What are essentials in their case, a typical case? It is necessary to get rid of all unnecessary materials in construction, necessary to use the mill to good advantage, necessary to eliminate, so far as possible, field labor which is always expensive. It is necessary to consolidate and simplify the three appurtenance systems—heating, lighting, and sanitation. At least this must be done if we are to achieve the sense of spaciousness and vista already necessary.

And it would be ideal to complete the building in one operation as it goes along, inside and outside. One operation and the house is finished inside as it is completed outside. There should be no complicated roofs. Every time a hip or valley or a dormer window is allowed to ruffle a roof the life of the building is threatened. The way windows are used is naturally the most useful resource to achieve the new characteristic sense of space. All of this fenestration can be made ready at the factory and set up as the walls. But there is no longer any sense in speaking of doors and windows. These walls are largely a system of fenestration having its own part in the building scheme—the system being as much a part of the design as eyes are a part of the face.

Now what can be eliminated?

1. Visible roofs are expensive and unnecessary.
2. A garage is no longer necessary as cars are made. A carport will do, with liberal overhead shelter and walls on two sides.
3. The old-fashioned basement, except for a fuel and heater space was always a plague spot. A steam-warmed concrete mat four inches thick laid directly on the ground over gravel filling, the walls set upon that, is better.
4. Interior "trim" is no longer necessary.
5. We need no radiators, no light fixtures. We will heat the house the Roman way—that is to say—in or beneath the floors, and make the wiring system itself be the light fixtures, throwing light upon the ceiling. Light will thus be indirect except for a few outlets for floor lamps.
6. Furniture, pictures and bric-a-brac are unnecessary except as the walls can be made to include them or be them.
7. No painting at all. Wood best preserves itself. Only the floor mat need be waxed.

8. No plastering in the building.
9. No gutters, no down spouts.

Now to assist in general planning, what must or may we use in our new construction? In this case five materials: wood, brick, cement, paper, glass. To simplify fabrication we must use the horizontal unit system in construction. (See lines crossing plans both ways making rectangles 2 x 4 feet.) We must also use a vertical unit system which will be the boards and batten-bands themselves, interlocking with the brick courses.

The walls will be wood board-walls the same inside as outside—three thickness of boards with paper placed between them, the boards fastened together with screws. These slab-walls of boards will be high in insulating value, be vermin proof, and practically fireproof. These walls like the fenestration may be prefabricated on the floor and raised up into place, or they may be made at the mill.

The appurtenance systems to avoid cutting and complications, must be an organic part of construction. Yes, we must have polished plate glass. It is one of the things we have at hand to gratify the designer of the truly modern house and bless its occupants.

The roof framing in this instance is laminated of 2 x 4's making the three offsets seen outside in the eaves of the roof and enabling the roof to be sufficiently pitched without the expense of "building up" the pitches. The middle offset may be used to ventilate the roof spaces in summer. These 2 x 4's sheathed and covered with a good asphalt roof are the top of the house, its shelter gratifying to the sense of shelter.

All this is in hand—no, it is in mind—as we will plan the disposition of the rooms.

What must we consider essential now? We have our corner lot—an acre—with a south and west exposure. We have a garden. The house is wrapped about two sides of this garden.

1. We must have as big a living room with as much garden coming into it as we can afford, with a fireplace in it, and book shelves, dining table, benches, and living room tables built in.

2. Convenient cooking and dining space adjacent to if not a part of the living room. This space may be set away from outside walls within the living area to make work easy. This is a new thought concerning a kitchen—taking it away from outside walls and letting it run up into overhead space with the chimney, thus connection to dining space is made immediate without unpleasant features and no outside wall space lost to the principal rooms. There are steps leading down from this space to a small cellar below for heater, fuel, and laundry. The bathroom is next so that plumbing features of both kitchen and bath may be combined.

3. Two bedrooms and, in this case, a workshop which may be a future bedroom. The single bathroom is not immediately connected to any single bedroom, for the sake of privacy. Bathrooms opening directly into a bedroom occupied by more than one person or two bedrooms opening into a single bathroom have been badly overdone. We will have as much garden and space in all these space appropriations as our money allows after we have simplified our construction as proposed by way of modern technique. . . .

[Here is] a modest house that has no feeling at all for the "grand" except as the house extends itself parallel to the ground, companion to the horizon. That kind of extension can hardly go too far for comfort or beauty of proportion. As a matter of course a home like this is an architect's creation. It is not a builder's nor an amateur's effort and there is considerable risk in exposing the scheme to that sort of imitation or emulation. This is true because it could not be built except as the architect oversees the building and the building would fail of proper effect unless the furnishing and planting were done by the architect.

[Discussing] it thus briefly may help to indicate how stifling the little colonial hot-boxes, hallowed by government or not, really are where Usonian family life is concerned. You might easily put two of them, each costing more, into the living space of this one and not go much outside the walls. Here is a moderate cost brick and wood house that by new technology of a lifetime has been greatly extended in scale and comfort. A single house. Imagine how the cost would come down were the technique familiar or if many were executed at one time—probably down to $3,500, according to number built and location. There is freedom of movement, and privacy too, afforded by the general arrangement here, unknown to the current boxment. Let us say nothing about beauty. It is an ambiguous term in the provinces of which our big cities are the largest. But I think a cultured American housewife will look well in it. The now inevitable car will seem part of it. Where does the garden leave off and the house begin? Where the garden begins and the house leaves off. Withal, it seems a thing loving the ground with the new sense of space—light—and freedom to which our U.S.A. is entitled.

NOTES

1. Wright refers here and below to "greenbelt towns," three New Deal communities planned in 1935 under the auspices of the Resettlement Administration and constructed shortly there after as Greenbelt, Maryland; Greendale, Wisconsin; and Greenhills, Ohio—as well as various sorts of housing elsewhere, ranging in style from stripped-down "internationalist" through Art Deco to simplified Georgian–Cape Cod "colonial."

2. The earlier (1936–37) of two residences for Herbert Jacobs at Westmoreland (now Madison), Wisconsin, is generally considered the first "Usonian" house. The second, known as the "Solar Hemicycle" in Middleton on the outskirts of Madison, designed in 1942 but not constructed until 1948, departs from the "true" or "phase one" Usonian format.

14c To the Blackbourns (1938)

To the Blackbourns:

Herewith the plans for a good time space for your family in a style to which you are, as yet, unaccustomed but one which you might truly call your own if you wanted to. We call the style Usonian meaning "of these United States." If the house seems a little open for your Northwest, that openness has been taken care of by building the house upon a paved concrete mat itself heated by steam pipes laid under it in the gravel filling beneath. This insures comfort no matter how cold outside and there are no radiators in sight. What looks like them in the drawings are really the folding screens between the several spaces opening into the central or general space—a kind of enclosed patio.

Space is characteristic of this free pattern for a freer life than you could possibly live in in the conventional house—separated into boxes; itself a big box.

One thing to mention at the beginning is the matter of the lot. No ten thousand dollar house should stand on less than 100 ft. so we have taken a thousand dollars off the cost of the house and put it into another lot—two lots 60 x 120 ft. on level land—$2,000 invested in that.

We have studied your little family and arranged for all including the dog. Each has his own privacy when needed and good time space for all together without any basement or an attic.

The swimming pool might not come within our appropriation, in which case a sunken garden or lawn would do very well.

Betty Jane has a telephone box and all the privacy by the fireplace in the sitting room any young girl has a right to expect before she owns her own home—or her own car.

The boys meantime have plenty of room for action.

The dining, sitting, and ground floor sleeping spaces can all be thrown into the central space which is, as before said, a kind of enclosed patio on occasion.

Mother has a convenient kitchen next the dining table—everything "on ballbearings" to save labor. It is all but automatic.

Father's office is next so mother can answer the telephone when he is away.

There is plenty of car space—not enclosed because cars—today—are not a horse and buggy anymore.

When Father and Mother want to get away from it all their sleeping room on the ground floor may be closed off for quiet and it opens to the garden which may be a zone of quiet with an outdoor fireplace.

There is one extended 9 ft. flat ceiling over everything on the ground floor with a continuous band of glass tubing running all around the house. This ceiling becomes open trellis over the terraces outside.

Betty Jane, Bruce, and Ramsey have their own little bailiwicks upstairs front.

American (I prefer to say Usonian) family life is unlike any other in the world and I think this plan recognizes it for pretty much what it is—at this stage of development—a little private club—with special privacies, ultra conveniences, and style all the while.

Concerning cost. It is idle to suppose any estimating concern could tell us what the cost of it all would be, never having built anything like it. For instance, the steam heated floor mat, walls of well-insulated plywood set up directly upon it—under a well-padded flat roof composed of laminated 2 x 4 framing without pitches—ready for a snow load to stay there as long as possible. No painting except wax inside. No interior trim—few interior doors, few windows, glass tubing used in bands about the house instead. Plate glass otherwise. No plastering—plywood ceiling instead and plywood walls exposed. The mat could be paved with either brick or stone and the chimneys built of either. The roofs are 4 ply tar and gravel over the entire house. There is only a small excavation for the heater in the basement (oil burner) and a small laundry. The space has a large ventilating shaft in the chimney. The kitchen extends above the roof and forms the kitchen into a large ventilating shaft for the house—a scheme working very well in other houses we have built.

We are sure, estimating from the several similar constructions we have completed, that this house could be built under our own supervision in Minneapolis for eight thousand dollars including an architect's fee of $750.

We have found that estimates (inexperienced as they must be and founded upon familiar construction) would run between $12,500 and $15,000. Much of this house should be prefabricated in shops and set up on the site.

No need to expatiate further at this preliminary stage. The drawings do that.

Of course we hope you will like it.

Frank Lloyd Wright: Taliesin: August 22nd, 1938

FIFTEEN

Acceptance Speech
(1949)

First awarded in 1907, the American Institute of Architects' Gold Medal is conferred on an individual "in recognition of a significant body of work of lasting influence on the theory and practice of architecture." Wright was the sixteenth recipient and is still the only non-member or non–honorary member to receive it other than Thomas Jefferson, and he 123 years after his death.

Previous winners included Victor Laloux, Milton Medary, and Ragnar Östberg, whose "lasting influence" is open to discussion. Of those whose influence is clear, George B. Post and Eliel Saarinen were seventy-four when honored, Charles McKim sixty-two, Aston Webb sixty, and Edwin Lutyens fifty-six. Wright's lasting influence is without question, but in March 1949 he was three months shy of his eighty-second birthday. So while much appreciating "this token of esteem from the home boys," he could not refrain from chiding the AIA for tardiness. "It's been a long time coming," he says with tongue barely in cheek, "but here it is at last."

In his speech he stresses his independence and integrity, his refusal to market himself, to hustle jobs, which meant he had spent years "sitting around, waiting, . . . hoping somebody would come and give me something to do." This is the "persecuted genius" speaking as patriarch, minimizing the persecution, maximizing his genius, unable to refrain from self-congratulation for his many accomplishments—

sometimes delicately, sometimes brazenly. After all, he happily admits, "I don't think humility is a very becoming state for me."

Eerily echoing the first text in this volume, "The Architect" from 1900, he again criticizes and challenges his colleagues, this time for lack of social responsibility. As he had done so often, he laments the sorry state of American democracy, wondering if it had not devolved into a "mobocracy" of "cowards" afraid in a cold-war climate of conformity to implement "the great freedom that we hoped for when we founded this nation." And not for the first or last time he offers his "principles" of organic architecture as guidelines for turning what "we call democracy" into the real thing.

Even if some in attendance perceived Wright to be an annoying, cantankerous old man who talked too much, the intensity of his convictions and the power of his work would likely have forced them to agree when Mies van der Rohe said that "in his undiminished power [he] resembles a giant tree in a wide landscape which year after year attains a more noble crown." Wright himself could not have put it better.

The "Acceptance Speech of Frank Lloyd Wright," delivered March 17, 1949 in Houston, was published in the Journal of the American Institute of Architects *(May 1949).*

Ladies and Gentlemen:

No man climbs so high or sinks so low that he isn't eager to receive the good will and admiration of his fellowmen. He may be reprehensible in many ways; he may seem to care nothing about it; he may hitch his wagon to his star and, however he may be circumstanced or whatever his ideals or his actions, he never loses the desire for the approbation of his kind.

So I feel humble and grateful. I don't think humility is a very becoming state for me, but I really feel touched by this token of esteem from the home boys. It has reached me from almost every great nation in the world. It's been a long time coming from home. But here it is at last, and very handsomely indeed. And I am extremely grateful.

I don't know what change it's going to effect upon my course in the future. It is bound to have an effect. I am not going to be the same man when I walk out of here that I was when I came in. Because, by this little token in my pocket, it seems to me that a battle has been won.

I felt that way when I was sitting in my little home in Arizona in '41, and the news came over the wire that the Gold Medal of the Royal Institute of British Architects had fallen to a lad out there in the Middle West, in the tall grass. Well, I felt then that the youngsters who have held, we will say, with me and who have believed and made sacrifices and taken the gaff with me, had won a worldwide fight. But it hadn't been won at home. The Cape Cod Colonial—by the way, have any of you observed what we fellows have done to the Colonial? Have you seen it come down, and its front open to the weather, and the wings extend and have it become more and more reconciled to the ground? It has; you notice it.

Well, anyway, it is very unbecoming on an occasion like this to boast. But I do want to say something that may account in a measure for the fact that I have not been a member of your professional body, that I have consistently maintained an amateur status.

Long ago, way back in the days of Oak Park, I set up a standard of payment for my services of ten per cent. I have consistently maintained it. I have always felt a competition for the services of an architect, who to me is a great creative artist, was a sacrilege, a shame, and pointed to history to prove that nothing good ever came of it. And I think nothing good ever *will* come of it.

Also, I think that to make sketches for anybody for nothing, to tender your services, to hawk yourself on the curb in any circumstances, is reprehensible.

Now, I know the ideals of this institute very well. I took them to heart years ago, and believe me, with this Medal in my pocket, I can assert truthfully that never have I sacrificed one iota of those ideals in any connection whatsoever.

The man does not live who can say that I sought his work. And I remember in the very early days, when the children were running around the streets without proper shoes, and Mr. Moore, across the way, wanted to build a house, a fine house.[1] A fine man, a great opportunity for a youngster like me. Well, I had these ideals at heart even then, and I never went to see Mr. Moore and I never asked anybody to say a word for me, because who was there who could say an honest one? They didn't know anything about me.

So I glanced up one day through the plate-glass door—and, by the way, I *started* the plate-glass door—there were Mr. and Mrs. Moore. Well, you can imagine how that heart of mine went pitty-pat. He came in and sat down opposite me.

"Now, Mr. Wright," he said, "I want to know why every architect I ever heard of, and a great many I *never* heard of, have come to ask me for the job of building my house?"

"Well," I said, "I can't answer that question, but I am curious to know did Mr. Patton come?" Mr. Patton was the President of The Institute—that is, of The A.I.A. at that time.[2]

"Why," he said, "he was the first man to come."

"Well now," Mr. Moore said, "why haven't you come to ask me to build my house? You live right across the road."

"Well," I said, "you are a lawyer, aren't you, Mr. Moore? You are a professional man. If you heard that somebody was in trouble, would you go to him and offer him your services?"

"Ah!" he said, "I thought that was it. You are going to build our house."

Well it began that way, and it began to get noised about. The next man was Mr. Baldwin, who was also a lawyer, and wanted to build a house.[3] Mr. Baldwin appeared several months afterward and laid a check on the table. It was not a big check. It was $350, but it would be $3,500 now. And you can imagine what this did to me. And he said, "Here is your retainer, Mr. Wright."

Well, now, that is how that began, and it has been that way ever since, and I've never in my life asked a man to say a good word for me to another man who was going to build. Well, now, as a consequence, I have been sitting around, waiting. I have spent a good many years of my life hoping somebody would come and give me something to do. And every job I ever had hit me out of the blue on the back of the head. Now, that's true. So, this Gold Medal—let's forget all about design, let's forget all about contributions to construction and all the rest of it—I feel I can stick it in my pocket and walk away with it just because I sat there waiting for a job.

Now, of course, architecture is in the gutter. It is. I have heard myself referred to as a great architect. I have heard myself referred to as the greatest living architect. I have heard myself referred to as the greatest architect who ever lived. Now, wouldn't you think that ought to move you? Well, it doesn't. Because in the first place they don't know. In the next place, no architect, in the sense that a man now has to be an architect, ever lived, and that's what these boys in front of me don't seem to know.

Architects as they existed in the ancient times were in possession of a state of society, as an instrument to build with. The guilds were well organized. The predetermined styles were well established, especially in the Gothic period. An architect in those days was pretty well furnished with everything he needed to work with. He didn't have to be a creator. He had to be a sentient artist, with a fine perception, let's say, and some knowledge of building, especially if he was going to engage in some monumental enterprise, but he didn't have to create as he does now.

Now we have an entirely different condition. We live by the machine. Most of us aren't much higher in our consciousness and mentality than the man in the garage, anyhow. We *do* live by the machine. We *do* have the great products of sciences as our tool box, and as a matter of fact science has ruined us as it has ruined religion, as it has made a monkey of philosophy, as it has practically destroyed us and sent us into perpetual war.

Now, that isn't our fault, but where, I ask you, were these new forms of building to come from that could make full use of these advantages that have proved to us so disadvantageous? Who is going to conceive these new buildings? Where from? How come?

Now, it's a great pity that the Greeks didn't have glass. A great pity that they didn't have steel, spider spinning, because if they had we wouldn't have to do any thinking, even now. We would copy them with gratitude. No, not with gratitude. We would not know even we were copying them. We would not know. We would not have the least gratitude.

But now what must an architect be if he is going to be really one worthwhile, if he is really going to be true to his profession? He *must* be a creator. He must perceive beyond the present. He must *see* pretty far ahead. Well, let's not say that, because we can all do that, but he must see into the life of things if he is going to build anything worth building in this day and generation.

And, do you know, we ought to be the greatest builders the world has ever seen? We have the riches, we have the materials, we have the greatest release ever found by man in steel and glass. We have everything, but. We have a freedom that never existed before. We profess democracy out of a "mobocracy" that is shocking, astounding and arresting. But we have built *nothing* for democracy. We have built *nothing* in the spirit of the freedom that has been ours. No. Look at Washington. Look anywhere. You can even go out and see the Shamrock. And, by the way, I want it recorded right here and now that that building is built in what is called the

"International Modern Style."[4] Let's give the devil his due. Let's put it where it belongs. And anyhow, while we are speaking of that exploit, why? It ought to be written in front of it, in great tall letters, in electric lights—W-H-Y—Why?

Well, Houston has it. And Houston is a good example of the capitalist city, the pattern of the capitalist city—one single, great broad pavement, skyscrapers erected at one end and, way out in the country at the other end, skyscraper, and in between, out on the prairie and in the mud, the people.

Well, now, we are prosecuting a cold war with people who declare with a fanatic faith that is pitiful in the have-nots. We declare a faith in the "haves," when we act. We declare a faith in the union of something beneficial to both the "haves" and the "have-nots" when we talk. When are we going to practise what we preach? When are we going to build for democracy? When are we going to understand the significance of the thing ourselves, and live up to it? When are we going to be willing to sit and wait for success? When are we going to be willing to take the great will and the great desire for the deed?

Now, we can do it. We have got enough "on the ball," as the slang phrase is, to go on within that direction if we will. But to me, the most serious lack, the thing we haven't got—and if you look over the political scene, of course it is obscene—of all this thing we are talking about. Honor? Nowhere. Now, what is the sense of honor? What would it be in architecture? What would it be in the building of buildings? What would it be in the living of a life, in a democracy, under freedom? Not mistaking license for freedom, not mistaking individuality for personality, which is our great error, and which characterizes a mobocracy instead of a true democracy. Now, what would a sense of honor be, that sense of honor that could save us now? As science has mowed us down and we are lying ready to be raked over the brink, what could save us but a sense of honor? And what would that sense of honor be?

Well, what is the honor of a brick? What would be an honorable brick? A *brick* brick, wouldn't it? A *good* brick. What would be the honor of a board? It would be a *good* board, wouldn't it? What is the honor of a man? To be a *true* individual, to live up to his ideal of individuality rather than his sense of personality. Now if we get that distinction straight in our minds, we'll be able to go on. We will last some time. If we don't get it, we might as well prepare for the brink. We are going over.

Now, I have been right about a good many things—that's the basis of a good deal of my errors. And it has a basis, that's one thing I can say for *my* errors. We can save ourselves. We're smart. We have rat-like perspicacity. But we have the same courage and that's what's the matter. I don't know of a more cowardly—well, I'm getting too deep in here and I cannot swear, not tonight. But we are certainly a great brand of cowards in America. We've got all our great opportunities to live a spiritual life, with great interior strength and nobility of purpose, and minds go by the board. Why? I have asked myself all these years—Why? You've all seen it. I am not telling you anything new. Churches—religion—what has it become? Philosophy—what is it? Education? What have you? Cowardice. What are the universities today? Overflowing with hungry minds and students. And yet, as I stand here now I am perfectly willing to admit and to confess that it's not the fault of the universities. It's not the fault of education. None of this is the fault of the systems that exist among us. They are our *own* fault. *We* make these things what they are. We allow them to be *as* they are. We've got the kind of buildings we deserve. We've got the kind of cities that are coming to us. This capitalist city, of which Houston is an example, we did it. It came to us because we are what we are, and don't forget it. If we are ever going to get anything better, if we are going to come by a more honorable expression of a civilization such as the world is entitled to from us—we put ourselves on a hill here, in a highlight, we talk about the highest standard of living the world has ever seen, we profess all these things, and we don't *deliver*.

Now why we don't isn't the fault of the institutions. It is not the fault of any class. It is not the fault of the big boys that make money and make the blunders and shove us over the brink, like this out here that we spoke of a minute ago. No. How would they learn better? How is the architect who built the building going to know any better? How are they going to find out? They can only find out by your disapproval. They can only find out by your telling the *truth*, first to yourselves and then out loud, wherever you can get a chance to tell it.

Now, we have got to find honor. You know the old sayings— we dislike them now because they are a reproach. We don't honor the people, really, the men who came over here with an ideal in their hearts and founded this basis, as they thought, for freedom. They couldn't forsee, by the way, its sudden riches and these new scientific powers put into our hands, that we would be so soon degenerate. No.

I think if we were to wake up and take a good look at ourselves *as ourselves*, without passing the buck, without trying to blame other people for what really is our own shortcoming and our own lack of character, we would be an example to the world that the world needs now. We wouldn't be pursuing a cold war. We would be pursuing a great endeavor to plant, rear and nurture a civilization, and we would have a culture that would convince the whole world. We'd have all the Russians in here on us, working for us, with us, not afraid that we were going to destroy them or destroy anybody else.

It is because of cowardice and political chicanery, because of the degradation to which we have fallen as men—well, a crack comes to mind, but I'll refrain. My wife knows what it is, I am not going to say it.

Well now, that's serious enough, and that is all I think I ought to say.

Now, I want to call your attention to one thing. I have built it. I have built it. Therein lies the source of my errors. Why I can stand here tonight, look you in the face and insult you—because, well, I don't think many of you realize what it is that has happened, or is happening in the world that is now coming toward us. A little place where we live, with 60 youngsters—we turned away 400 in the past two years—and they come from 26 different nations.[5] They all come as volunteers because this thought that we call organic architecture has gone abroad. It has won abroad, under different names. A singular thing. We will never take an original thought or an idea until we have diluted it, until we have passed it around and given it a good many names. After that takes place, then we can go, and we do go.

Well, that has happened. This thing has been named different names all over the world. It has come back home and I use the word—I say come back home advisedly—because here is where it was born. Here it was born in this cradle—as we are fond of calling it—of liberty which has degenerated into license. Now, what are we going to do with it? Are we going to let it become a commonplace and shove it into the gutter, or are we really going to look up to it, use it, honor it—and believe me, if we do, we have found the centerline of a democracy. Because the principles of an organic architecture, once you comprehend them, naturally grow and expand into this great freedom that we hoped for when we founded this nation and that we call democracy.

Well it's enough, isn't it?

NOTES

1. Nathan G. Moore House (1895), Oak Park, Illinois, expanded and remodeled by Wright in 1923.

2. Norman S. Patton (1852–1915) lived in Oak Park and was treasurer of the Illinois chapter of the AIA in 1893–94.

3. Hiram Baldwin House (1905), Kenilworth, Illinois.

4. Since the Shamrock Hotel (1946–49, demolished 1985), Houston, by Fort Worth architect Wyatt C. Hedrick was a conservatively styled building not in the "International Style," Wright was having a bit of fun with his Houston hosts.

5. Wright refers here and above to the "youngsters" of his Taliesin Fellowship. See Document 13, n. 2.

For Further Reading

There are hundreds of books about all aspects of Frank Lloyd Wright's life and work, far too many to list here. Most are monographs on segments or themes of his career, pictorial or literary monographs on individual buildings, types thereof, or on his art glass, furniture, and other design accoutrements.

Of numerous compilations of his literary work, the most comprehensive is Bruce Brooks Pfeiffer (ed.), *Frank Lloyd Wright: Collected Writings*, 5 vols. (New York: Rizzoli International Publications, 1992–95). His recent *The Essential Frank Lloyd Wright: Critical Writings on Architecture* (Princeton, NJ: Princeton University Press, 2008) is an abridged (453-page) version of *Collected Writings*.

The most comprehensive collection of his renderings is Yukio Futagawa, ed., *Frank Lloyd Wright Monograph,* 12 vols. (Tokyo: A.D.A. EDITA, 1984–88).

By far the best of several guides to the built work is Thomas A. Heinz, *Frank Lloyd Wright Field Guide* (Evanston, IL: Northwestern University Press, 2005).

Wright published *Frank Lloyd Wright: An Autobiography* (New York: Longmans, Green, 1932), revised and expanded (New York: Duell, Sloan & Pearce, 1943), revised and expanded again and published in 1977 by Horizon Press in New York.

For biographies consult Robert C. Twombly, *Frank Lloyd Wright: His Life and His Architecture* (New York: John Wiley & Sons, 1979); Brendan Gill, *Man of Many Masks: A Life of Frank Lloyd Wright* (New York: G. P. Putnam's Sons, 1987); and Meryle Secrest, *Frank Lloyd Wright* (New York: Alfred A. Knopf, 1992).

Index